Choose Retirement Series

# CHOOSE THE
# SOUTHWEST
## FOR RETIREMENT

### Third Edition

## Retirement Discoveries for Every Budget

JOHN HOWELLS

The
Globe
Pequot
Press

Guilford, Connecticut

The prices and rates listed in this guidebook were confirmed at press time. We recommend, however, that you call establishments before traveling to obtain current information.

Cover and text design: Laura Augustine
Cover photos: Chris Corrie and John Warden/Index Stock
Maps by Lisa Reneson

**Library of Congress Cataloging-in-Publication Data**

Howells, John, 1928–
    Choose the Southwest for retirement : retirement discoveries for every budget / John Howells.—3rd ed.
        p. cm. — (Choose retirement series)
    Includes index.
    ISBN 0–7627–0801–8
    1. Southwest, New—Guidebooks.    2. Retirement, Places of—
Southwest, New—Guidebooks.    3. Cost and standard of living—
Southwest, New.    I. Title.    II. Series.

F785.3.H69    2000                                               00–056174
917.904'34—dc21

Manufactured in the United States of America
Third Edition/Third Printing

# CONTENTS

# THE SOUTHWEST

# Introduction to the Southwest

If you've bought this book, it's safe to bet that you or someone close to you is looking into possible retirement choices. Some of you may find that as you narrow your choices to a certain section of the country, more detailed information is needed to make final decisions. Others of you may already know where you want to retire and want to zero in on that particular area from the beginning.

So, to better inform readers who want to sharpen their focus on the retirement aspects of the Southwest, my wife and I started out on another odyssey of research and enjoyable travel, visiting new towns and revisiting familiar places. Towing our fifth-wheel trailer, we stayed several days in each town to assimilate the flavor of what it's like to live in a community, something that studying statistics and chamber of commerce handouts can't convey. As a result, this third edition of *Choose the Southwest for Retirement* contains descriptions of many new retirement locations, some not covered in other publications, plus more in-depth information about previously discussed communities. We've evaluated more than fifty different towns for your consideration and, by extension, many more places in surrounding localities.

## What We Mean by the "Southwest"

Most people will agree, the "West" begins in Texas and ends at the Pacific Ocean. However, to sharpen our definition of the "Southwest," let us agree to exclude the eastern half of Texas. Why? Because east Texas is culturally, climactically, and conceptually part of the South and/or Midwest. In east Texas, we're talking swampy bayous, cotton fields, prairies, and folks who don't even own a pair of cowboy boots. In west Texas, you'll find sagebrush, dry hills, cactus-fed cattle, and people who wear cowboy boots even if they come from New Jersey. For our purposes, then, a north-south line through San Antonio marks the easternmost boundary of our research.

Wait a minute, you say. What about California? Clearly, you can't travel any farther west than California without renting a boat or donning water wings. Yet think about it: California differs from neighboring Nevada and Arizona in the same way as west Texas differs from Louisiana and Arkansas. That is, California differs culturally, geographically, and conceptually from Arizona and Nevada. It's true that California's eastern deserts mirror Nevada and Arizona landscapes, but few people live here. Most retirees prefer California's unique climates along the Pacific or the traditional central areas of the state. These are as different from Nevada and Arizona deserts as east Texas is from west Texas. Retirement in California is the subject of another book.

How far north does the Southwest extend? Even though the top portions of Colorado and Utah extend northward, into what some might consider the Northwestern part of the country, this book considers the entire states of Colorado and Utah as part of the Southwest. Their climates and geography blend with their southern neighbors and present a unified landscape of retirement possibilities. Readers looking for a particular lifestyle and quality of life typical of New Mexico, Arizona, or Nevada might well investigate Colorado or Utah before making a choice.

One thing all Southwest areas have in common is a dry climate. Vast areas are in semidesert or arid mountain country. Rainfall is scarce, often just a tenth of that expected in the Midwestern and Eastern states. Temperatures are dependent on altitude here, and mountains receive more rain than low-country deserts. Higher altitudes, of course, mean more livable summers and winter snows that can range between light and incredible, depending on the location.

The Southwest's low humidity turns out to be the key to its success in attracting retirees. Humidity's influence on climate can't be exaggerated. If you've ever spent time in a low-humidity location, you'll know that cold days don't seem nearly as chilly, and hot days are much more bearable.

The term *desert* incorrectly conjures images of Sahara-like sand dunes and desolate sweeps of barren land. True, North American deserts can be like that, but they rarely are. You'll find plenty of vegetation but of a different nature. Over eons, plants and animals have adapted to living in dry country—even in places with 4 inches of rainfall per year. Trees and bushes have learned to survive on little water, flourishing miraculously in a dry desert or mountain environment. The first spring storm makes the desert bloom with an unforgettable explosion of colorful flowers and shades of green, all of which disappear when the plants withdraw into their water-conserving mode for the summer. Some plants have developed tough outer layers that prevent precious water from evaporating and thus stay green year-round.

Animals, too, have adapted. An amazing variety of reptiles, mammals, and birds do perfectly well in the desert. Some survive the fierce summers by conserving body energy during the heat of the day, then foraging and exercising in the cooler hours of the morning and evening. Other species have developed patterns of migration, spending summers in higher altitudes where the weather is cool and damp, then wintering in the pleasant warmth of the desert.

It should come as no surprise, then, that we humans, the most adaptable of all organisms, have also adapted to dry mountain and desert living. When residing in the desert, we've learned to conserve body energy by living in air-conditioned homes, driving air-conditioned cars, and foraging at air-conditioned shopping malls. We exercise by riding bikes or playing golf in the cooler hours of the morning and evening. Midday is for naps. Instead of developing tough outer layers that prevent precious water from evaporating, we develop suntanned skins and sip cool drinks. Forget about evaporation!

Higher altitudes and naturally colder Southwestern climes offer comfortable springs, summers, and falls. There you'll appreciate shirt-sleeve days and sweater evenings. In August, you can play golf at noon if you please. The obvious high-altitude trade-off is a true winter season in place of the low desert's balmy, sun-filled Januarys and Februarys. So, when winter arrives, cold-weather Southwesterners enthusiastically pull on heavy clothes and strap on snowshoes or skis to enjoy their crisp, dry winter wonderlands. Others drive an hour or so to the low desert and go swimming.

Unlike the middle section of the United States, where frozen ground, ice, and slush last all winter, Southwestern winters are livable. In all but the highest and most snow-prone areas, Southwestern winter is an on-again, off-again affair. For example, Denver isn't much colder in winter than Sacramento, California; the key is that because of their different altitudes, Sacramento gets winter rains, whereas Denver gets snow. Denver's overnight snowfall can be dramatic (a foot or more is common), yet the snow rarely stays around for more than a day or two. It's often gone by the next afternoon. A big plus is that Denver's dry air makes cold days much more bearable than Sacramento's humid, river-chilled atmosphere. A fifty degree, 85 percent humidity day in Sacramento will make you wish you were in Denver.

## Where Do the Statistics Come From?

When available, *weather statistics* from the database of the National Oceanic and Atmospheric Administration are listed at the end of each retirement location. Average high and low temperatures are listed for the four seasons, as well as yearly rainfall and snowfall. When no official data were available, information could often be obtained from local chambers of commerce. If no weather figures are listed, you'll get a good idea of the weather by looking at a chart from a nearby town.

*Crime statistics* come from the latest edition of the FBI's yearly publication: *Uniform Crime Reports, Crime in the United States.* The entire report is in my database. I've ranked several hundred towns and cities, those I consider the better retirement locations, for personal safety using the FBI's crime statistics. Because only cities with populations of more than 10,000 are included in the report, because many cities either don't file reports or file inadequate data, and because the latest available information is for 1997–1998, I don't refer to the data unless the results are unusual. All towns and cities discussed in this book have above average safety.

When available, *cost-of-living statistics* are included with the review of the retirement locations. These figures come from the American Chamber of Commerce Researchers Association's latest issue of their *Cost of Living Index.* Again, they are only available for select cities, but they tend to reflect the cost of living in similar or nearby cities. Listed are the percentage of the national average prices of housing, medical, utilities, and groceries as well as an overall ranking, with one hundred being the average.

## Quality of Life

Our travels have taken us through hundreds of communities, and we checked out many, many local conditions before making the final selections for this book. However, because a town is not described here doesn't necessarily mean it wouldn't be a great place to retire. The bottom line: There is no "best" place to retire for everyone. Selecting your ideal retirement home is a highly individual decision and depends on personal lifestyle, future aspirations, and, most importantly, your definition of an ideal quality of life.

The phrase "quality of life" means something different for every individual. When you ask New York City residents about their quality of life, you might hear them rave about the plethora of cultural events available to them. They enjoy everything from opera performances, jazz clubs, and Broadway plays to world-class restaurants, museums, and Fifth Avenue shops. They'll tell you they can't imagine living without all the excitement that is characteristic of urban life. Existence would be boring without Manhattan's highly charged atmosphere of culture, entertainment, and conveniences.

When you ask the same question of residents in a small Southwestern town, "quality of life" might be defined in terms of peace and quiet, outdoor activities, and low-key cultural events. People here prize the crystal-clear quality of the air they breathe, their sense of security, and their connection to their neighbors and community. Their quality of life is enhanced every time they're treated to the sight of a doe and her fawn grazing in a forest glade. Miles of hiking and bicycle trails, winter skiing, and summer gold-panning replace world-class symphonies, gourmet restaurants, and museums.

Yet Southwestern retirement doesn't mean just outdoor activities. Many communities provide exciting cultural events and entertainment that rival those found back East. True, you probably won't see world-renowned personalities appearing in a musical, but the fact that your hairdresser is performing in the amateur theater guild's play or your next-door neighbor works on set design makes up for the lack of professionalism.

## Southwestern Lifestyles

Because the Southwest provides such a wide range of climates and a variety of cities and towns, different lifestyles are possible. There's something to fit any personality or appetite and plenty of opportunity to acquire a taste for some new hobby, skill, or whatever endeavor you'd care to try. Many activities listed throughout this book can, of course, be enjoyed in Eastern or Midwestern settings, but not as easily, and not as a regular part of your routine.

Hunting and fishing are much easier to do in most Southwestern environs, because most open lands, forests, and streams are public property. Instead of being fenced and posted with KEEP OUT signs, most undeveloped land belongs to the U.S. Forest Service or the Bureau of Land Management. It belongs to all of us.

River rafting is another common sport in the Southwest, simply because of the many white-water rivers here, and because they are much longer than those back East. Most Eastern white-water rapids are a few miles long and can be covered in a matter of hours. Some Western rivers can take as long as two weeks to explore, rafting by day and camping at night. Again, since most of the land traversed is public, you can pretty much launch your boat and set up your tent wherever you darn well please.

Rock hunting and prospecting are popular hobbies in the Southwest, something not often done in the rest of the country. Again, because so much land is public, you can wander about at your pleasure. You can pan most streams for gold, break open rocks in search of ore, or collect gemstones where you find them. Because vegetation is usually sparse, rocks and minerals are exposed for easy examination. The exciting part is, should you by chance stumble across something valuable, you can stake a claim and start mining. Don't laugh; my brother once found a silver and lead mine and took out $2 million from the first 85 feet of digging. However, be aware that Congress may change the laws concerning mining and prospecting.

Jewelry making is a popular avocation out West; hobbyists often use semiprecious stones they've collected in the desert and polished themselves. Another popular hobby is photography. The lone Western ghost towns, abundant wildlife, and sensational landscapes that cannot be found elsewhere are frequent subjects of shutterbugs.

Most other social and recreational activities available to Easterners are enjoyed in the Southwest. Bridge clubs, literary groups, travel clubs— whatever you enjoyed before will entertain you here. If you can't find your niche, you can usually develop one at the local senior citizens' center.

## None of the Above

You may be one of those easy-to-please types whose interests are limited to watching television and gossiping with neighbors. We all know people who arrange their lives to fit the television schedule. Sunday is for football, weekdays for soap operas, and weeknights for sitcoms. Making trips to the supermarket, browsing downtown stores, and visiting neighbors have to fit into the time between programs.

While some folks would view such a lifestyle as boring, others see it as a perfectly natural way to live; after all, this is the way they've lived all their lives. When they had jobs, they couldn't afford the luxury of staying up late to watch David Letterman, and since they worked during the daytime, soaps were something they only heard others talk about. Now, when they can do anything they care to, they choose to indulge themselves.

However, I suspect these folks won't be reading this book. For them, it doesn't make sense to move away for their retirement years since they have everything they need right where they live. Before moving, then, consider the recreational and social opportunities of your old and new home bases. Changing where you live is an opportunity to change your entire lifestyle. Your retirement can be a new beginning, not just a continuation of the same old groove in the same old rut.

## Real Estate Prices

Throughout this book, I've tried to give readers a sense of local housing costs and real estate prices. Aside from the probability that my estimates may soon be outdated, I've had grave doubts about the wisdom of including prices. They can be misleading in the extreme. Why? Because it's virtually impossible to convey an accurate picture of a housing market. It seems as if it should be a simple job: State the average sales prices in a region, and let readers extrapolate from there. Readers are thus prepared to pay an average price for an average home, an above-average price for an above-average home, or a below-average price for a below-average home, whatever the pocketbook can stand. What's the problem?

Part of the problem is defining the terms "average house" and "average sales price." Suppose we agree that an average house is a 1,500-square-foot, three-bedroom, two-bath home in a safe neighborhood. That's the easy part. What's difficult is determining the average cost of that average house. Statistics tell how many homes were sold in a given community and how much money changed hands. Now, if my junior high school math serves me correctly, we find the average sales price by dividing the total sales by the number of homes sold. But how many of those houses sold fit our definition of an "average house"? If there's been an unusual number of expensive homes sold—in a new, upscale subdivision, for example—we would have a misleading figure.

A further problem arises when an author interviews real estate brokers about values of local property. Some realtors will quote the average "selling price" as the cost of the average home, which, as we've seen, can be misleading. Others, realizing that the average selling price is unrealistic, will estimate the cost of an "average" home. And others, anxious to entice buyers to the community, may exaggerate and quote the lowest-offered price as the "average."

The biggest problem of all in trying to pin down elusive housing costs is that the figures most commonly available are the median figures for the current month. Unless the exact same number of homes sell for the exact same prices, next month's statistics will be different. Next month's prices could be 10 percent higher or lower. That means nothing, because the following month they will be different again. Over the course of a year, there may be little or no change in property values, even though monthly figures vary widely.

In this book, I've tried to steer a center course between the tilts, but I'll be the first to admit that prices quoted here are quite subjective. Furthermore, inflation and changing market conditions could make them obsolete before this book is ready for its next edition.

## Private Retirement Communities

Year by year, retirement becomes more of a big business, prompting impressive corporate investment. Planned retirement communities, often of astounding size, are popping up all over the country. Arkansas, Tennessee, and North Carolina lead the trend, with other states following suit. Arizona's Sun City West, for example, has 7,100 acres, with more than 15,000 homes. Often these places are "hermetically sealed" developments; that is, to enter a property, you must be a member of that development or have good reason to be there. (Wanting to price property is usually a good enough reason to allow you entry, however.) Round-the-clock guards staff the gates, scrutinizing everyone who enters. Occasionally, after the project is sold out, the original developers are no longer interested in staffing the gates with expensive security guards. It then becomes the responsibility of the owners' association.

Many complexes restrict buyers to age fifty-five and older. Children and younger adults may visit but not live there. This affects the community in two ways. Obviously, your life will be more tranquil without gangs of kids riding bikes, playing boom boxes, and knocking baseballs through your living room window. And you'll probably enjoy a lower crime rate. FBI statistics indicate that burglaries, vandalism, and theft usually occur in direct proportion to the number of teenagers in the neighborhood. On the other hand, many retirees prefer living in mixed-age neighborhoods; they find children and younger people fun to be with.

Developers look for inexpensive land for their new complexes, so they buy square miles of desert or large tracts of forested land. They can then afford to put in roads and utilities, dam up streams to create lakes and ponds, lay out a golf course or two—all at a fraction of what land alone would have cost in other parts of the country. Since rural wages are generally lower than in large cities, quality housing becomes relatively inexpensive.

There are two caveats to keep in mind: First, make sure you are going to be satisfied with the location of your new home. Many retirement developments we've visited are located several miles from the nearest town. Why? Because that's where the corporation found the cheapest land. This could mean a 20- or 30-mile drive into town to shop at the supermarket or to buy a bit of hardware for the shed you are building.

Second, beware of glib promises and supersalesmanship. When a retirement project is in its initial phase, a beautiful, to-scale plan of the development shows the future shopping mall, the clubhouses, the swimming pools, and all the wonderful amenities to come. An enormous supermarket and hardware store are clearly part of the plan. Believe this when you see it. Sometimes, when and if the "mall" is completed, the supermarket turns out to be a convenience store. (This doesn't happen as often with the more established developers.)

After you visit a development, check with a real estate office and the local newspaper's classified section to see what resales in the development are selling for. If homes are offered at prices drastically below those of the development's sales office, you may have trouble getting your price if you need to sell later. Also, if you like the development, you could save money by buying a resale instead of a newly built unit.

An advantage to getting in on the early stages of a retirement complex is that it's easier to become involved socially and to make new friends with neighbors as they move in. You might, however, prefer a well-established neighborhood, where you can join existing clubs and activities instead of having to form them. Another point to keep in mind is that *membership fees,* either yearly or monthly, are involved in planned communities. These fees can be reasonable or considerable, depending on the situation. By the way, the rule of thumb is that $100 in monthly fees is a financial commitment roughly equivalent to an additional $10,000 mortgage.

## Retirees Welcome!

Many communities actively seek retirees, doing everything possible to lure them into the area. For good reason: According to a study done by the Alabama Department of Economic and Community Affairs, when fifty new retirees locate in a small community, the impact is equivalent to a $10 million industry moving in. Retirees spend money. About 90 percent of their income goes for local goods and services. They actually create jobs rather than take jobs. With a half million retirees relocating each year, we're seeing a massive redistribution of wealth, flowing from industrial metropolitan areas to rural and small-town America. A sign of the times: A McDonald's restaurant in Florida recently replaced its kids' playground with a shuffleboard court. The welcome mat is definitely out for retirees.

Today's senior citizens, as a group, are more affluent than at any time in recent U.S. history. Because of the fantastic real estate appreciation of the 1970s and '80s, those of us who happened to buy homes when they were cheap now have tremendous equities with which to finance our retirement. Unfortunately, we may be the last of the affluent retirees. Our children and grandchildren have to struggle to become homeowners; low down payments and $100-a-month mortgages are faded memories. Today's average retired couple has $225,000 in total assets, much of it in home equity. These unused funds, when released and used for retirement, can permit retirees to upgrade their lifestyles dramatically. When spent in a new community, this money benefits local residents. That's why so many small towns are begging retirees to join them.

## Bargain Opportunities!

Local boosters too often place undue emphasis on a low cost of living and cheap real estate as prime attractions of their area. True, these items go hand in hand; that is, when you find low-cost housing, you'll also find economical living costs in general. In our travels, we've encountered real estate markets where $30,000 will buy a three-bedroom home, where carpenters will remodel for $10.00 an hour, and where haircuts are still $5.00. Remember, however, that inexpensive living isn't necessarily the same as quality living. Some low-cost areas are exceptional bargains, combining a high quality of life with welcoming neighbors and affordable living costs. Yet other low-cost areas are intensely dreary and boring, places you'd only visit under a witness protection program.

Why is the cost of living and housing so much less in some localities? Basically, you'll find two reasons for cheap real estate and low rents. The most common reason is that the area's an undesirable place to live. The town has been steadily losing population because it has absolutely nothing going for it—no jobs, no charm. Homes sell for rock-bottom prices because eager sellers outnumber reluctant buyers. Unless you are sincerely dedicated to boredom, bad weather, and cable TV, the area is not a place you would seek out for retirement.

The second reason is that an unforeseen, disastrous business slump or trend has caused the local job market to disintegrate. In this event, people don't necessarily want to leave the area and seek work elsewhere; they have to. Homes go on the real estate market at giveaway prices. There's no other choice.

Although situations like this are personal tragedies for displaced families, they open windows of opportunity for retirees. Since working for a living and a regular weekly paycheck aren't essential for most retired couples, bargain real estate is theirs for a fraction of what similar housing would cost elsewhere. As younger couples with children move away, over-sixty people move in and raise the ratio between retired and working people to impressive levels. The over-sixty crowd becomes a majority and wields appreciable influence over local government and political processes.

We've visited a few of these towns and reported on them in the first and second editions, places like Ajo and Bisbee in Arizona, where mines closed, and Colorado's Grand Junction, whose economy toppled when the oil shale industry collapsed. As you might imagine, opportunities like these don't last forever. As retirees move in and snap up the bargains, prices naturally rise, yet they rarely rise to the level they were at before the problem occurred.

## Doing Your Own Research

Authors of magazine articles and guidebooks commonly grade retirement communities, ranking the top places from one to ten, as if they were rating major league baseball teams. With a baseball team, we can check the scores; can't argue with that. But cities and towns don't receive scores except in somebody's mind. The fact that a freelance writer likes a city and ranks it number one in a magazine article doesn't prove a thing. For all we know, maybe the writer has never even seen the place.

Favorable ratings are too often awarded on the basis of conditions that don't affect retirees. For example, good schools, high employment, and a booming business climate will boost a town's popularity rating, while horrible weather and high taxes are often ignored. Quality grammar schools and juvenile recreational programs matter less to retirees than quality senior citizens' centers and safe neighborhoods. Full employment and thriving business conditions spell high prices and expensive housing. Also, cultural amenities, such as museums and opera companies, receive high marks in retirement analysis. Yet how many times a month will you be going to the opera? The museum? Would you rather live in a town with two golf courses and no museums or two museums and no golf courses? To find your ideal location, you're going to have to do your own ranking.

Ideally, you'll start your retirement analysis early. A great way to do this is by combining research with your vacations while you are still working. Instead of visiting the same old place each year, try different parts of the country. Even if you are already retired, you need to do some traveling if you plan on moving to another area of the country. Your travels needn't be expensive, however. Pick up some camping equipment at the next garage sale in your neighborhood—a tent, sleeping bags, and a cooking stove. Just about anywhere you want to visit will have either state parks with campgrounds or commercial camps where you can pitch a tent. Many RV parks have special spots for tent camping. Your local library will have a campground directory to help you locate a place in or near your target town.

Check out local real estate prices. Look into apartment and house rentals. Also consider the kinds of entertainment and cultural activities offered in the area. These could be anything from performances by light opera companies to conveniently located corner taverns. The question is, will you be happy you moved there? Just looking closely, as if you truly intended to move to the area, will tell you a lot.

While you are there, be sure to drop in on the local senior citizens' center. Talk to the director and the members of the center to see just what services will be available should you decide to move to the area. A dynamic and full-service senior center could make a world of difference in your everyday life.

When investigating a town, one of your first stops should be at the local chamber of commerce office. The level of enthusiasm and retirement advice offered by the chamber staff clearly tells you something about the community's attitude toward retirees. Most chamber offices love to see retirees; they recognize the advantages of retirement money coming into the economy and the valuable contributions retirees can make to the community. Their chambers of commerce will do just about anything to help you get settled and to convince you that living in their town is next to paradise. Sometimes, though, you may experience chamber staff who aren't the least bit interested in your upcoming move. When this is the case, you might guess that the level of services and senior citizen participation in local affairs is somewhat inadequate.

## Internet and Newspaper Research

Between periods of travel, do some research at the local library or by mail. Another excellent way of finding out about a community is by using the Internet. Almost every chamber of commerce now has a Web site, as do most towns. Often you'll find pages specially dedicated to retirement and relocation guidance. Real estate prices, recreation and entertainment attractions, and weather information can be found via links to those pages. Newspapers are often on-line, so you can get local news and a real flavor of town life. Almost all libraries have out-of-town newspapers. The larger the library, the greater the variety of papers. If you live in a small town where your library can't provide the newspapers you want (particularly those from another state or from smaller towns some distance away), write to the chamber of commerce for the area you are interested in and explain that you need a copy or two to make decisions about retiring there. You can also contact the newspaper itself (your librarian can help you track down the name of the paper). Some real estate brokers will gladly mail you copies of the local newspaper, hoping you will use their services when and if you decide to buy. We once had a real estate office send us a three-month subscription to the local paper to help us make up our minds.

The most important part of an out-of-town paper is the classified section. Check prices for land parcels, homes and condominiums, rentals, and mobile home parks; compare them with those listed in your hometown newspaper to get a picture of relative costs. Contrast help wanted ads with work wanted ads. This tells you wage rates, should you consider working part-time, and offers you clues on the kind of competition you will have for jobs. A scarcity of help wanted ads indicates unemployment.

This won't matter if you don't plan on working, but it's important if you need to work part-time.

Mobile home parks advertise monthly park rentals, giving you an idea of what that style of living costs. Should there be an undersupply of vacancies, you can expect rentals to be expensive. Comparing prices of used items such as furniture, appliances, and cars against your local paper's classifieds can tell you a great deal about local living costs.

Display advertisements provide supermarket and department store specials to compare, particularly if national chains operate both there and in your hometown. Sometimes identical specials will be priced differently from one locality to another, a further measure of costs. Ads will tell you whether large discount stores are available for shopping convenience and economy.

A newspaper's editorial page broadcasts the publisher's political stance. A paper that slants news stories to match its owner's opinions makes uncomfortable reading if you happen to be on the other side of the political fence. A publisher can profoundly influence the thinking of a community. When the newspaper is the only source of local news, the publisher's opinions are often accepted as clear truths by your neighbors. Being the only conservative in a neighborhood of liberals (or vice versa) can make you feel lonely. Particularly revealing are newspaper campaigns for or against services and spending for senior citizens.

You learn a lot about how safe a community is by the way crime is reported in the news columns. If a bicycle theft or a reckless-driving arrest makes front page headlines, rest assured, the crime situation isn't too serious—assuming, of course, you aren't a bicycle thief and don't occasionally drive your Buick on the sidewalk. But if chain saw murders, carjackings, and drive-by shootings are buried on page 27, look out!

A good newspaper will list senior citizens' activities, cultural events, community college classes, and other undertakings that might interest you. A paper with a large section devoted to senior citizens' news reflects a high level of interest in seniors' well-being. Look for news about retiree political action groups; when seniors band together to vote, the level of services and benefits rises in proportion to their voting strength.

Libraries also have out-of-town telephone books, full of valuable information. The yellow pages paint an unabridged picture of a town's business life: banks, supermarkets, shopping centers, and other commercial enterprises. Check for local and intercity bus service and taxi companies. Look under the listing for "airlines" or "airports" to see if there is a local airport and which airlines service it. See how many hospitals there are. A telephone book also gives an up-to-date listing for the chamber of commerce office and the senior citizens' center.

## Continuing Education

A growing trend in the country is the return of seniors to the classroom. Everywhere, community colleges, adult education centers, and universities are adding classes and programs expressly tailored to older adults' needs. More than two-thirds of U.S. colleges and universities offer reduced rates or even free tuition to older citizens. You won't feel like the proverbial sore thumb in a setting where you have company your own age.

But continuing education for retirees is more than a pleasant learning experience; the classroom is a tool for retirement adjustment. Signing up for a class in Chinese cooking, fly tying, or rock polishing puts you in contact with others from the community. An adult classroom is a great place to make friends with lively, stimulating people who share your interests. Taking classes is a surefire way of becoming part of your new community.

Most schools have loads of interesting, not-for-credit classes, and many allow you to audit the more serious courses—that is, take the class without the worry about quizzes, tests, finals, or term papers. You get the intellectual benefit and fun without having to do the homework or participate in class discussions.

If you have a trade or special skill of some sort, an even faster way of getting known is to offer to teach a class. Community colleges and adult education programs often can't afford to hire full-time teachers and therefore welcome the opportunity to add classes with part-time or volunteer teachers. If your skills are needed, schools often don't require a teaching degree, just experience and the ability to communicate it to others.

Once, when my wife and I moved to a small Oregon city, I taught a couple of community college classes in freelance writing. It wasn't for the money—which was almost nothing—but for the opportunity to meet townspeople with a common interest in writing. The class was a resounding success, and my wife and I made a half dozen friends and received an invitation to join a local writers' group. Our entrance into the town's social life was immediate and satisfying.

Even if you have no intention to take classes, a community college or university can be important to your lifestyle. Most schools provide the community at large with a wide selection of social and cultural activities. You don't have to be a registered student to attend advertised lectures and speeches given by famous scholars and scientists, politicians, visiting artists, and other well-known personalities. Concerts, ranging from Beethoven to boogie-woogie, are presented by guest artists as well as the university's music department. Dramas, comedies, and musicals are produced by the theater department, with season tickets often costing less than a single performance at a Broadway theater. Some schools make special provisions to allow seniors to use their recreational facilities, and art exhibits, panel discussions, and a well-stocked library are often available to the public.

## What to Look For

The following is a list of requirements that my wife and I consider essential for a successful retirement relocation. Your needs may be different; feel free to add or subtract from the list, then use it to measure communities against your standards.

- *Safety.* Can you walk through your neighborhood without glancing anxiously over your shoulder? Can you leave your home for a few weeks without dreading a break-in? Most retirees feel that safety is the most important condition of all in selecting a new home.
- *Climate.* Will temperatures and weather patterns match your lifestyle? Will you be tempted to go outdoors and exercise year-round, or will harsh winters and suffocating summers confine you to an easy chair in front of the television set?
- *Housing.* Is quality housing available at prices you're willing and able to pay? Is the area visually pleasing, free of pollution and traffic snarls? Will you feel proud to live in the neighborhood?
- *Nourishment for Your Interests.* Does your retirement choice offer facilities for your favorite pastimes, cultural events, and hobbies?
- *Social Compatibility.* Will you find common interests with your neighbors? Will you fit in and make friends easily? Will there be others from your own cultural, social, and political background?
- *Affordability.* Are goods and services reasonable? Can you afford to hire help from time to time when you need to? Will your income be significantly affected by state income taxes? Will taxes on your pension make a big difference?

- *Medical Care.* Are local physicians accepting new patients? Does the area have an adequate hospital? Do you have a medical problem that requires a specialist?

- *Distance from Family and Friends.* Are you going to be too far away from those you care for, or in a location where nobody wants to visit? If you would rather they wouldn't visit, you may do better moving even farther away.

- *Transportation.* Does your new location enjoy intercity bus transportation? Many small towns have none, which makes you totally dependent on a car or taxis. How far is the nearest airport with major airline connections? Can friends and family visit without driving?

- *Senior Services.* Are there senior citizens' centers and programs in the area? Do they offer dynamic opportunities for travel, volunteer work, and education? Are there continuing education programs at the local college or adult education classes at the local high school?

# ARIZONA

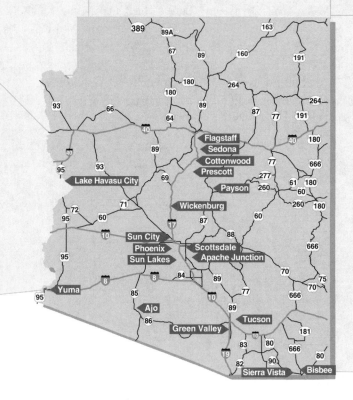

# ARIZONA

Arizona is the third most popular state in the nation for those seeking new horizons for their retirement. (Florida is first; California, second.) It's interesting to note that of all the states that send retirees to Arizona, California sends the most. You'll also find many retirees making a second relocation move, to Arizona from Florida, having tried Florida retirement first. In fact, so many retirees are choosing Arizona retirement that 25 percent of the state's residents are older than fifty-five. That's one out of four—most of them voters—so you can be sure senior citizens' issues garner a fair share of attention, from the local city council to the governor's office.

So, what's the big attraction? The answer is Arizona's pleasant weather and gorgeous scenery. Arizona's low property taxes and abundant cultural and recreational opportunities are frosting on the cake.

Arizona is a great place to play tourist whenever the mood strikes. There's no need to sit at home, not when Arizona has more national parks and monuments than any other state. You can also visit the state's innumerable golf and tennis resorts, Native American villages, natural scenic splendors, dude ranches, and desert and mountain playgrounds.

The nice thing about Arizona weather is that retirees have a wide range of climates from which to choose. That's one of the benefits of being retired: You no longer have to put up with the weather in your hometown. Whether you like it hot or cold, Arizona has the right weather for you.

Hot-weather fans (I happen to be one of them) can't do better than southern Arizona. If you like year-round summer, try Phoenix, Tucson, or Yuma. It's true that during July and August, afternoons can top one hundred degrees, but it's also true that December and January afternoons are always balmy, often seventy degrees or higher. No matter how hot it gets during the day, Arizona's dry air allows the heat to radiate rapidly so that the nights are usually cool. With more than 300 days of sunshine each year and almost no rain, you have loads of opportunities to get outdoors. And just think about it: no snow shovels, tire chains, rubber boots, or windshield scrapers!

Since most places you go will be air-conditioned, from the shopping mall to the racetrack grandstand, there's no need to suffer during the hottest part of the day. Most people hit golf balls or play tennis early in the morning and take their deserved naps in the afternoon. It's never too hot (or too cold) to get out in the evening for a brisk walk or enjoy the famous Arizona sunsets.

One reason many people choose to retire to Arizona's hot, dry areas is for health concerns. The arid climate seems to alleviate symptoms of chronic diseases such as arthritis and asthma. Some find they're able to cut down on medication; others eliminate taking drugs entirely.

Other people prefer cooler weather (as does my wife). They dislike air-conditioning and don't mind a little snow. Many find continuous summer boring; they adore the invigorating changes in seasons. The place for them is the Arizona mountains, any of a dozen cool locations where air-conditioning is optional or even absurd. Arizona's amazingly diverse topography offers residents a wide choice of climates, ranging from those found in the warmest regions of the Southwest to habitats similar to the coolest Rocky Mountain regions of Canada. When Flagstaff thermometers climb out of the seventies in the summertime, it's considered warm; on rare occasions when it tops ninety, it's a heat wave. In Phoenix or Yuma, on the other hand, a ninety-degree August day might indicate a cold front passing through. This book lists a number of Arizona mountain communities that feature four-season climates—without excessive snow—and pleasant summers.

Arizona receives very little rain because the high Pacific Coast mountains block moisture-laden clouds from the ocean. This is particularly true in the southern reaches of the state. Most rain clouds that reach the dryer sections of Arizona are blown up from the Gulf of Mexico in the summer months, and not very often at that. The mountain and northern parts of the state receive considerably more rain and snow, but compared to Eastern states or California, even the wettest parts of Arizona seem arid.

Despite scanty rainfall, the state has a fascinating variety of plant and animal life. Characteristic plants in the desert regions are cactus, mesquite, yucca, agave, creosote bush, and sagebrush. More than a hundred varieties of cactus are found in Arizona, ranging from the little prickly pears to the giant saguaro cactus that can tower 50 feet above the desert floor. Many plants remain dormant during the long dry spells only to burst forth in blossom at the first hardy rain shower.

Coyotes, mountain lions, antelope, deer, and wildcats range mountain and desert alike. The desert is the home of creatures such as rattlesnakes, scorpions, and the venomous gila monsters, whose bite is fatal to small animals, but who are so shy and sluggish that it's extremely rare to hear of one attacking a human. Higher altitudes are often covered with forests of pine, juniper, and ponderosa, great habitat for deer, raccoons, and other denizens of the woods. The best part about both desert and mountain landscapes is they're accessible to everyone. About 45 percent of Arizona's land is owned by the federal government. It isn't fenced, and you won't see any KEEP OUT signs. If you feel like strolling through government-owned deserts or forests, you can do so.

Much of the state's wealth lies in its mineral deposits. Rich mineral veins make Arizona one of the great copper-producing areas of the world. Arizona also ranks among the leading states in the production of gold, lead, and silver. Most of the uranium mined in the United States comes from the Colorado Plateau region. Unless the rules change, you are permitted to prospect on federal land and stake a claim if you hit it rich. The chances of your doing so are extremely small; you probably wouldn't recognize a valuable mineral if you stubbed your toe on it, and most land has already been prospected. Your chances of winning the lottery are better, but there's always that possibility, and it's a healthy way of getting outdoors.

## Arizona's "West Coast"

After the wild Colorado River exits the Grand Canyon, it heads south toward Mexico and the Gulf of California. Along the way, it is captured by a series of dams that provide peaceful lakes to contrast nicely with the wild desert hills and canyons that enclose the river. Over the years, the river's rush to the sea has carved fantastic sculptures from sandstone, making this one of the more scenic stretches of river highway in the West. Sand brought from the West's hinterlands, carried by rapid currents and deposited by lazy eddies over eons, has left sandy beaches along the length of the river. Residents like to refer to this ancient length of sandy riverbank as Arizona's "West Coast."

Along this stretch of waterway—from the Arizona town of Parker to the Nevada town of Laughlin—growing numbers of retirees and snowbirds settle in every winter. The numbers increase each year, with more and more buying homes and staying year-round. Nestled between the rugged Mohave and Chemehuevi Mountains, with wide open desert vistas, the shimmering waters of Lake Havasu reflect the nearby peaks. The

## Arizona Tax Profile

Sales tax:
5% to 7%; food and drugs exempt

State income tax:
graduated from 3.8% to 7% over $150,000

Property taxes:
from 0.8% to 1%

Intangibles tax:
none

Social Security tax:
none

Pension taxes:
private employer pensions fully taxed; government pensions receive $2,500
exemption; personal tax credits allowed

Gasoline tax:
18¢ per gallon

lake's 45 miles of fishing, boating, and water recreation bring vacationers back again and again. Naturally, their thoughts turn to this desert lake when time comes for retirement.

For years, commerce along the river consisted of basic services opening seasonally to supply anglers with bait and beer, but that was about all there was. Once development took off, however, there was no stopping it. Places like Lake Havasu have grown from small clusters of trailers and fishing shacks, with catfish and mallards as the major attractions, into small cities, with all the facilities needed for comfortable retirement. This is one of the fastest-growing areas of its kind in the country.

# History

The first settlers here were Native Americans who erected some rather sophisticated, multistory buildings. The settlement at Oraibi dates from A.D. 1200, making it one of the oldest Native American communities in what is now the continental United States. The first Europeans came in 1528, when Cabeza de Vaca, who was shipwrecked off the coast of the Gulf of Mexico, meandered through what is now Arizona on his way back to Mexico. His stories about golden cities sparked the interest of the Spanish conquistadores, who mounted an expedition into the territory in 1539.

The Spanish explorers wasted no time in settling the area, doing some farming and lots of mining. They discovered silver in what is now Arizona and New Mexico and several valuable copper deposits that are still mined to this day. In 1821, when Mexico won independence from Spain, Arizona became part of the New Mexico Territory and permitted American traders to enter the region. When war with the United States broke out in 1846, the Mormon Battalion captured Tucson, and the territory became part of the United States.

Until the late 1800s, when Arizona's mining and agriculture became significant to its new owners, immigrants were mainly interested in finding ways to cross Arizona and get to California without losing their scalps to Apache war parties. The returning 49ers, now armed with a knowledge of mining, began locating valuable gold and silver deposits and rediscovering mines worked by the Spanish two centuries earlier. Tales of the fabulous wealth to be found were spread by wagon drivers who had crossed the region, bringing many of the first settlers. The wagon and stagecoach routes used by the Arizona pioneers later became the network over which the modern state highway system was developed.

# Phoenix

Let's start our investigation of Arizona with the most popular area in the state for retirees: Phoenix.

Located in the appropriately named Valley of the Sun, Phoenix is Arizona's largest city as well as the state's capital. It sprawls over miles of desert terrain, covering a variety of neighborhoods that cater to all budgets and lifestyles. The metropolitan area encompasses more than twenty other smaller cities. The size of this area alone allows for a number of possible retirement choices.

Retirees who relocate here usually do so because of the more than 300 days of sunshine they can count on each year. Rarely will they get rained out at one of the area's more than 130 golf courses. All types of outdoor recreation are available year-round in the Phoenix area. You'll find tennis courts in almost every neighborhood, miles of hiking trails, and access to some of the country's best spectator sporting events. It never gets too warm for outdoor fun, because you can always get out in the morning or evening, then stay indoors, in air-conditioned comfort, during the afternoon.

Phoenix is named for the bird of myth that rises from the ashes of its destruction, and appropriately so, because European settlers in the 1860s founded the city on the ruins of an ancient Native American settlement. The newcomers restored the sophisticated irrigation systems left by the mysterious Hohokam tribe, who had abandoned them four centuries earlier. Within the city limits today you can visit an archaeological dig at Pueblo Grande, the site of a Hohokam village that was deserted about 1450. A few miles southeast are the ruins of Casa Grande, a four-story housing complex built of layers of caliche mud. This, too, was abandoned in the mid-1400s for reasons that remain unclear to this day.

Some say the image of a bird rising from the ashes of a fire is also an appropriate description of Phoenix in the summertime. In July and August, temperatures can match those of the glowing ashes of a medium-size bonfire. It makes you wonder how people survived the intense heat before the days of air-conditioning. It's easy to say that folks get used to heat, and they do to a certain extent in a dry climate, but when the thermometer hits 115, as it sometimes does here, that's more than just heat. Best stay inside and keep the air conditioner going. But with relative humidity in July and August at only 20 percent, and with air-conditioned homes, cars, and shopping centers, there's no need to be uncomfortable in Phoenix.

## Recreation and Culture

One benefit of living in or near a major metropolitan area like Phoenix is the variety of cultural, recreational, and social opportunities available to residents. Professional sports fans are in heaven here, with the NFL Cardinals playing big-league football at Sun Devil Stadium, the Phoenix Roadrunners of the International Hockey League duking it out at Memorial Coliseum, and the NBA Phoenix Suns playing at America West Arena. A recent addition is the National League Arizona Diamondbacks, with their new Banc One Park in downtown Phoenix. Spring baseball training camps host the Oakland Athletics, the Chicago Cubs, the Milwaukee Brewers, the California Angels, and the San Francisco Giants. Local fans get a chance to enjoy exhibition games well in advance of the regular season.

## Making a Choice

Because of Phoenix's size, it's difficult to generalize or choose only a few neighborhoods that invite retirement living. Because retirement is such a big deal here, you not only have hundreds of neighborhoods, but also small towns in all directions, any of which may suit your particular lifestyle. It's up to you to investigate.

Every imaginable lifestyle is available to retirees here. Some people prefer elegant "gated" communities, where every facet of their social and recreational needs is met by professional social directors. Usually these developments restrict residents to fifty years of age or older and provide snazzy recreation centers and country club facilities. Other retirees prefer open, multigenerational neighborhoods where they can make their own friends and choose their own recreational activities. Satisfactory retirement neighborhoods come in all flavors and price ranges, from expensive to moderate to downright cheap. Mobile home living is popular here and covers everything from luxurious, golf course developments with clubhouses to incredibly inexpensive parks where you can purchase an older, 8-foot-wide unit for less than $2,000. You may not love the neighborhood, however.

Therefore, if Phoenix weather and amenities are what you're looking for, you'll have to do a lot of investigating on your own. It would take an entire book to evaluate every neighborhood. Rent a car, if you didn't bring one with you, and spend a few days looking around. You have lots of choices.

To give you some clues, first consider a couple of traditional, well-organized, seniors-only retirement communities in the Phoenix area: Sun City and Sun Lakes. Then look at two open, multigenerational communities: Scottsdale on the high end of the scale and Apache Junction on the economical end. When you visit, don't confine your investigation to just these communities. Take your time and make sure you're making the correct decision.

## Phoenix Area Weather

| | In degrees Fahrenheit | | | | | |
| --- | --- | --- | --- | --- | --- | --- |
| | Jan. | April | July | Oct. | Rain | Snow |
| DAILY HIGHS | 67 | 84 | 105 | 88 | 7" | — |
| DAILY LOWS | 38 | 52 | 78 | 57 | | |

## Phoenix Area Cost of Living

| (percentage of national average) | | | | |
|---|---|---|---|---|
| Overall | Housing | Medical | Groceries | Utilities |
| 103% | 101% | 114% | 104% | 103% |

# Two Sun Cities

In 1960, on New Year's Day, a new concept in retirement made a dramatic appearance in the Arizona desert. The Del Webb Corporation unveiled its first retirement-oriented model homes in a newly created community called Sun City. One of the first retirement developments, a large-scale, self-contained city restricted to mature residents, Sun City promised "an active way of life" for retirees. Before a single home was put on the market, a shopping center, golf course, and recreational facilities were in place. The shopping center provided space for a supermarket, variety store, laundromat, barber shop, drug store, and service station. These facilities were essential, for at that time Sun City sat way out in the desert, a long way from the city. (Today, it's been swallowed up by Phoenix's expanding metro area.)

Del Webb officials expected as many as 10,000 curious visitors that first day. To their surprise, 100,000 showed up. Immediately, 237 homes were snapped up by the public, and by the end of the year sales reached 1,250. Prices were as low as $8,000, but it wasn't price alone that sold the buyers. They bought the concept of Sun City's invigorating lifestyle, with year-round golfing, shuffleboard, dance clubs, socializing, and volunteerism. By the time all 8,900 acres had been developed and sold, Sun City's population had reached 46,000.

Sun City's seven recreation centers and eleven golf courses are owned and operated by residents who pay a yearly membership. A few other amenities at Sun City are a forty-acre recreation center, the 7,169-seat Sundome Center, a library, seven medical complexes, restaurants, banks, and many other business conveniences.

Developers around the nation monitored Sun City's rapid growth and soon began jumping on the bandwagon. Today, you'll find 2,400 adult retirement communities around the nation. More Sun City developments in the Southwest are under way in Tucson; Las Vegas; Hilton Head, South Carolina; and Georgetown, Texas. This concept of over-fifty, organized communities changed the way many people view retirement.

Riding the wave of success, the Del Webb Corporation purchased another 7,100 acres a few miles west of Sun City and named it Sun City West. The community quickly sold out, with more than 30,000 residents enjoying the benefits of four multimillion-dollar recreation centers, nine eighteen-hole golf courses, a 203-bed hospital, and a 7,169-seat performing arts center.

Not everyone will enjoy the homogeneity of planned retirement; some prefer a multigenerational neighborhood. But obviously, many others like the idea of having neighbors and friends of their own age who share the same values and worldviews. When they want to play golf, their neighbors aren't busy working, hosting a Cub Scout meeting, or playing baseball with the kids.

An added benefit is not having hordes of teenagers roaming the streets on skateboards or speeding through on motorcycles or hot rods. (Relatives younger than age nineteen are only permitted to visit here. We're told this has cut teenage vandalism and crime to almost nothing.) Without a population of children, property tax dollars instead go toward community upkeep and improvements, rather than to support schools.

This prearranged lifestyle particularly suits those moving from another area, who have no acquaintances here and who don't want to invest a lot of time trying to make friends and develop recreational interests. It's all right here in one package. For some people, not having youngsters around is a drawback, but others find it a blessing. "If I want to hear the pitter-patter of little feet," said one lady, "I'll put shoes on my cat."

## Recreation and Culture

In addition to the marvelous activities always going on next door in Phoenix, Sun City residents participate in more than 250 community, service, and social organizations. The Sundome Center for the Performing Arts is the country's largest single-level theater and presents some spectacular entertainment, ranging from one-man shows by Kenny Rogers to concerts by a ninety-five–piece symphony orchestra.

Arizona State University offers noncredit enrichment courses in Sun City and credit courses at ASU West. Rio Salado Community College offers special-interest classes at various convenient locations.

## Real Estate

One reason homes in the original Sun City sold so quickly is they were priced right. Starting at $8,000, the more expensive ones topped out at about $15,000. As development continued, a need for more features and more square footage pushed prices a bit higher. When the supply of homes dried up and development started at Sun City West, buyers moved in that direction.

This made homes in the original Sun City a great buy, especially for those with low budgets. Perfectly nice two-bedroom homes on no-maintenance lots sell for as little as $40,000. Townhouses go for even less. In fact, 90 percent of the old Sun City homes are priced in the $50,000 to $130,000 range. Buy one, and you are part of the community, with access to all facilities.

Sun City West offers a higher-quality home, and prices follow the quality, as you might expect. Low-end, two-bedroom townhouses start at about $70,000, with luxurious four-bedroom homes going for more than $250,000.

Sun City Grand is the newest development and is the fastest-growing of all Del Webb properties. On 4,000 acres, 1,000 homes a year are selling from the low $100,000s to the mid-$200,000s. An eighteen-hole champion golf course was added in 1997 and still another in January 2000.

After just one tour through the model homes, one feels tempted to buy immediately. The architecture is bold and imaginative (to match the payments); the furniture is top quality and luxurious. A word of caution: It's terribly easy to stand in the middle of one of these well-lighted and professionally furnished places and imagine how happy you might feel living there. Try to picture how the place will look furnished with your pink sofa (the one with the stained cushions), that comfortable but threadbare recliner, and that wooden floor lamp that was a wedding present from your sister-in-law. If the place still feels like your dream home, then buy it.

## When Grandkids Visit

Take them to see one of the big-league sports teams. Just about any time of the year, you'll find football, baseball, basketball, and hockey games going on. Several major league baseball teams hold spring training camps here, with numerous regularly scheduled exhibition games for the public. Indianapolis race cars thrill crowds here, as well as stock car racing, and even dragboat racing.

## Addresses and Connections

*Chamber of Commerce:* 12425 West Bell Road, Suite C305, Surprise, AZ 85372

*Newspapers: Sun City Daily News,* 10102 Santa Fe Drive, Sun City, AZ 85372; *Phoenix Arizona Republic,* 120 East Van Buren Street, P.O. Box 2243, Phoenix, AZ 85004

*Airport:* Phoenix Sky Harbor, a half hour away
*Bus/Train:* Greyhound and Amtrak serve the vicinity

# Sun Lakes

South of Phoenix is another example of a planned retirement development, but with a more expensive, luxurious tone. In several respects, this is the Scottsdale of seniors-only communities. It comes as no accident that Sun Lakes bears more than a passing resemblance to its counterparts west of Phoenix. Why? Because this miniature Sun City was founded by Ed Robson, who got his start in construction working for Del Webb. He scouted a location about 23 miles south of downtown Phoenix and started off with mobile homes in 1972. Soon he realized that he could construct a quality home for little more than the cost of a double-wide mobile, so he switched to luxury homes. The result is today's community of 12,000 residents, divided into four country club neighborhoods, each with its own golf course and clubhouse. Although golf is Sun Lakes's central theme, residents enjoy a multitude of other activities such as tennis, swimming, fitness, and arts and crafts. Nine conveniently located courts make tennis the second most popular outdoor recreation.

Sun Lakes is out in the country, with a quiet atmosphere similar to that which must have characterized Sun City when it began years ago. However, the way Phoenix is growing, it's just a matter of time before the megalopolis swallows Sun Lakes as well. This is a place for those who want country club living and who will make use of the facilities. An impressive number of shopping facilities make it unnecessary to travel to Phoenix, not even for major purchases. But when you want to go to the big city, Interstate 10 access is just 2 miles away. The fact that Phoenix is nearby and is an easy drive over the interstate is one of the features about Sun Lakes that many retirees most admire. "It's a straight shot up the interstate to the airport," said one man, "so it's no problem when our children visit."

The crime rate here is said to be exceptionally low; several residents maintain that this is one of the safest places they've ever lived. For those who want to be extra safe, two of the four Sun Lakes neighborhoods are gated. Only those with legitimate business are allowed in.

## Recreation and Culture

Golf is why many people retire to Sun Lakes, and that's why they buy homesites on the course. For them, there is no other sport. However, one of the nice things about being so close to Phoenix is that you can participate in any or all events available to Phoenix residents.

For continuing education, Chandler Community College is just a hop, skip, and a jump away. Arizona State University is also conveniently reached by freeways.

## Real Estate

The cost of living is about the same as Phoenix; however, housing costs are considerably higher. The homes here emphasize luxury and quality, and the result is higher home prices than many locations. New homes currently cost between $130,000 and $300,000. In many ways, Sun Lakes resembles the much larger Sun City complexes north of Phoenix, but prices are much higher, with prices starting at $130,000 as opposed to Sun City West's $95,000. Resales of conventional homes range from $80,000 to $350,000, and mobile home resales start at about $60,000.

## When Grandkids Visit

If you're ready to retire, you are old enough to have clear memories of World War II, so take the grandkids to the Champlin Fighter Museum and the Confederate Air Force. The Champlin Museum features fighter planes from both world wars; the Confederate Air Force specializes in keeping WWII planes in flying order, with bombers being the specialty. The kids can climb up into a genuine B-17, past machine guns and ammunition belts, and into the bomb bay.

## Addresses and Connections

*Chamber of Commerce/Senior Center:* Sun Lakes Homeowners Association, inside each development

*Newspaper: Sun Lakes Splash,* 9532 East Riggs Road, Sun Lakes, AZ 85248

*Airport:* twenty minutes to Phoenix Sky Harbor Airport

*Bus:* no local bus; private shuttle company to Phoenix airport

# Scottsdale

In Arizona, Scottsdale is synonymous with high-class, luxurious, expensive. This gilt-edged city of 135,000 on Phoenix's eastern limits is to Arizona what Palm Springs or Beverly Hills is to California. As such, it has become a retirement haven for those who don't mind paying more in return for sophistication, Saks Fifth Avenue–style shopping, and gourmet restaurants galore. Obviously, a lot of well-heeled retirees fall into this category, because 90 percent of Scottsdale's population is older than fifty years of age. Billing itself as "Arizona's Playground," the city is also proud of its vast recreational opportunities.

The accent on retirement here is away from Sun City–style, closed, seniors-only communities. Instead, Scottsdale retirees choose neighborhoods in which they blend with residents of mixed ages, similar to the settings they left in their hometowns. This gives Scottsdale a different look, a distinct residential countenance that avoids mile after mile of similar dwellings. Most homes are custom built or are constructed in small enough numbers to look stylistically different from one another.

Scottsdale has some of the most elegant and opulent shopping districts and residential neighborhoods we've encountered anywhere in the country. Majestically landscaped boulevards are lined with so many fabulous, prestige-name stores that your credit card vibrates as you drive past. Sumptuous residential neighborhoods display homes so elegant and palatial that you'll hate yourself for not being able to afford one. Scottsdale may have a poor neighborhood, but we've never stumbled across it. Well, we did find one "ghetto" area where people drove Buicks instead of BMWs.

An additional boost to Scottsdale's reputation as a place to retire comes from the FBI's crime report, which ranks the city in the upper 25 percent for personal safety. This is the best score of any of the Arizona towns reviewed in this book.

Lest you write off Scottsdale as a place for only the ultra-rich and snobbish, let's take a look at some surprising statistics. First, Scottsdale's cost of living is only slightly above Phoenix's and is not far above the national average. While real estate prices are higher than most other Phoenix locations, median sales prices in Scottsdale are still below Sedona and Prescott markets and, in fact, are below many of the more mundane Southwestern locations covered in this book. This lower median sales price doesn't mean that homes in Scottsdale are cheaper than in Prescott; it just means that Scottsdale has a much larger inventory of homes in less-expensive ranges. When many more homes in the $100,000 to $130,000 range sell than in the $500,000-plus class, the median sales price drops.

## The West's Most Western Town

In addition to its spiffy, upscale reputation, Scottsdale cultivates yet another image by calling itself "The West's Most Western Town." This concept manifests itself in the original town center that used to be an elegant shopping district before the name-brand stores moved to more opulent quarters on Scottsdale or Camelback Roads. Today, this older area affects Western storefronts that house upscale bars and restaurants or sell expensive Western-style clothing and souvenirs. Every January the city celebrates this heritage with thirty days of parades, street dances, and the inevitable hokey staged shoot-outs on Main Street. Local residents seem to take this Old West theme to heart; you'll see more ex–New Yorkers wearing wide Stetsons, snakeskin boots, and expensive Western shirts than any place this side of Las Vegas.

But Scottsdale isn't all glitz and rodeos. It's one of the Southwest's leading art centers, with 120 galleries displaying works of local and international artists. Once the shoot-out on Main Street ends, the Scottsdale Celebration of Fine Arts takes over until April, with exhibits of oil, watercolor, and pastel paintings; sculpture; jewelry; and ceramics, all by local artisans.

## Cave Creek and Carefree

On Scottsdale's northeastern edge, the communities of Cave Creek and Carefree epitomize tasteful desert-living lifestyles. The area is in the foothills, sitting above Scottsdale and Phoenix. The extra altitude makes an enormous difference in the temperature as well as the scenery. Most homes are on large lots that are beautifully landscaped with natural desert plants. Large cacti of all descriptions, flowering desert trees, and gnarled shrubbery surround well-tended homes. Mountains loom in the background, and the air is pristine. This is one of our favorite retirement locations; we highly recommend it for those who can afford it.

Prices are as high as the quality, with most homes selling from $250,000. Shopping and commercial establishments are also upscale, with excellent restaurants and boutiques drawing patronage from Phoenix and Scottsdale. Two excellent golf clubs are center points for duffers.

## Recreation and Culture

If the Phoenix area sounds like a golfer's paradise, with 130 golf courses, consider that twenty of these courses are in Scottsdale, and several new layouts are under construction. Fourteen golf courses are public, including the Tournament Players Club of Scottsdale (permanent home of the PGA Phoenix Open and the Senior PGA Golf Tournament). Nineteen driving ranges await to help keep your swing in shape. Tennis buffs will find fifty public courts at numerous city parks, with lessons given at Indian School and Scottsdale Ranch Parks.

When you live in Scottsdale, you'll want to take full advantage of the mountain views and pristine environment by getting outdoors as often as possible. Scottsdale maintains a green belt with nearly 40 miles of city-maintained, multiuse paths. Residents regularly use them for biking, jogging, hiking, strolling, or, in some cases, limping. There are also 200 miles of unpaved recreational trails for hiking and horseback riding.

The city's park system offers a variety of facilities that appeal to folks of retirement age, such as full-size swimming pools, exercise rooms, and dance studios. Daily admission to swimming pools is $1.00 for adults. Programs include swimming lessons, diving instruction, and synchronized swimming teams.

Scottsdale and surrounding communities offer many adult lifelong learning programs, with interesting classes in just about anything you might imagine. The Scottsdale Community College offers an Elderhostel program as well as a great continuing education program. Those older than sixty-two get a 50 percent discount for certain courses.

Senior citizens are invited to join the Older Adult Service and Information System (OASIS), in which adult volunteers are trained to enhance the reading, writing, and communication skills of grade-school students.

With the University of Arizona located next door in Tempe, Scottsdale is exposed to the cultural influences of a large school. It has its own symphony orchestra, which performs at the Scottsdale Center for the Arts. The center also offers theatrical productions, concerts, and other cultural events.

## Real Estate

Scottsdale spreads out over 185 square miles, with hundreds of distinct neighborhoods. It's impossible to characterize all of them. Suffice it to say that just about anywhere you might wish to live will be in quality surroundings, although some areas will be more polished than others. Deliberately or accidentally, Scottsdale has managed to keep neighborhoods tasteful, with Southwestern or Mediterranean architecture, and for the most part has avoided the tract-house look that plagues many fast-growing communities.

We were surprised to find a few homes offered in acceptable neighborhoods for around $100,000. Average three-bedroom homes in average neighborhoods were offered at $114,000 to $159,000. The average sales price is about $130,000, which shows there is a large market of lower priced homes. Older condos and townhouses can be found for $65,000 and up.

## Medical Care

With such a high percentage of the population of Scottsdale near or older than retirement age, health care servers have responded by providing some of the best facilities in the region. In addition to three excellent hospitals, this is the home of the $50 million Mayo Clinic. Numerous other medical establishments are scattered around the Phoenix area. Scottsdale has more than 600 doctors, about 150 dentists, and more than 20 nursing homes.

## When Grandkids Visit

Try a picnic at the McCormick Railroad Park on East Indian Bend Road. In addition to a mile-long train ride, you'll enjoy seeing old railroad cars, a turn-of-the-twentieth-century locomotive, and two restored train depots. When the kids get tired of trains, they can ride an old-fashioned merry-go-round.

## Addresses and Connections

*Chamber of Commerce:* 7343 Scottsdale Mall, Scottsdale, AZ 85251

*Senior Services:* Scottsdale Senior Center, 10440 East Via Linda, Scottsdale, AZ 85258

*Newspaper: Scottsdale Progress Tribune,* 7525 East Camelback, Scottsdale, AZ 85251

*Airport:* Phoenix Sky Harbor International is practically next door

*Bus/Train:* Scottsdale is served by its own city buses and Phoenix bus service, as well as Greyhound and Amtrak; complimentary Dial-a-Ride is available for the elderly or disabled

## Scottsdale Area Cost of Living

| (percentage of national average) | | | | |
|---|---|---|---|---|
| Overall | Housing | Medical | Groceries | Utilities |
| **110%** | **118%** | **115%** | **112%** | **105%** |

# Apache Junction

Not far from Scottsdale is the more reasonably priced Apache Junction. It doesn't have the charisma or charm of Scottsdale (few places do), but it also doesn't have the price tag. One of Phoenix's many commuter bedroom communities, Apache Junction is fast acquiring another reputation, that of a popular retirement destination for both permanent and temporary residents. Retirees from the Midwest and East are ending their retirement search when they discover Apache Junction's laid-back attitude and the area's year-round summer. Over the last few years, the permanent population has doubled, almost to 20,000. Most of this increase can be attributed to retirees.

Only a half-hour drive via the fast-moving Superstition Freeway from downtown Phoenix and Sky Harbor Airport, the town can almost claim rural status due to its position on the border between city and desert. In the distance, the Superstition Mountains rise above the desert floor, presenting a mysterious, fortresslike appearance. Once the stronghold of fierce Apache warriors, these mountains also are the source of the most famous "lost gold mine" story of all times. The Lost Dutchman's Mine has drawn adventurers for a century, searching and exploring the canyons and cliffs of the Superstitions in hopes of finding the treasure. According to legend, at least eight men have died mysteriously in their quest for the Lost Dutchman. But don't let this discourage you; by all means, have a look. (By the way, the mine was lost, not the Dutchman.) Every February, the Lost Dutchman Days festival is celebrated with concerts, a rodeo, a parade, and a carnival.

Apache Junction sits on the western end of the famous Apache Trail, which is also known by the mundane name of Highway 88. This 78-mile stretch of winding, scenic road follows the ancient trail used by Apaches to traverse the canyons of the Salt River to present-day Roosevelt Lake. This road is a slow but interesting route to the lake. About 25 miles of the road is gravel, with occasional steep dropoffs at the road's edge, and it can be impassable in wet weather.

## Snowbird Heaven

The town of Apache Junction has long been a favorite with RV enthusiasts and snowbirds who travel to Arizona each winter. They enjoy it here because the town welcomes them (and their money) so warmly and because the city of Phoenix is easy to visit. More than forty mobile home and RV parks accommodate some of these visitors. Their number approaches 35,000 for the season. The main complaint we hear from full-time residents is that many businesses cater to snowbirds and close their doors for the summer season. Fortunately, other communities and Phoenix itself have any type of business connections you might need without regard to season.

Regular retirees, looking for a permanent place to live, are also moving here, finding that year-round residence is easier than traveling back and forth with the change of seasons. In addition to a warm welcome, retirees find some of the best real estate buys in the state here. A variety of lifestyles are available in Apache Junction: living on rural acreage, quiet single-family neighborhoods, mobile home living, and over-fifty-five-only retirement complexes. The town ranks in the top 25 percent of safe places as reported by FBI statistics.

## Recreation and Culture

In addition to the many golf courses available in the Phoenix area, seven more golf courses are within a short drive of Apache Junction. Since I'm not a golfer, I must admit that something puzzles me—some of the courses listed specifically mention grass. Maybe I'm wrong, but this leads me to believe that some Arizona courses are mostly sand.

Fishing enthusiasts can travel to several lakes within a 16- to 30-mile range of Apache Junction, and the Tonto National Forest lies due north, with trout streams, game-filled woods, and endless hiking trails and campgrounds.

For hardy adventurers with tough bottoms, Central Arizona College offers a five-day horseback trek into the Superstition Wilderness. The school also is host to Elderhostel programs for people older than fifty-five, with courses in liberal arts and sciences.

## Real Estate

Most homes in Apache Junction range from $60,000 to $100,000, with excellent value for the dollar. Mobile homes are plentiful and reasonably priced. The higher the elevation in the foothills, the more expensive the property. Homes with acreage, nice views, and stables for horses routinely top $200,000, still bargain priced when compared to similar properties around Scottsdale. The more expensive places are found at or near the "fence line"—that is, as close to the Tonto National Forest as possible, for you can't build on that land. Local people claim that just this small difference in elevation causes an amazing drop in temperature. It's still hot in the middle of a July or August day, but not as hot as the valley floor.

## Medical Care

Valley Lutheran Hospital is just 6 miles west of Apache Junction, and numerous other hospitals are available in the Tempe, Mesa, and Phoenix metropolitan area. Scottsdale's Mayo Clinic is less than 20 miles away.

## When Grandkids Visit

Take them to the Goldfield Ghost Town, about 3½ miles outside Apache Junction. The place features fake gun battles and tours through an old mine. At one time the town boasted three saloons. Today there's still one saloon open, where you can duck inside to down a stiff one while the kiddies watch fake gunmen shoot it out in the street with those god-awful loud blank cartridges. You might want to have more than one drink at this point.

## Addresses and Connections

*Chamber of Commerce:* 1001 North Idaho Road, Apache Junction, AZ 85217

*Senior Center:* 1177 North Idaho Road, Apache Junction, AZ 85219

*Newspaper: Apache Junction Daily Bulletin,* 860 South Saguaro Drive, Apache Junction, AZ 85220

*Airport:* Phoenix Airport is about twenty minutes away

*Bus:* Greyhound connects with Phoenix

# Flagstaff

This northern Arizona city sits near the base of the San Francisco Peaks, which rise to 12,670 feet in the distance. The mountains provide a breathtaking backdrop for Flagstaff and its 61,000 inhabitants. This is an excellent example of Arizona's diversity in climate and outdoor activities. Only two and a half hours north of Phoenix—"where summer stays all year round"—Flagstaff is proud of its four distinct seasons. One of these seasons is definitely winter. The 7,000-foot altitude here guarantees full mountain winters, with copious snow—as much as 20 inches in some months and more than 100 inches for the year. To some folks, snow is an attraction; for others, a pain in the neck. This is one Arizona location where you want to keep your snow shovel handy.

Summers are delightful, with temperatures seldom topping ninety degrees, while Phoenix cooks at more than one hundred degrees. Summer evenings are always cool (air-conditioning is not needed here), and you'll sleep under blankets every night. A profusion of spring wildflowers makes hiking trails delightful, and fall is punctuated by aspens displaying brilliant yellows to complement the reds and purples of deciduous trees and the deep green of the evergreens.

Flagstaff is small enough to avoid being a metropolis, yet large enough to supply all the shops, restaurants, churches, and service organizations you'd ever need. A large mall offers sixty-five indoor shops with chain department stores such as Sears and J. C. Penney. The city received its name from a large flagstaff that was erected for a Fourth of July celebration back in the 1870s, and the downtown shopping area capitalizes on this with an old-town motif. Quaint shops, galleries, and bistros are the order of the day here.

## Recreation and Culture

Outdoor enthusiasts will find fishing and hunting opportunities without equal. Fishing in nearby streams and several recreational lakes yields great catches. For hunters the area is excellent, with annual hunts for deer and elk. Just 136 miles north is Lake Powell, with its long shoreline. Flagstaff has numerous golf courses—one public, several private—and dozens of tennis courts for spring, summer, and fall recreation. Horse racing is popular in the summer, as are dog sled races in the winter. A 15,000-seat indoor multipurpose dome hosts Division IAA Big Sky varsity football games as well as other sporting events. Skiing is 15 miles away at the Snow Bowl on San Francisco Peaks. Cross-country skiing is also available closer to town.

Northern Arizona University, a well-regarded institution, hosts numerous fine-arts presentations. From theatrical productions to museums, the university makes Flagstaff one of the cultural centers of the Southwest. Coconino Community College, just a few years old, enhances continuing education in Flagstaff. Joining the schools in filling a culture and arts schedule is summer's Festival of Arts, which includes concerts, theater productions, film showings, and visual-arts offerings. The Festival in the Pines features superb arts and crafts that are for sale. The Flagstaff Symphony hosts several fine performances from October through April. And Flagstaff's Winter Festival stages events from competitive skiing and skating to dog sled races.

## Real Estate

A variety of homes are available here for both rental and sale. Although housing costs are almost 28 percent above the national average, all price ranges, tastes, and budgets are accommodated, from log cabins in the pines to luxury homes on the golf course. Utility costs are low, bringing the overall cost of living down to about 7 percent above average. Curiously, average selling prices for real estate are higher here than I would expect. The median sales price is about $145,000, which could mean that a larger-than-average number of high-ticket homes are selling. Some of the less expensive areas are the Grandview and Bow and Arrows subdivisions, where homes sell in the $70,000 to $100,000 range. You'll also find expensive locations such as Lakeside Acres, where homes range from $220,000 to more than $1 million. Apartment rentals average $630 a month.

## Medical Care

Because of its position as the largest town in the area, Flagstaff has developed a strong base of medical facilities and health professionals. A 126-bed hospital offers most medical specialties, everything from neurosurgery to plastic surgery. A cancer center is equipped with the latest technology. Two air shuttles and a fleet of ground ambulances bring emergency cases within a 130-mile radius of Flagstaff to the hospital.

## When Grandkids Visit

A trip to the Grand Canyon might be in order. It's about an hour and forty-five minutes away, but several tour companies will take you by bus if you prefer not to drive. Tours include visits to early-day and contemporary Native American cultural sites. In town, the Coconino Center for the Arts offers ever-changing exhibits, including the Festival of Native American Arts. A third possibility, for summer, is the ski lift at Snow Bowl. It features a 6,450-foot-long chairlift that climbs to a panoramic vista at 11,500 feet. Residents say you can see the Grand Canyon from the top.

## Addresses and Connections

*Chamber of Commerce:* 101 West Route 66, Flagstaff, AZ 86001
*Adult Center:* 245 West Thorpe Road, Flagstaff, AZ 86001
*Newspaper: Arizona Daily Sun,* P.O. Box 1849, Flagstaff, AZ 86002
*Airport:* Pulliam Airport, with daily commuter flights to Phoenix
*Bus:* both a city bus and Greyhound serve the area

## Flagstaff Area Weather

|  | In degrees Fahrenheit | | | | | |
|---|---|---|---|---|---|---|
|  | Jan. | April | July | Oct. | Rain | Snow |
| DAILY HIGHS | 42 | 58 | 82 | 64 | 22" | 108" |
| DAILY LOWS | 15 | 26 | 51 | 31 | | |

## Flagstaff Area Cost of Living

| (percentage of national average) | | | | |
|---|---|---|---|---|
| Overall | Housing | Medical | Groceries | Utilities |
| 112% | 128% | 113% | 112% | 109% |

# Prescott

The picturesque city of Prescott, often compared with Sedona as a premier Arizona retirement location, consistently receives glowing recommendations from guidebook writers. Indeed, Prescott does compare well with Sedona, yielding all the desired features for gracious retirement plus a gorgeous mountain setting.

Surrounded by a majestic backdrop of foothills and a ponderosa pine forest, the city is characterized by tastefully designed homes that cling to gentle slopes on large, tree-covered lots. Its ambience permits the region to stand head and shoulders above most other Southwestern mountain locations. Away from downtown, homesites are architecturally designed to take advantage of the forest and mountain settings. Close to the center, Prescott is mature, one of Arizona's oldest communities, with many turn-of-the-twentieth-century homes.

Residents are proud of Prescott's image of small-town America, with its conservative architecture, proud Victorian homes, and more than 450 buildings listed on the National Register of Historic Places. The town was founded in 1863 after gold was discovered in the headwaters of the

Hassayampa River. The following year it was already large enough to be named the capital of the Arizona Territory.

Self-proclaimed "Everybody's Home Town," Prescott does indeed have a hometown feeling, even though its business district indicates a small city rather than a small town. With a population of 38,000 (120,000 in the immediate area), it's anything but smallish. Prescott's downtown area centers on an old-fashioned square, complete with a traditional courthouse and bronze statues. The parklike setting seems to invite residents to gather during numerous community celebrations and ceremonies. It's a place where you can park your car and walk to shops and restaurants instead of driving to each destination. (Residents don't worry too much about crime here, since Prescott ranks in the upper 30 percent of the FBI's crime safety charts.) One side of the square faces a heritage of the early mining-town days, "Whiskey Row," once a block-long string of saloons, gambling palaces, and places of lesser fame, today a charming collection of antiques shops, fine restaurants, and boutiques. The chamber of commerce is also located on the square, and its staff is unusually helpful to potential retirees.

Prescott is surrounded by jagged peaks, often snow-covered, and a forest of ponderosa pines (reputedly the largest tract in the world) overlooks the city. Not only does Prescott's movie-set panorama rival Sedona's, but residents claim the weather is better here and that the four seasons are more sharply delineated. The elevation averages about 5,400 feet, which means cooler summers than in most of Arizona, with daily highs rarely climbing out of the eighties, then dropping into the sixties every evening. On the other hand, winters are colder, with several good snowfalls each year. Winter lows are in the twenties at night, but it almost always warms into the fifties by noon.

Our last visit to Prescott was in January, two days after a 3-inch snow. The sky was brilliant, and most of the snow was gone after two sixty-degree afternoons, although it still looked pretty on the ground and clinging to the needles of the gracious ponderosa pines.

## Recreation and Culture

Prescott's activity calendar has something going on every month of the year, from art shows and horse racing to music festivals and a Cowboy Poetry gathering. Especially popular are the summer-long horse racing, a Frontier Days celebration, a bluegrass festival, and the famous

Christmas tree–lighting ceremony and parade. Prescott's holiday lighting events have earned it the title of "Christmas City."

For golf, Antelope Hills is a municipal course that features two eighteen-hole courses. Three other country clubs have eighteen-hole, semiprivate layouts nearby. The city has public tennis and racquetball courts and both indoor and outdoor Olympic-size pools, along with hiking trails, camping and fishing areas, and horse trails. Trail maps are available at the U.S. Forest Service office and from the chamber of commerce. Should you be unable to control the urge, 7,600-foot Granite Mountain offers exciting rock-climbing opportunities. Local lakes are stocked with trout, bluegill, bass, and catfish. There's even a gambling casino on the Yavapai Indian reservation.

Yavapai College, a two-year school, offers a noncredit "retirement college" with hundreds of students older than sixty-five. Other cultural activities include musical performances by the visiting Phoenix Symphony, community theater groups, and several museums.

As you might expect, the rugged mountains, soaring pines, and sparkling lakes inspire local artists. Their work can be enjoyed at galleries at Yavapai College, the Mountain Artists Guild, the Southwest Artist Association, and the Prescott Fine Arts Association. The latter group also presents a full season of theater, ranging from musicals to drama, comedy to melodrama.

## Real Estate

Housing prices for the Prescott and Prescott Valley area seem to be near the national average, although around the city of Prescott, prices are somewhat higher. Average selling prices are around $167,000, which reflects the popularity of high-end homes tucked away in the forested hills. There appears to be an abundance of rentals, however, for those who want to try the area for a few months before making any decisions. I predict that with Prescott's growing popularity, housing prices will continue to creep up. Occasionally an acceptable place can be found for as low as $75,000, but most homes sell for more than $113,000, and those places with views overlooking the valley can easily cost $200,000 or more.

In the older parts of the city, you'll find several neighborhoods of Victorians and areas of modest, lower-priced homes. Most of Prescott has been built on rolling, uneven terrain, not suitable for mass-produced tract houses, so most buildings tend to be custom-designed to fit on individual lots.

The median price of a condo is $90,000, with more modest ones priced several thousand dollars less. Rentals in Prescott range from $561 for a one-bedroom apartment to $675 to $1,200 for a three-bedroom house.

## Prescott Valley

For those seeking less costly housing, the place to look is in nearby Prescott Valley. This is a quickly growing community, in the process of developing its own reputation as a retirement destination.

With fewer steep hills, Prescott Valley permits cluster construction, which keeps prices down and quality high. The valley is literally sprouting with new, more affordable homes. New homes here start in the $85,000 range and offer more square footage, larger lots, and more amenities than similar prices will buy in Prescott. Of course, you sacrifice view for more housing for the dollar. But the city of Prescott is only twenty minutes away, and large-scale shopping is even closer.

## Medical Care

Health care is above average here, with nearly 130 physicians and surgeons serving the community, and private doctors are accepting new patients. The 127-bed Yavapai Regional Medical Center and a large Veterans Affairs Medical Center are both conveniently located.

## When Grandkids Visit

They'll enjoy Prescott Animal Park, 6 miles north in Heritage Park Zoo, where you'll see exotic animals in their natural settings. Or try any number of museums, not the least of which is Sharlot Hall, which is filled with Arizona pioneer memorabilia as well as prehistoric Native American artifacts. The three-acre grounds feature pioneer buildings, an old-time locomotive, and demonstrations of early-day Arizona handicrafts and ways of life.

## Addresses and Connections

*Chamber of Commerce:* P.O. Box 1147, Prescott, AZ 86302

*Newspapers: Prescott Daily Courier,* 147 North Cortez, P.O. Box 312, Prescott, AZ 86032; twice-weekly: *Prescott Sun,* 238 North Marina, Prescott, AZ 86301

*Senior Center:* Lloyd Roe Center, 335 East Aubrey, Prescott, AZ 86301

*Airport:* Prescott Municipal, with commuter service to Phoenix

*Bus:* Greyhound provides service to Cottonwood and Phoenix, and the Prescott Transit Authority serves the local area

## Prescott Area Weather

| | Jan. | April | July | Oct. | Rain | Snow |
|---|---|---|---|---|---|---|
| | | In degrees Fahrenheit | | | | |
| DAILY HIGHS | 50 | 67 | 89 | 72 | 18" | 20" |
| DAILY LOWS | 20 | 33 | 56 | 36 | | |

## Prescott–Prescott Valley Area Cost of Living

| Overall | Housing | Medical | Groceries | Utilities |
|---|---|---|---|---|
| (percentage of national average) | | | | |
| 100% | 116% | 108% | 113% | 98% |

# Cottonwood

Midway between Prescott and Sedona is a strategically located retirement possibility in the picturesque Verde Valley. News about Cottonwood and nearby Clarkdale seems to be spreading by word of mouth, for the area receives scant coverage in retirement publications. But the word is apparently getting around, because 26 percent of the Verde Valley's population is older than sixty-five.

Although Cottonwood's scenic values pale when compared to nearby Sedona or Prescott, most Verde Valley homes enjoy mountain vistas in almost any direction. The rolling hills around Cottonwood itself aren't wooded, as they are in Prescott or Sedona, yet the valley is completely surrounded by the Prescott National Forest. Cottonwood is the largest community here, the commercial and shopping center for the entire valley.

Cottonwood and Verde Villages, right on Cottonwood's city limits, have a combined population of about 16,000. Clarkdale has around 8,500 inhabitants. This population supports adequate shopping, and because it's only 17 miles from Interstate 17, transportation is better than many areas of central Arizona. A local bus service, called CATS (Cottonwood Area Transit System), operates six days a week and picks up door-to-door in response to phone calls. Greyhound buses stop at Camp Verde, 14 miles away, and daily shuttles take you to the Phoenix airport.

The Verde Valley sits at a much lower altitude than either Prescott or Sedona—at an elevation of 3,300 feet—so Cottonwood receives much less snow. Nevertheless, the Verde Valley's air is just as crystal clear and crisp. Its location puts it close to many natural wonders: desert trails, mountain forests, rivers, and lakes. A big attraction is that property prices are far lower than in the large, congested areas in and around Phoenix.

## Recreation and Culture

More than 150 miles of rivers and streams wind through the Verde Valley, so opportunities for fishing, hunting, canoeing, and river rafting are essentially unlimited. Golf and tennis facilities are abundant in nearby Sedona. Yavapai College has a branch, Verde Valley Campus in Clarkdale, that offers classes for continuing education.

## Real Estate

Homes here are bargain priced when compared with Cottonwood's expensive neighbors, Sedona and Prescott. Since most growth here has occurred in the past ten years, the majority of homes are fairly new. Prices range from mobile homes on individual lots and fixer-uppers in the $40,000 range to elegant hillside homes at $150,000 and up.

## Medical Care

Cottonwood's 104-bed Marcus J. Lawrence Hospital is known as one of the finest diagnostic and treatment centers in northern Arizona. It has a large medical staff and an excellent emergency department, which is equipped with the latest technology. The facility serves a wide area and is the nearest emergency clinic for Sedona.

## When Grandkids Visit

Don't miss a trip to Jerome, a ghost town located between Cottonwood and Sedona. It's picturesque and quaint enough to become a retirement location for some people. Nicknamed "The City in the Sky," Jerome deserves the description, for it clings to the brink of an incredibly steep mountainside and extends downward a breathtaking 1,500 feet. Streets wind and switchback from the brink to the valley below in an almost gravity-defying manner. Substantial brick buildings, homes, and businesses—mostly abandoned today—are reminders of Jerome's colorful past. At its peak in 1929, when 15,000 lived in this roaring, violent town, it had the reputation of being "the most wicked city in America." Today the town is making a comeback: up to 400 residents from its low point of 100 in 1955.

## Addresses and Connections

*Chamber of Commerce:* 1010 South Main Street, Cottonwood, AZ 86326

*Senior Services:* 102 East Pima Street, Cottonwood, AZ 86326

*Newspaper: Verde Independent-Bugle,* 116 South Main, Cottonwood, AZ 86326

*Airport:* nearest is Phoenix Sky Harbor

*Bus:* shuttles take you to Phoenix, plus there's local bus service and door-to-door service on call

## Cottonwood Area Weather

| | Jan. | April | July | Oct. | Rain | Snow |
|---|---|---|---|---|---|---|
| | | In degrees Fahrenheit | | | | |
| DAILY HIGHS | 58 | 77 | 95 | 82 | 13" | 5" |
| DAILY LOWS | 28 | 42 | 66 | 64 | | |

# Payson

The Western writer Zane Grey, once a Payson resident, had this to say about the region: "And the sun was setting in a blaze of gold. From the Rim I took a last lingering look and did not marvel that I loved this wonderland of Arizona."

Located in the center of the world's largest stand of virgin ponderosa pines, nestled in a breathtaking valley just below Arizona's majestic 7,000-foot Mogollon Rim, the town of Payson is another favorite candidate for mid-Arizona retirement. And, it's an easy ninety-minute drive north of Phoenix. Payson sits at about the same altitude as Prescott, at 5,200 feet, and offers the same four-season climate as Prescott and similar spectacular scenery. Local boosters like to refer to Payson as the Rodeo Capital of Arizona.

Payson was never a well-kept secret with Phoenix residents. This little mountain town, with cool breezes, pine trees, and gorgeous scenery, has been a favorite summer getaway for decades. With July and August temperatures fifteen to twenty degrees below those in Phoenix, you can understand Payson's popularity. When the Phoenix pavement bakes in

110 degree August days, Payson residents play golf in 89 degree sunshine. In the evening they'll be wearing sweaters, for temperatures always drop below sixty degrees.

Yet Payson's altitude isn't so high that winters aren't mild enough for hiking, fishing, and horseback riding, with occasional snows for cross-country ski treks. During the three coldest months, temperatures always approach sixty degrees by afternoon.

Payson started out with a split personality. On the one hand were summer residents who delighted in their part-time homes tucked away among the pines. They loved to design their places as Swiss chalets, complete with frilly curlicues along the roof lines, Swiss-style shutters, and other artsy-craftsy touches. On the other hand were local folks, those who lived here all year, who preferred to define their image as rugged outdoorspeople, proud of rodeos and their Old West heritage. The result is an interesting mixture of architectural styles. Western log cabins, with wagon-wheel and longhorn motifs, sit cheek to jowl by alpine cottages with pink-and-green wooden scallops around the windows and split front doors painted with bouquets of flowers. Oddly enough, because the neighborhoods are so woodsy, the homes exude charm instead of clashing. Even Swiss-style mobile homes don't look out of place in such a lovely setting.

Zane Grey was one of Payson's earliest boosters. He wrote several books while living in his dream cabin in Payson and intended to make his permanent home here. Grey wrote in 1920 (in *Under the Tonto Rim*), "I love the great pine and spruce forests, with their spicy tang and dreamy pace, murmuring streams and wild creatures."

Unfortunately, Grey became furious when local officials wouldn't allow him to hunt bears out of season. So, despite the murmuring streams, wild creatures, and dreamy pace, Grey left Payson in a huff, never to return. For years his cabin was a tourist attraction, but it burned to the ground in 1990, presumably torched by a gang of vindictive bears.

Retirees here have plenty of folks their own age to play with. Almost 60 percent of the population is older than fifty-five. The chamber of commerce utilizes retirees, with twenty-nine volunteers working in the chamber office. "We couldn't operate without 'em," said the local chamber CEO. The retired community is quite active here, with many projects going on at one time to keep everyone who wants to work busy. One popular community project is the Humane Society. Volunteers work hard trying to find a home for every stray dog or cat that comes into the shelter. They dread having to put animals to sleep. They dread it so much, in fact, that they simply don't do it. The result is that the Humane Society shelter grows larger and larger every year as new strays take up residence in the Payson retirement home for animals. Should you move to Payson, don't be surprised if the first group to call on you is not Welcome Wagon but rather representatives from the Humane Society, begging you to take in a pet or two.

## Recreation and Culture

With mild year-round weather, Payson is the place for outdoor sports. The spectacular Mogollon Rim is just a few miles north of town, where hunting, fishing, hiking, and sight-seeing are legendary. Roosevelt Lake is only 30 miles from Payson, a popular place for boating and fishing that's famous for championship bass tournaments.

Payson is the site of the world's oldest continuous rodeo. The event has grown from a local contest between cowhands to a world- class event attended by top rodeo hands from all over the country. The community celebrates with a rodeo dance, a parade, and a fiesta.

Adding to the Western-outdoor theme is the State Championship Old Time Fiddlers Contest as well as a blues festival. The Tonto Community Concert Association presents an impressive schedule that features classical and folk music and dance performances. The Rim Civic Orchestra, an all-volunteer group of musicians, presents two concerts a year and performs at various civic functions. Programs consist of everything from Bach to ragtime.

For indoor sports, a nearby gambling casino, operated by the Tonto Apache tribe, brings revenues to the community as well as affordable entertainment at the casino's 476 slot machines. The casino is a welcome source of employment for Payson residents, providing 381 jobs for citizens of the Rim Country.

Eastern Arizona College has offered classes here since 1976 and has completed the first phase of a permanent campus. Senior citizens can enjoy continuing education experiences in a small school setting.

## Real Estate

Although some upscale neighborhoods feature expensive homes, most neighborhoods are relaxed, with more affordable housing. Mobile homes are interspersed with conventional housing, particularly in the less-expensive areas, but with lots of trees and natural landscaping, they blend in just fine.

In the last several years the development of Chaparral Pines Golf Club and the Rim Golf Club has contributed to the relocation of corporate executives to the region; homes in these areas start at $350,000. Because of Payson's natural beauty, more and more people are relocating here, so the cost of all housing continues to escalate.

## Medical Care

Because of the mature population, the local hospital has enlarged and is becoming a cancer treatment center for northern Arizona. Facilities are excellent; the Payson Regional Medical Center is the only round-the-clock hospital for nearly 25,000 full- and part-time residents of the Rim Country area, including the Tonto Apache Reservation. Payson has attracted many top medical professionals in the past couple of years, and the hospital has added a number of state-of-the-art departments. It is less than a two-hour drive to the Mayo Clinic in Scottsdale, as well as to numerous excellent medical facilities in Phoenix.

## When Grandkids Visit

Be sure to visit the Payson Zoo. It started out with a dozen studio animals left over from movies and TV commercials but soon started taking in cast-off zoo animals, retired circus beasts, and injured local wildlife. Randy, the zoo's manager, just couldn't turn away any animal. Today the zoo is home to about sixty animal refugees and is still growing. A local society takes collections for their support. Randy says that when animals come into his life before he has accommodations ready for them, he takes them into his one-bedroom trailer. At one time he was living with three baboons, a deer, and a bobcat. The zoo features a lion and at least one tiger.

## Addresses and Connections

*Rim Country Regional Chamber of Commerce:* 100 West Main Street, Payson, AZ 85547

*Senior Center:* 130 West Main Street, Payson, AZ 85547

*Newspaper: Payson Roundup/Mogollon Advisor,* 708 North Beeline Highway, Payson, AZ 85541

*Airport:* shuttle service is available to Phoenix Sky Harbor

*Bus:* bus service connects the area with Phoenix, some 94 miles to the south

## Payson Area Weather

| | In degrees Fahrenheit | | | | | |
| | Jan. | April | July | Oct. | Rain | Snow |
|---|---|---|---|---|---|---|
| DAILY HIGHS | 53 | 70 | 93 | 76 | 21" | 25" |
| DAILY LOWS | 24 | 35 | 59 | 40 | | |

# Sedona

Most popular retirement locations offer much the same kinds of services, housing, shopping, and other amenities necessary for everyday living. The major differences are price variations, transportation sources, and recreational and cultural opportunities. Some have prettier scenery than others; sometimes the weather is better. Occasionally you'll find a retirement town that stands out in one category or another. Rarely will you run across a town that stands out across the board. Sedona is one of these places. Its incomparable scenic wonders rank it among a half-dozen retirement destinations that soar high above the ordinary. Your first view of Sedona is guaranteed to take your breath away, and you'll never get over that initial shock. A friend who lives there says, "Every morning when we wake up, we look outside, drink in the view, feel joyful, and congratulate ourselves for being able to live in Sedona."

The best way to experience Sedona's impact is by driving from Flagstaff over slow, 27-mile Oak Creek Canyon Road. This is often described as one of the most scenic highways in North America. The pavement winds and twists through thick pine forests and gnarled oaks, with distant glimpses of deep gorges and arroyos embellished with enormous natural stone sculptures. Fantastic shapes of spires, chimneys, and buttes never fail to bring sighs of amazement.

When you reach Sedona, the canyon broadens and drops into a wide amphitheater overshadowed by enormous red, pink, and orange rock formations. Brilliantly hued cliffs and rugged spires of florid sandstone ascend majestically above the town. The rich greens of Arizona cypress, junipers, and piñon pines contrast dramatically with the red background framed by the deep blue Arizona sky—a sight not easily forgotten.

On our first visit to Sedona several years ago, we felt a curious feeling of déjà vu. The place seemed strangely familiar, as if we'd visited here often. This odd feeling kept nagging until it suddenly hit us: Western movies! We've seen this exact scenery in innumerable shoot-'em-up films. Countless bands of backlot Apache warriors have attacked wagon trains as they lumbered past these red rock formations. Cavalry troop extras have galloped along the trails, and stagecoaches have surrendered so many strongboxes full of fake treasure that we half expected to see a posse arrive at any moment.

Hollywood discovered Sedona and Oak Creek Canyon in the 1920s, beginning a relationship that continues to this day. With all this astounding scenery, it is quite understandable. Actually, Zane Grey was the first to portray Sedona artistically; he fell in love with the place, describing it in his popular novel *Call of the Canyon*. When Hollywood was ready to film the story, Grey insisted that it be shot on the Sedona location. Since that time hundreds of films and television shows have capitalized on the dramatic rock formations as background settings. A local group, the Sedona Film Commission, is engaged in promoting the area for more productions.

Hollywood artists and technicians came so often that many decided to relocate; some still call Sedona home. This "Red Rock Country" has long attracted artists of all dimensions, who draw inspiration from the area's fantastic vistas. New Age settlers and spiritual seekers also find Sedona a desirable location for healing and emotional rejuvenation. In the mid-1970s they proclaimed their discovery in the area of four electromagnetic energy sources called vortexes. Today a community of alternative healing practitioners provide a varied schedule of workshops and events here.

The number of retirees who select Sedona as their home base is truly impressive. The head of the senior citizens' center estimates that around 40 percent of the population are retired. "This makes for an interesting mix of retired folks, artists, New Age devotees, and businesspeople," she said.

The town has around 10,000 residents, although the business district and facilities make the town seem much larger. Tourism is big here, and tourist money supports an unusually large number of quality restaurants. Since growth has been recent, most construction is new and well maintained. People understand the beauty and practicality of natural landscaping, blending their homes into Sedona's beauty. A bonus is that desert landscaping doesn't include lawns that continually need mowing.

Sedona's altitude is 4,300 feet—that's 3,200 feet higher than Phoenix, which is only two hours away by car, and 2,700 feet lower than Flagstaff, which is less than an hour away. (Some guidebooks list Sedona as being at a 4,400-foot altitude. Since the town slopes downward, it all depends on where you measure.) This altitude means warmer winters than Flagstaff and cooler summers than Phoenix.

Lest I make Sedona sound like paradise on Earth and start a stampede, let's take a look at two downsides frequently mentioned by residents. First, this is an expensive place for property. Second, traffic is unusually heavy on Sedona's few main thoroughfares. Traffic is aggravated by the continuous flow of tourists gawking at the scenery, grabbing parking spaces, and generally getting in everybody's way. On the other hand, Sedona's quality of life and stunning landscape greatly lessen the impact of these inconveniences.

## Recreation and Culture

Sedona golfers can choose among two nine-hole and two eighteen-hole courses. The unique settings provide enthusiasts with breathtaking views at every turn. Courses stay open year-round. The area also supports five tennis-club resorts. Camping, fishing, and hiking are exceptionally popular and accessible because 77 percent of the countryside is U.S. Forest Service land. The wilderness begins at the edge of town. Hiking and horseback riding trails abound, with or without tour guides.

Sedona surely is a place to cultivate latent talents or to appreciate the artistic talents of others. There are between 200 and 300 resident artists, which accounts for the thirty-five art galleries and exceptionally active community art center. Two theater groups present dramas year-round, and a senior citizens' center group offers several "ad hoc" performances. Another theater group presents outdoor performances on summer evenings.

New on the scene is the Sedona Cultural Park, which will feature symphony, opera, ballet, and guest artists. The Theater and Music wing of the Artists and Craftsmen Guild presents programs that range from jazz to the classics, as well as monthly art exhibitions to augment the many art galleries in town. Other highlights of the seasons are the

Internatonal Film Festival, Red Rock Fantasy (with a million lights in themed displays, held every evening from Thanksgiving through January), the Sedona Arts Festival, and the Sedona Chamber Music Festival. Each fall, internationally renowned musicians gather to present a full day of musical celebration called Jazz on the Rocks.

## Real Estate

Sedona has grown rapidly in recent years, with affluent retirees and successful artists a large segment of new residents. As a result, property prices have kept pace with growth. This is not a place to look for bargain-basement real estate; views like this do not come dirt cheap. Some are expensive showplaces, constructed to take full advantage of the natural beauty of the panorama, but you'll also find less costly homes that do quite the same. Manufactured homes start at $45,000 and go up to $130,000; conventional homes on quarter-acre lots start at $160,000. For a nice view, add $30,000. One prestigious development asks $315,000 for its entry-level homes and $900,000 for its top-of-the-line places, with building lots starting at $160,000. Expect to pay from $800 to $1,200 a month for house rentals and $600 and up for apartments, which aren't too plentiful. The popular Village of Oak Creek, 8 miles south of Sedona, often has available rentals, but overall, rentals in the area may be difficult to find.

## Medical Care

A new medical facility has taken some of the pressure off the medical care situation. Recently opened is Sedona Urgent Care, a walk-in medical clinic, open seven days a week. Previously, the nearest centers were in nearby Cottonwood and another in Flagstaff, 27 miles to the north. But the area does have paramedics, ambulances, an outpatient health care center, and a medical evacuation helicopter. Also, an adequate number of doctors, dentists, and optometrists are available to take care of local residents.

## When Grandkids Visit

Take them to Red Rock State Park. The park offers three main trails designed to suit whatever energy level you care to expend. The Smoke Trail follows Oak Creek through lush wooded areas, always with spectacular views of the red rock formations along an easy ½-mile hike. You might want to bring a fishing rod and try to hook a trout.

Overnight camping isn't permitted here, and you must pack out what you bring in.

## Addresses and Connections

*Chamber of Commerce:* P.O. Box 478, Sedona, AZ 86339
*Senior Services:* 331 Forest Road, Sedona, AZ 86336
*Newspaper: Sedona Red Rock News,* P.O. Box 2894, Sedona, AZ 86339
*Airport:* commuter flights to Phoenix
*Bus:* van shuttle to Phoenix Airport

## Sedona Area Weather

| | Jan. | April | July | Oct. | Rain | Snow |
|---|---|---|---|---|---|---|
| | | In degrees Fahrenheit | | | | |
| DAILY HIGHS | 55 | 72 | 95 | 78 | 18" | 9" |
| DAILY LOWS | 30 | 42 | 65 | 49 | | |

# Bisbee

Tucked away in a steep canyon in the rugged Mule Mountains of southern Arizona—the domain of the great Apache warriors Geronimo and Cochise—the town once called "Queen of the Copper Camps" is making a dramatic comeback. When I first wrote about Bisbee in 1987, it had just suffered a jolting financial disaster. Some homes were selling, completely furnished, for as little as $500. If nobody had the $500, houses were sometimes abandoned, with their owners not even bothering to lock the doors. By the time we visited, things had taken a turn for the better, with retirees coming in to buy the cheap real estate and rebuild the town. Since then Bisbee has made a dramatic switch in direction, from a semi-abandoned mining town to its newer role as an enchanting retirement "discovery."

Once a wild, wide-open city of 25,000 miners, merchants, and adventurers intent upon making their fortunes, Bisbee today is slow and quiet. Since the town is off the standard tourist track, not that many visitors disturb the peace. A stroll through Bisbee's narrow streets is like stepping into the past. Daytime sounds are muted; after midnight the streets are all but deserted. Although ghosts of the past can almost be seen, Bisbee is far from being a ghost town. Residents express great satisfaction with Bisbee's balance between quiet leisure and fulfilling activities.

More than just a source of bargain housing, Bisbee's colorful history matches its picturesque desert-mountain setting, only a few miles from the Mexican border. Its narrow, winding streets epitomize a classic style of mining towns of the late nineteenth century; it's a place frozen in time. The town's architectural style is appropriate, a mixture of authentic Victorian and Western mining camp, with brick and clapboard construction dating from the 1890s and even earlier. Because of steep hills and ornate Victorian construction, people often describe the town as having a certain San Francisco atmosphere—without the cable cars, of course.

What happened to Bisbee? Disaster struck quite suddenly, back in 1975, when Phelps-Dodge, the mining company that sustained Bisbee's economy, ceased operations. Panic and despair struck the canyon's households. Families began leaving in droves. If Bisbee hadn't been the county seat, disaster would have been total.

This collapse happened near the end of the "flower child" movement of the 1960s and '70s. Word circulated through the underground that Bisbee was a great place to "be." Young adventurers, intellectuals, artists, and a few loafers floated into town on a wave of fading idealism. Some bought furnished homes for almost nothing; others squatted in vacant houses.

When retirees heard about these bargains, they created a new wave of immigration to Bisbee. Gradually, members of the Love Generation decided that making money was really "where it's at," so they sold their homes to retirees for profits and moved on to join the Yuppie Generation. One needs big bucks to buy the obligatory BMW; that kind of money isn't easily earned in Bisbee.

Fortunately, many of the new wave didn't want to leave; they had fallen in love with Bisbee. These "kids" are now in their forties and fifties, with graying hair, moving inevitably toward senior citizen status. Fortunately for Bisbee, those who stayed were loaded with talent: artists, writers, and intellectuals. Enough creative people stayed to give Bisbee the reputation and flavor of an artists' colony.

Today's population has stabilized a little more than 8,000. You'll no longer find boarded-up storefronts downtown, either. They are all occupied and bustling with profitable businesses. Numerous shops and boutiques dispense antiques, gifts, crafts, jewelry, and tourist goods, and galleries display the works of local artists.

This colorful downtown section, known as "Old Bisbee," happens to be one of the area's major tourist attractions. In its heyday, forty-seven saloons watered the thirsty center of town, affectionately known as "Brewery Gulch." Historians consider Bisbee to have been the "liveliest spot between El Paso and San Francisco." The fame of Brewery Gulch's dance-hall girls lives on today with stories of Crazy Horse Lill, Kate Elder (Doc Holliday's mistress), and Black "Jack," who dressed as a man and robbed stages. A few saloons remain, enough for atmosphere, but most have been converted into art galleries and studios.

Revisiting today, we find even more retirees have selected Bisbee for permanent homes. An increase in the retiree population and income always creates a healthy snowball effect on commerce, services, and organizations that serve the community. Prosperity has gradually returned to Bisbee. Naturally, the latest wave of bargain-hunting home buyers has pushed up selling prices. But since prices started at an incredibly low level, real estate is still an excellent buy. Turn-of-the-twentieth-century homes and well-preserved Victorians are available in town, as well as more conventional housing in the outlying districts of Warren and San Jose.

Bisbee's climate is excellent, with a high enough altitude (5,300 feet) to keep the summers pleasant, plus low humidity to make the winters brisk but not bitter. During our January visit the thermometer dropped into the forties by midnight, yet we walked around town in light sweaters, feeling perfectly comfortable. Many summer residents come here from Phoenix and Tucson, fleeing the baking, one hundred-degree-plus, July–August season. One reason for the cooler summer temperatures is that the steep canyon walls cast early shadows across the town to block the afternoon heat of the desert sun. A sign painted prominently on one of the downtown buildings proclaims that Bisbee has the "best climate in the world."

Shopping is adequate, with additional shopping in Douglas, 23 miles to the east. Douglas is on the Mexican border, across from Agua Prieta, where some locals like to shop for bargains. Just a few miles south is the town of Naco, also a place to browse for south-of-the-border items.

## Recreation and Culture

Bisbee has an eighteen-hole golf course at Turquoise Valley Golf & RV Park; this course is one of the oldest in the Southwest.

Bird-watchers enjoy the San Pedro Riparian National Conservation Area,

15 miles from Bisbee, and Ramsey Canyon, some 25 miles distant. Not limited to birds, watchers are treated to sightings of all sorts of wildlife: mule deer, javelina, coyotes, and of course the ubiquitous desert jackrabbit.

The cultural ambience here centers on the creative colony of artists and craftspeople. Various galleries feature works by Southwest and local artists, poetry readings, dinner theater, and Old West melodramas. The Bisbee Arts Coalition is a community-based volunteer organization dedicated to promoting art, humanities, and cultural activities. Cochise College, based in Douglas, has a branch in Bisbee. The school provides personal-growth opportunities in continuing education and lifelong learning.

## Real Estate

Be aware that the days of bargain homes are long gone. Of course, fixer-uppers can occasionally be found, and satisfactory housing can still be located for less than $50,000. Mid-range housing runs between $60,000 and $100,000. At one time, the really old, historic places were bargains, and retirees had fun remodeling to bring them up to acceptable standards. For many people, renovating and rejuvenating an old house is enjoyable, a chance to allow artistic and creative abilities to run rampant. However, prices for old homes have skyrocketed in the past few years. You'll pay much more per square foot for an old Victorian than for a brand-new place. This is because not much new construction is under way. There's no room and no infrastructure for many more residences. For this reason, too, rentals are difficult to find. Places that used to be for rent are now owner occupied.

## Medical Care

Medical facilities are noteworthy for a small town: the forty-nine-bed hospital—with eight full-time doctors and an ambulance service—is ranked among the best in towns of 6,000 or less. Other medical professionals include five dentists, two optometrists, a chiropractor, and an osteopath.

## When Grandkids Visit

A trip to the old Copper Queen Mine is in order. The mine is right in the center of town. A mining ore car takes you underground for a one-hour tour of the copper mine. Visitors, wearing helmets and headlamps, can see how miners worked this famous ore deposit.

## Addresses and Connections

*Chamber of Commerce:* 31 Subway Street, P.O. Box BA, Bisbee, AZ 85603

*Senior Center:* 300 Collins Road, Bisbee, AZ, 85603

*Newspaper: Bisbee Daily Review,* 12 Main Street, Bisbee, AZ 85603

*Airport:* commuter airlines fly out of Bisbee–Douglas International Airport, 17 miles away

*Bus:* there's a local bus operated by Catholic Community Services and a shuttle service to Tucson Airport

## Bisbee Area Weather

|  | In degrees Fahrenheit | | | | | |
|---|---|---|---|---|---|---|
|  | Jan. | April | July | Oct. | Rain | Snow |
| DAILY HIGHS | 57 | 74 | 89 | 77 | 16" | 4" |
| DAILY LOWS | 33 | 47 | 65 | 51 | | |

# Sierra Vista

Near Bisbee—just 26 miles west—the high desert town of Sierra Vista is emerging as a popular retirement destination and one of Arizona's fastest growing communities. With abundant sunshine, crystal clear air, and an elevation of 4,600 feet, Sierra Vista enjoys an enviable climate. July high temperatures average eighty-nine degrees and July lows average sixty-seven degrees.

The town's picturesque setting among the Huachuca, Dragoon, Mule, and Whetstone Mountains justify Sierra Vista's Spanish name: "mountain view." The town owes its existence to Fort Huachuca (pronounced waa-CHOO-ca), established in 1877 as a cavalry post to secure the southern border and protect settlers from attacks by the Apache chieftain Geronimo. This was the home base for the famous Black troopers, known as "Buffalo Soldiers," of the 9th and 10th Cavalries. They pursued Pancho Villa's army in the 1916 expedition into Mexico led by Gen. John H. Pershing.

From a small townsite around the fort, Sierra Vista has grown to more than 40,000 residents, including 11,700 military and civilian workers employed at Fort Huachuca. Several major commands now operate on Fort Huachuca, including the U.S. Army Information Systems Command, the Army Intelligence Center and School, and the Electronic

Proving Grounds. Because of the military presence here and amenities available to retired personnel, Sierra Vista is naturally popular with military retirees and families.

Sierra Vista is the commercial center for Cochise County and parts of northern Mexico. To meet the area's growing needs, a 400,000-square-foot mall opened in late 1999 with all major retailers represented. Fine dining is also available throughout the area.

## Recreation and Culture

Sierra Vista's mild winters and warm summers encourage outdoor sports such as golf, tennis, hiking, and bike riding. Two championship golf courses are located here, and nine other golf facilities are within easy driving distance of town. You'll also find first-class bowling lanes, public and private tennis courts, and an Olympic-size swimming pool.

Great saltwater fishing can be found less than five hours away, along well-maintained roads, on Mexico's Sea of Cortez. Actually, the Mexican border is only 20 miles to the south of here. Freshwater fishing and boating areas are closer at hand, and hunters have the opportunity to stalk white-tailed and mule deer, javelina (wild pig), a variety of game birds, and even the cagey wild turkey.

Sierra Vista offers cultural and family-oriented activities throughout the year. The Winter Arts Festival and Arts Discovery Series present plays, concerts, musicals, dances, readings, and recitals. Annual events include the Arizona Junior Rodeo, the Thunder Mountain Marathon, the Buffalo Soldier Celebration, the Fourth of July Celebration, the Southwest Wings Birding Festival, the Art in the Park arts and craft festival, the Family Festival, and the Cinco de Mayo Festival.

Two modern community centers host active seniors and present community programs. A beautiful new 31,000 square foot public library is well-equipped to service the community's information needs.

## Real Estate

Housing is affordable and diverse, including country-club settings with golf-course homes, ranchettes, apartments, and condos, as well as traditional neighborhoods. In early 2000 the median sales price of a three-bedroom home was $110,000, with half of the sales falling below that figure. A gated retirement community for fifty-five-plus residents were going for $124,000. One RV park has a section of "park models" (mobile homes) that people use for either summer or winter getaways.

## Medical Care

Sierra Vista Community Hospital, with eighty-three beds, offers twenty-four hour emergency service. The Raymond W. Bliss Army Health Center takes care of Fort Huachaca and veterans. The town has fifty physicians, twenty-two dentists, and eight chiropractors in practice.

## When Grandkids Visit

Take them to the famous Tombstone, a living history museum of the Old West, nicknamed the "town too tough to die." It's only 16 miles away. Here the grandkids can see a reenactment of the shoot-out at the OK Corral, in which Wyatt Earp, his brothers, and Doc Holliday fought the Clanton gang. Take a stroll along the boardwalks on Allen Street or stop in at the Birdcage Theater, a notorious saloon and dance hall that opened in 1881. Bullet holes from sixteen gunfights riddle the walls and floors.

## Addresses and Connections

*Chamber of Commerce:* 21 East Wilcox Drive, Sierra Vista, AZ 85635
*Senior Services:* 3020 Tacoma Street, Sierra Vista, AZ 85635
*Daily Newspaper: Sierra Vista Herald,* 102 Fab Avenue, Sierra Vista, AZ 85635
*Airport:* municipal airport, regular commuter connections via Mesa Airlines
*Bus/Train:* Greyhound bus connections from Tucson (Tucson Rapidos Bus Line), 75 miles away; Amtrak stops daily in Benson, 35 miles north

## Sierra Vista Area Weather

| | In degrees Fahrenheit | | | | | |
|---|---|---|---|---|---|---|
| | Jan. | April | July | Oct. | Rain | Snow |
| DAILY HIGHS | 58 | 74 | 89 | 77 | 11" | 4" |
| DAILY LOWS | 34 | 47 | 66 | 52 | | |

# Ajo

One of my favorite retirement success stories took place in a little mining town in the Arizona desert. The setting was Ajo, about 120 miles west of Tucson and 110 miles south of Phoenix. Ajo's economic mainstay was a huge open-pit copper mine that provided employment and good wages. This was a thriving community with more than 10,000 inhabitants. Suddenly, without warning, the mining company shut down the Ajo copper works.

Caught without regular paychecks, families wasted little time in packing their belongings and heading out for greener pastures. Almost overnight, Ajo dwindled to a skeleton of its former self, down to 2,800 residents and dropping toward ghost-town status. Many homes in Ajo that were owned by the mining company were dumped on the real estate market and offered for as low as $13,000. Privately owned properties were sacrificed at giveaway prices. One real estate broker remembered, "At one time we had 600 houses listed for sale and nobody interested in buying."

Those residents who remained in Ajo were determined to make a go of it. They embarked on a campaign to encourage retirees to join them and save Ajo from becoming an abandoned wreckage. One of my earlier books—*Retirement Choices*—highlighted Ajo, described the situation, and urged retirees to take a look as a possible place for inexpensive desert retirement. The word soon got out, and buyers eager for affordable retirement property visited, liked what they saw, and began snapping up bargains.

Once low-cost company housing was disposed of, the real estate market stabilized. But prices leveled out at what most people would still consider rock bottom. As of our last visit in 1997, the listing price of homes on the Ajo market ranged from $25,000 to $149,500. Many homes were offered for around $45,000. This would be for a substantial, three-bedroom place on a nice-size lot.

Because retirees purchased the vast majority of these homes, Ajo embarked on a new career: from mining center to retirement center. The reverse shift in population created a satisfying snowball effect on the economy. One couple remarked, "We moved from California five years ago, and it's been amazing how new folks moving into Ajo have changed the look of the town, by planting trees, landscaping, and sprucing up their properties." Retirees moving into Ajo also put pressure on the community for more goods and services, thus creating jobs and bringing working-class families back into Ajo to fill these jobs. Today's population approaches 5,000, more than half of them retirees.

Another shift in Ajo's place in the universe has occured as several thousand retired snowbirds have started flocking into town to enjoy a few weeks or months of warm desert winter, something they wouldn't have done back when Ajo was an industrial mining town. The extra money they've spent here further enhances the economy, creating even more jobs for younger, working-class families. "One nice thing about Ajo," said one retired couple, "is that we have a mixture of young and old. We have about 600 children in our school and many young adults to balance out the social scene."

Originally, Ajo was located a short distance from its present site, but in 1916 a rich ore deposit was discovered below the town, so the mining company decided to move the town to its current location. Now, the term "company town" often creates negative pictures, visions of smokestacks, clapboard row houses, and company-controlled stores. This isn't always the case, and certainly these images are incorrect in Ajo. Because the town needed to be moved, a decision was made to rebuild with refinement and style.

The mining superintendent in charge at that time hired an architect to design a "garden city." The result is an unusually tasteful palm-lined plaza, an oasis that looks more as if it belongs to a desert spa than an Arizona mining camp. The Ajo Community Health Center replaced the company hospital and does a creditable job of taking care of local residents, with two doctors on staff and one doctor on call. Further legacies of the company town are facilities originally built for corporate executives but now available for public use. One example is the country club, with its golf course and other amenities. It's now operated as a nonprofit organization for the benefit of Ajo residents.

The plaza is quite livable, a place where local retirees congregate to exchange greetings and comment on the earthshaking events that rarely happen here. Crime? Hardly. I can't imagine a place with more personal safety than Ajo.

Residents keep in touch with the world via cable TV (with about ten channels), a weekly newspaper, and daily delivery of the Phoenix and Tucson papers. An interesting transportation development is La Tortuga Transit, a rural transportation bus project that connects the town with Tucson and points between. Whenever enough local people get the urge, they arrange for La Tortuga Transit to run them up to Laughlin, Nevada, to challenge the gambling casinos there.

The weather is typical of the Arizona desert. Even though the town is situated at 1,750 feet, it still gets hot in the summer. The local chamber of commerce describes Ajo as "the place where summer spends the winter" and "the town where warm winters and friendly smiles await you." The chamber also claims that Ajo is noted for having the best climate in the country, with warm winters and continuous sunshine that other parts of Arizona cannot equal.

## Recreation and Culture

The country club's nine-hole golf course is supplemented by lighted tennis courts, a swimming pool, bowling alley, rifle range, an equestrian center, and numerous parks and picnic grounds. Although the golf course is only nine holes, it's rated by the Arizona Golf Association as an eighteen-holer (rating 68.1, slope 111). The club has a lounge and restaurant.

There are a surprising number of social and cultural events here. Besides a Fine Arts Guild, music club, and amateur theater, the old high school is used for talent shows, vaudeville presentations, and dances.

## Medical Care

The Ajo Community Health Center is open daily from 8:00 A.M. to 5:00 P.M., with a doctor on call around the clock. This is an outpatient clinic providing primary care, laboratory, X-ray, and pharmacy services. On-call emergency care is also available, with plane or helicopter ambulance transportation to Phoenix and Tucson. Two doctors and two dentists maintain practices in Ajo.

## When Grandkids Visit

Take them to the Organ Pipe Cactus National Monument, just south of town, where they can see enormous stands of organ pipe cactus. This is virtually the only place in the United States where this variety can be found. Spectacular saguaro cacti, with their soaring, uplifted arms, and other desert vegetation also decorate this unspoiled desert land. Your grandkids might also enjoy a visit to Puerto Peñasco, Mexico, a couple of hours' drive down to the Gulf of California, on Cholla Bay. The town of Puerto Peñasco isn't too spectacular, but beaches here are uncrowded and seem to go on forever, with great swimming and fishing fun for all.

## Addresses and Connections

*Chamber of Commerce:* 321 Taladro, Ajo, AZ 85321
*Senior Center:* 1215 Center Street, Ajo, AZ 85321
*Newspaper: Ajo Copper News,* 33 Plaza, Ajo, AZ 85321
*Airport:* Tucson is the nearest connection
*Bus:* service to Tucson three times a week

## Ajo Area Weather

| | | | | | | |
|---|---|---|---|---|---|---|
| | Jan. | April | July | Oct. | Rain | Snow |
| DAILY HIGHS | 64 | 82 | 103 | 88 | 6" | 2" |
| DAILY LOWS | 50 | 56 | 78 | 61 | | |

In degrees Fahrenheit

# Tucson

Tucson sits in a high-desert valley, with the majestic Catalina Mountains to the north, the Santa Rita Mountains to the south, and the Rincon Mountains to the east. Dry, crisp air and Sonoran desert landscaping qualify Tucson as one of the nation's better winter destinations. The valley's elevation at 2,300 feet guarantees an agreeable year-round climate, with summer temperatures about 5 degrees cooler than Phoenix. In fact, an inch or two of snow usually touches down in the winter. Summers are still hot, just not as hot as Phoenix.

Many neighborhoods are as Southwestern chic as you'll find anywhere in the state. This is particularly true in the northern environs, where the land rises into gentle hills with a Palm Springs or Scottsdale look. The city's Mexican and Pueblo heritage is evident in house styles; low, adobe houses with red-tiled roofs are interspersed with modern ranch and Spanish-colonial homes. These influences go further than house styles: Spanish is widely spoken—for many, a first language—and a plethora of restaurants specialize in cuisine from nearby Mexico.

Its 450,000 inhabitants qualify Tucson as a moderately large city, and it is still growing. The fastest-increasing age group here is the over-sixty crowd, which used to account for 20 percent of the population but is now more than 30 percent. Since it's the over-sixty group who are most likely to vote, it's no surprise that senior citizens get fair treatment in this city. The well-appointed Tucson Senior Citizens' Center clearly evidences the attention that city politicians show retired people.

Retirees will find living costs in Tucson about average, with a slightly below-average housing market. Warm and pleasant winters don't demand much in the way of heating costs, but this is offset by obligatory air-conditioning in the summer. Crime levels are admittedly higher than many Southwestern cities, but police point out that high numbers of offenses in certain areas raise the averages for the entire city. As is generally the case, the better the neighborhood, the lower the crime rates.

Tucson has its share of organized retirement and over-fifty-five residential developments. With beautifully designed homes, extensive sports centers, and shopping and medical facilities, these complexes are small cities in themselves. One adult community, Saddle Brooke, calls itself the "youngest adult community" because it sets its lower age limit at forty-five years of age instead of the usual fifty-five. Housing prices in these adult communities range from $70,000 to $170,000. Typically, these retirement retreats feature eighteen-hole golf courses, shuffleboard, tennis courts, jogging tracks, and clubhouses complete with card rooms, dance floors, exercise rooms, and swimming pools.

Twelve miles northwest of Tucson's downtown, one of the newer Sun Cities is under construction. Currently about 3,600 residents live in this upscale development, with a projected 5,000 inhabitants when finished. This 1,000-acre active adult community is even closer to the Catalina Mountains—you feel as if you can reach out and touch them—and is surrounded by natural desert vegetation and a golf course with impressive views of the nearby mountains. This is one of the highest-quality Sun City settings, and homes are priced accordingly.

Many smaller, apartment-type retirement quarters are available in and around Tucson. They range from places where renters must be "active" to those offering "senior care" concepts, a euphemism for "nursing home." You'll also find the growing concept of "life care" centers, in which apartments are provided for those who are still active, then rooms with housekeeping care, and eventually nursing care for those who need it.

The Armory Park Senior Citizens Recreation Center (in downtown Tucson) is a model of its kind. Senior citizens take an energetic part in running the center and have no trouble getting all the volunteer help they need. At any one time several hundred volunteers are on call, as organizers try to use everyone's special skills. For example, retired accountants and tax practitioners give free income-tax assistance, and other retirees teach handicrafts such as jewelry making, crocheting, and painting. A senior citizens' housing authority high-rise is across the street from the center and another is planned, making it convenient for everyone to participate.

## Recreation and Culture

Golfers enjoy the thirty-five golf courses in Tucson's immediate vicinity, some played in deep canyons, others in open desert. City and county parks have handball and racquetball courts, swimming pools, and organized recreational programs. There are more than 300 tennis courts in the Tucson area, and many of them lighted for night play. It may come as a surprise that winter skiing is available just 30 miles away at Mount Lemmon Ski Valley, the southernmost place to ski in the nation.

The Colorado Rockies major league baseball team holds spring training here, with the attendant exhibition games. There's also a AAA Pacific Coast League team that plays through the season. For other organized sports, fans can drive two hours to Phoenix. A greyhound track operates year-round.

The University of Arizona, located in Tucson, greatly enriches the community's educational, cultural, and recreational life. Classes, lectures, plays, and concerts are an ongoing boon to retirees. Probably due to the university's influence, Tucson is the only city in the state with its own opera company, and it also has a light opera company that stages Broadway musicals. The Tucson Symphony Orchestra, Ballet Arizona, and the Arizona Theatre Company add to the community's cultural offerings.

## Real Estate

Living costs here are about the same as for most Arizona cities, about average nationally, but the wide range of real estate prices makes Tucson practical for almost any budget. Buyers can choose from a wide selection of neighborhoods, ranging from inexpensive to out-of-touch-with-reality. Condos start in the $65,000 range and continue on up. Most neighborhoods feature housing between $80,000 and $125,000. Apartment rents average $548.

Tucson is also a popular place for mobile home living. The local newspaper's classified section usually has listings from mobile home parks that are advertising spaces for rent, something rare in many metropolitan areas. A space in one of Tucson's adult mobile home parks can be found for as low as $150 a month. The nicer ones charge more, with $200 considered a fairly high rent. Compare this with $350 to $400 in some cities, and you'll understand what a bargain mobile home living is in Tucson.

With so many parks to choose from, you would be well advised to do some shopping. Some parks are primarily for working people, and their interests and social lives are intertwined with friends who live somewhere else. These parks will seem cold—not that people are unfriendly, but they prefer their lives to be more private. Other parks have mostly retired folks, where you'll find plenty of activities and neighborly retirees. Visiting a park residents' meeting or attending one of the bingo sessions can tell you a lot about who your new neighbors might be.

## Medical Care

Arizona's only state medical school is located here, with a teaching hospital at the University Medical Center. Fifteen hospitals in the area offer excellent medical care, with about 3,000 beds in all.

## When Grandkids Visit

It's absolutely obligatory to visit Old Tucson Studios, about a dozen miles west of the city. It'll look familiar to you and the kids, since more than 300 films and television thrillers have been made here. You'll see where John Wayne held off the Indians and where countless bad guys bit the dust in the middle of Main Street. Stunt men dressed as outlaws and lawmen demonstrate how movie shoot-outs are done, and a museum shows other cinematic effects. You might want to bring ear plugs for the shooting sprees.

## Addresses and Connections

*Chamber of Commerce:* 130 Scott Avenue, Tucson, AZ 85701
*Senior Services:* 900 Randolph Way, Tucson, AZ 85700
*Newspapers: Tucson Daily Star,* and *Tucson Citizen,* 450 South Park Avenue, Tucson, AZ 85714
*Airport:* Tucson International
*Bus/Train:* Greyhound and city bus service, as well as Amtrak

## Tucson Area Weather

| | In degrees Fahrenheit | | | | | |
| --- | --- | --- | --- | --- | --- | --- |
| | Jan. | April | July | Oct. | Rain | Snow |
| DAILY HIGHS | 65 | 81 | 98 | 82 | 12" | 2" |
| DAILY LOWS | 38 | 50 | 71 | 56 | | |

## Tucson Area Cost of Living

| (percentage of national average) | | | | |
| --- | --- | --- | --- | --- |
| Overall | Housing | Medical | Groceries | Utilities |
| 102% | 92% | 103% | 110% | 133% |

# Green Valley

Most exceptionally successful retirement communities became popular by accident—either as a by-product of tourism or because of unusually pretty surroundings—and are almost always situated near a good-size shopping area or large city. Green Valley is an exception to the general rule, for it stands complete as a partially age-restricted retirement center and was planned to be that way from its inception.

Originally an unlikely development dream on a slightly elevated piece of desert land, 25 miles south of Tucson on Interstate 19, Green Valley turned out to be not so unlikely after all. Today more than 25,000 people, the overwhelming majority of whom are retired, call Green Valley home. One source reports that the average age here is in the upper sixties. One resident said, "When I was a schoolteacher, I used to spend my summer vacations visiting friends here in Green Valley. When I retired, I just knew I had to move here."

Green Valley is unincorporated, and folks seem to prefer it that way—lower taxes, fewer bureaucrats, more time for golf. The town sits at an altitude of 2,900 feet at the foot of the Santa Rita Mountains and is 40 miles north of Nogales and Old Mexico. It's about 8 miles long and 2 miles wide and is divided by the interstate. One advantage Green Valley has over nearby Tucson and Phoenix is its higher elevation. Residents claim that summer temperatures are consistently five degrees cooler than Tucson and ten degrees cooler than Phoenix. On the hottest July and August days, low humidity permits night temperatures to drop by thirty to forty degrees. An escape from summer's hottest days can be found 20 miles away in the 9,000-foot elevation of the Santa Rita Mountains. Temperatures in the pine-shaded Madera Canyon, with an elevation of 4,000 feet, average twenty degrees cooler than Green Valley. But Green Valley winter daytime temperatures are similar to Tucson's and Phoenix's, averaging from the mid-sixties to the low seventies.

A study of the local telephone directory demonstrates the "melting pot" character of Green Valley. In addition to phone numbers and addresses, the directory lists the residents' former hometowns as well as their occupations before retirement. All fifty states and the ten Canadian provinces are represented. Residents from many foreign countries also make Green Valley their home. Your neighbors could come from

Australia, Costa Rica, England, France, Ireland, Germany, Sweden, or any of twenty-six other foreign countries from six continents. For the United States, California and Illinois each account for fourteen columns of names in the phone directory, with Michigan filling eleven columns and Minnesota and Wisconsin seven columns each. Green Valley residents take advantage of this diversity by forming clubs based on their place of origin. You'll find clubs for the Dakotas, Michigan, and Tennessee—most states are covered. A large number of retirees are Canadians, some spending only the winters here. There's even a British Women's Teapot Club.

Complete facilities include several large shopping centers, and the rec center for Green Valley is quite comprehensive, with facilities for arts and crafts, sewing, lapidary work, and photography. A swimming pool, Jacuzzi, sauna, and exercise room complete the recreational picture.

Not all of Green Valley is restricted to over-fifty folks. There's a sprinkling of young people around, just enough to keep the make up of the community from becoming one-dimensional. Instead of a Retired Seniors Volunteer Program (RSVP), seniors are served by a volunteer organization called Friends In Deed, which fills much the same function.

## Recreation and Culture

Golf is Green Valley's traditional outdoor sport; after all, it started as a development around a golf course. Today there are eight local courses, three of which are open for public play. They range from traditional wide layouts to tournament-quality designs. Tennis is also popular here, with thirteen courts, eight of them lighted for night play in specially designed facilities at recreational centers run by Green Valley Recreation. For less strenuous exercise, Green Valley offers shuffleboard and swimming at twenty-five pool facilities, some of which require membership. There's also a bowling alley.

Surprisingly, fishing is possible, even in the middle of the desert. Three fish-filled lakes are within an hour's drive from Green Valley. Less than twenty minutes from the community is one of the nation's best-known bird-watching sites at Madera Canyon.

Many seniors take advantage of the noncredit courses at Pima Community College, with interesting classes given in art, dance, history, language arts, and literature. For art classes in painting, woodworking, and ceramics, many residents depend on Green Valley Recreation. Also of interest are classes in jewelry making, quilting, and ballroom dancing. Just a short drive away is Tucson, a city that has been called "a cultural oasis in the desert." Green Valley residents regularly travel there to hear the Tucson Symphony, the Tucson Pops Orchestra, and the Arizona Light Opera Company.

## Real Estate

Living costs here are about the same as most Arizona towns, about average nationally, but the wide range of real estate prices makes it possible for those with any budget to make a selection. Although some inexpensive property can be found here, most of the area is more upscale than you might expect. The average household income here is surprisingly high for a retirement community: more than $44,000. Thirty-one percent of Green Valley households have incomes higher than $50,000.

According to the chamber of commerce, sale prices of homes in the past few years varied widely, with places selling from as low as $50,000 to more than $300,000. Rentals for unfurnished apartments start at $325 a month, with an annual lease, and $900 and up for furnished units on a seasonal contract. Two full-service retirement apartment complexes are available.

The low end of the housing market consists of the original town homes that were built by the first developer. They were intended for buyers to live in while their golf-course homes were built. They are perfectly livable and attractive, if somewhat small. The one-bedroom town homes can usually be purchased for as little as $40,000, with two-bedroom units another $10,000. Larger, conventional housing in excellent neighborhoods starts at $85,000. The interesting thing about Green Valley neighborhoods is that they are all nice looking, well kept, and delightfully landscaped with low-maintenance desert plants, cacti, and ornamental rocks. Lawnmower salespeople would starve here.

## Medical Care

Green Valley has two highly rated nursing homes, two private clinics, and a sixty-bed health care center. Four ambulances with trained emergency medical technicians are standing by, and Tucson hospitals are 20 miles away by Interstate 19.

## When Grandkids Visit

Check out the San Xavier Del Bac Mission on Tohono O'Odham Indian Reservation. Of all the sites founded by Jesuit missionary Eusebio Francisco Kino, this is the only one still in active use. Today it's operated by the Franciscans. Another possibility is the Titan Missile Museum, once a launching site for Intercontinental Ballistic Missiles, now an interesting museum with tours deep into the workings. The missiles are gone nowadays.

## Addresses and Connections

*Chamber of Commerce:* P.O. Box 566, Green Valley, AZ 85622

*Senior Services:* Green Valley Recreation, P.O. Box 586, Green Valley, AZ 85622

*Newspaper: Green Valley News,* P.O. Box 567, Green Valley, AZ 85622

*Airport:* Tucson International, 23 miles north, with shuttle service

*Bus:* Crucere provides service to Tucson

## Green Valley Area Weather

| | In degrees Fahrenheit | | | | | |
|---|---|---|---|---|---|---|
| | Jan. | April | July | Oct. | Rain | Snow |
| DAILY HIGHS | 67 | 84 | 101 | 88 | 12" | 2" |
| DAILY LOWS | 38 | 50 | 71 | 56 | | |

# Wickenburg

Wickenburg has a population of 6,000 and is the shopping center for 20,000 in the area. An impressive 30 percent of the town's population are retired. About an hour's drive northwest from Phoenix, the town of Wickenburg is attracting retirees who don't want to accept the neatly arranged, orderly, and secure life of Sun City or the bustle of traffic-bound Phoenix. A measure of big-city life has found Wickenburg, however, with the installation of a traffic light a couple of years ago.

In small-town Wickenburg, residents savor the tang of the Old West. The town has been famous for years for its guest ranches (they used to call them dude ranches), which go way beyond being simply ranches. They come complete with amenities such as swimming pools, tennis courts, and sometimes a golf course. Although guest ranches are still popular with tourists, the retirement emphasis is on small-acreage places where you can keep riding horses and live year-round.

This area is highly mineralized and was the site of a considerable gold rush back in the late 1800s. Several rich mines encircled the town, with millions of dollars' worth of the glittering mineral taken from the ground. Although most of the richest locations have been worked out over the years, enough remains to keep the local people busy prospecting and panning for the gold that the old-timers may have missed. Not only gold: Other valuable minerals such as silver, copper, turquoise, mercury, nickel, and tungsten crop up within a 25-mile radius of Wickenburg. Don't expect to become rich panning for gold, however, because yesteryear's miners were pretty busy. The town celebrates its Wild West past every February with Gold Rush Days, a weekend of rodeos, gold panning, and dressing up in period costumes.

It does get hot in the summertime, with July and August posting highs of one hundred degrees and above. But like most Arizona desert country, low humidity takes much of the sting from the high temperatures. Winter nights can be cold, with frost common, but day temperatures are quite pleasant, with shirtsleeve weather being the noonday norm and January days averaging sixty-three degrees at midday.

## Recreation and Culture

To play golf in Wickenburg, you must belong to a club. The Wickenburg Country Club is the least expensive, with monthly membership costing less than $100. The pricey spread is Los Caballeros Golf Club. However, avid golfers claim it's worth the more costly fees, because it's supposed to be one of the top ten courses in the state.

Wickenburg simply isn't large enough to provide a wide variety of cultural offerings, although several art galleries display the work of local artists and the local community center hosts Sunday-afternoon concerts by a civic group called Friends of Music. For theater, symphony concerts, and other major cultural events, it's necessary to travel an hour away to Phoenix.

## Real Estate

The cost of living here is about on par with Phoenix's, which is slightly above the national average. However, land here is abundant and fairly inexpensive, so building lots typically are sold by the acre, and you get more land for your money than you could expect in

Phoenix. You may keep horses in your yard if you care to; the local horse population is considerable. You can saddle up and go for a ride through open desert and brush country in almost any direction you care to ride. Since almost all of the surrounding land is owned by the federal Bureau of Land Management, nobody can interfere with your rides. You don't know how to ride horseback? No problem; local saddle clubs with friendly members will help you get started. The clubs organize numerous social activities centered on horseback riding, from afternoon rides for beginners to the grueling Desert Caballeros Ride for seasoned riders, who come from all over the country to participate.

Wickenburg has several mobile home parks, with many living units used only part of the year, their owners choosing to live elsewhere during the hot summer months. At one time it was possible to buy a lot and install a mobile home, but nowadays this is frowned upon by the city council.

## Medical Care

Because of the large number of seniors, health care is adequate, with a thirty-four-bed hospital and many doctors in private practice. Fifty minutes of driving takes you to excellent Sun City hospitals that specialize in, and cater to, problems of the elderly.

## When Grandkids Visit

Tour the Desert Caballeros Western Museum in downtown Wickenburg. There you'll find a collection of minerals, fossils, and artifacts from ancient Native American tribes who used to inhabit the region. Or you might want to picnic south of town where the normally dry Hassayampa River surfaces to form an unusual oasis of green willows and cottonwoods.

## Addresses and Connections

*Chamber of Commerce:* 216 North Frontier Street, Wickenburg, AZ 85390

*Senior Services:* 255 North Washington Street, Wickenburg, AZ 85390

*Newspaper: The Sun,* 179 North Washington Street, Wickenburg, AZ 85390

*Airport:* Phoenix Airport

*Bus:* Greyhound; no local bus service

## Wickenburg Area Weather

| | In degrees Fahrenheit | | | | | |
| | Jan. | April | July | Oct. | Rain | Snow |
|---|---|---|---|---|---|---|
| DAILY HIGHS | 67 | 79 | 103 | 82 | 11" | 2" |
| DAILY LOWS | 30 | 48 | 70 | 52 | | |

# Lake Havasu City

Before it became Lake Havasu City, the shore here was just plain Lake Havasu, a quiet, inexpensive location to escape the rigors of winter. Snowbirds would enjoy the winter, acquire a deep tan, then pack up their RVs and head north for the spring. Of course, those who visited always returned the following year to enjoy the quiet lake, good fishing, and delightful, summerlike winter.

The catalyst for change was Robert P. McCulloch, who flew over the area one day in search of a good place to test his outboard motors. He spotted an abandoned Army Air Corps landing strip, which is now the airport of Lake Havasu City. He started to dream, and plan.

In August 1963, McCulloch purchased 16,630 acres of virgin territory on the Arizona side of the lake and began to design a city. At first, the idea of relocating a manufacturing enterprise in an isolated desert hamlet seemed outlandish. But it worked out just as McCulloch dreamed, and the plant brought prosperity and growth. Gradually the economy bootstrapped itself, and outsiders started buying lots and building winter homes.

McCulloch's next wild idea occurred when he discovered that the famous London Bridge was for sale. Stone by stone the 170-year-old Tudor bridge was dismantled in London, shipped through the Panama Canal to Long Beach, California, and trucked to its new location on the shore of Lake Havasu. A problem developed when it turned out the bridge was too short to span the engorged Colorado River at this point. The problem was solved when part of the river was simply diverted under the bridge. The promotional effort paid off, for today the bridge is a surefire tourist attraction and a plus for the economy of the region.

From its original, unpretentious beginnings, Lake Havasu City has boomed to more than 36,000 full-time residents. Homes and condos, trailers and mobile homes, businesses and services of all descriptions have appeared as if by magic. An estimated 6,000 to 8,000 additional winter residents swell the population and add to the general prosperity.

Of all the Southwestern retirement destinations we've investigated in the past several years, we have to admit that Lake Havasu City is one of the most surprising. Every time we come here we're struck by the amount of innovative construction, new businesses, and nice restaurants, as well as the increased number of full-time retirees who choose to live on the treeless banks of a desert lake. The amazing thing is the touch of quality in all of this. The city has grown gracefully, and it's obvious that care has been taken with this expansion. Lake Havasu City combines all the convenience of a much larger population center with quality surroundings worthy of a high-class spa or resort. Adding touches of class are the spectacular scenic sculptures—cliffs, canyons, and ragged peaks—that never fail to draw gasps of astonishment from us when we pass through the area.

True, in July and August, you'll bake, but not much more than in Phoenix. And like Phoenix, winter's balminess and gentle warmth make you forget the rotisserie of summer. For some reason, Lake Havasu City is a bit warmer in the winter than rival Bullhead City, farther north. January averages five degrees warmer, with sixty-seven degrees as a high, yet summer highs are about the same, only a little above 108 degrees. Yes, that's 108 degrees—but air-conditioning quickly drops the thermometer down to seventy-two degrees, so, as they say, don't sweat it.

Lake Havasu City, as a retirement choice, is different from many popular locations. The economy doesn't count on retirees for sustenance. On the contrary; the region's booming economy attracts so many working-class families, many with children, that retirees are a true minority. There's no question about Lake Havasu's having a multigenerational, hometown feeling. As the chamber of commerce director pointed out, "Lake Havasu City isn't just another walled-in senior community. It's multigenerational, vibrant, yet easy-paced at the same time."

According to the FBI's statistics, the Lake Havasu area is one of the safest in the country, ranking in the top 20 percent of low-crime areas. The police department's fifty-six law officers are supplemented by the Citizens Volunteer Program, whose thirty-seven members donate thousands of hours each year to maintain the area's reputation for safety.

## Recreation and Culture

Some fishing enthusiasts insist on living as close to the source of prey as possible, so mobile home parks right on the river become their choice. RV parks dot the riverbanks, each with its own boat-loading ramp and nearby bait shop. By the way, boating and fishing aren't the only sports enjoyed here. Four golf courses, five tennis facilities, and at least one bowling alley will keep you active.

Those who like slot machines and roulette wheels will feel at home here. It isn't necessary to drive to Las Vegas; gambling palaces on the Nevada side of the lake draw throngs of senior citizens who can't wait to contribute their money. Five times daily, ferry boats obligingly shuttle rich passengers to the casinos on the Chemehuevi Indian Reservation on the California side, then fetch poorer but wiser passengers back to the Arizona side. Free buses will carry you to the Nevada gambling town of Laughlin. The casinos there will also cheerfully accept your money.

Attending to higher cultural needs than blackjack and poker are the Lake Havasu Art Guild, the Drury Lane Theater Company, the Havasu Light Opera Company, and a community choir and orchestra. For those interested in continuing education, Mohave Community College offers unique and challenging course options. A gem and mineral society provides outlets for rock hounds and collectors.

Year-round events crowd the calendar here. Golf and tennis tournaments, art festivals, and a Dixieland jazz festival are among the many happenings in the area. A Snowbird Jamboree takes place in the winter, as you might imagine, while the Hava Salsa Challenge and the Blue Water Invitational Regatta break the routine in the summer. October is time for the yearly celebration to commemorate the opening of the London Bridge.

A bustling senior center provides a dial-a-ride service in addition to the customary bridge games, arts and crafts, health maintenance, and nutrition programs. The Lake Havasu Senior Center holds line dancing classes three times a week, has a wheelchair lift van, and sponsors home delivery of meals. The community college offers fee discounts to senior citizens, and some activities are coordinated with Arizona State University, including drama performances, concerts, and lectures.

## Real Estate

The cost of living here barely tops the national average. High utilities and medical care costs are offset by low home prices. Despite this growth, housing costs generally are lower than in other metropolitan areas of Arizona and are markedly lower than comparable housing in California. According to the Lake Havasu Board of Realtors, single-family detached homes range in price from $45,000 to $400,000 (for golf course sites). Most neighborhoods have homes selling between $77,700 and $111,000. Town homes and condominiums are available from $35,000. Apartments and home rentals are plentiful and available from $545 to $700 a month. Residential lots average around $9,000.

## Medical Care

Because of the high number of retirees, the Lake Havasu area enjoys a more complete health care system than that ordinarily found in communities of similar size. A ninety-nine-bed acute-care hospital, staffed by thirty-five physicians, and a 120-bed nursing center serve the community. The hospital is in the process of expanding by half. For unusual medical problems, a state-certified life support/air evac system is available around the clock.

## When Grandkids Visit

They'll be interested in the London Bridge, a roller rink, and all of the great things to do at the Aquatic Center. Boating, waterskiing, and jet skiing are popular with the younger set, as well as swimming and cane-pole fishing for catfish from the banks of the Colorado River. Several boat tours entertain and inform as they cruise the waters. For that special treat, you and your grandkids might like to try parasailing, soaring 300 feet above the waters of the lake below, like eagles on high and . . . on second thought, maybe you wouldn't like that.

## Addresses and Connections

*Chamber of Commerce:* 420 English Village, Lake Havasu City, AZ 86403

*Senior Center:* 2223 Swanson Avenue, Lake Havasu City, AZ 86403

*Newspapers: Lake Havasu City Herald,* 2225 West Acoma Boulevard, Lake Havasu City, AZ 86403; *Today's Daily News,* 1890 West Acoma Boulevard, Lake Havasu City, AZ 86403

*Airport:* Lake Havasu City Airport, with several commuter connections to Los Angeles and Phoenix

*Bus:* none

## Lake Havasu City Area Weather

| | In degrees Fahrenheit | | | | | |
| | Jan. | April | July | Oct. | Rain | Snow |
|---|---|---|---|---|---|---|
| DAILY HIGHS | 67 | 87 | 109 | 91 | 3.8" | — |
| DAILY LOWS | 37 | 54 | 79 | 58 | | |

## Lake Havasu City Area Cost of Living

| (percentage of national average) | | | | |
| Overall | Housing | Medical | Groceries | Utilities |
|---|---|---|---|---|
| 102% | 87% | 107% | 112% | 113% |

# Yuma

Yuma, the last of the Colorado River towns, anchors Arizona's southwest corner, where the mighty Colorado crosses into Mexico on its way to the Gulf of California. At this point, the river loses some of its majesty. Much of its flow has been siphoned off along the way to irrigate truck farms, supply drinking water for dozens of communities, and make ice cubes for gambling casinos. A sleepy little desert town just a few years ago, Yuma's development can be described as explosive. Its present population is 57,000.

Only the central part, or "old town," shows evidence of its age and historic past. Everything else looks brand new. Originally described as "the great crossing place of a very wide and treacherous river," this was a trading center for early adventurers and settlers. In those days, Yuma's most noted landmark was its infamous Territorial Prison, a place as grim and dreaded as modern-day Barstow, California. (Well, almost as grim.) Of the prisoners who attempted escape, twenty-six were successful and eight died from gunshot wounds. Fortunately, escaping from Barstow is much easier; you simply tromp on the accelerator pedal and away you go. Actually, prison life wasn't all that bad; because of the massive adobe walls, the cells were one of the cooler places in a Yuma summer. In 1907 the prison was closed. It became a high school for a while, then free lodging for hobos during the depression of the 1930s, and finally a museum.

Because of its low-desert altitude (only 138 feet), summers here are exceptionally hot. Throughout the year, residents expect just a little more than 3 inches of rain. Think about that for a moment; 3 inches of rain is what most Eastern cities receive in one moderate rainstorm. Make no mistake, this is desert!

Yuma's winter population triples as snowbirds from all over the country descend on the area, bringing motor homes, trailers, and campers. But like the Rio Grande Valley area, Yuma convinces many snowbirds to nest for year-round retirement. We have friends who've purchased a lot in an RV park on the outskirts of Yuma. They say, "We love Yuma as our winter home. When it looks like rain in Oregon, we start packing our motor home and know we're going to have great summer weather while our Oregon neighbors are getting wet."

Many retirees take advantage of nearby Mexico for inexpensive prescription drugs, dental care, and experimental medications not yet approved in the United States (although many of these drugs have been okayed in Europe). A U.S. Marine Corps base is located within the city limits, sharing its runways with private and commercial aircraft. Residents are treated to an interesting display of Marine fighter jets and airliners alternating on takeoff. This base provides PX, commissary, and medical care for military retirees.

## Recreation and Culture

For gaming activity, Yuma Greyhound Park presents dog racing and pari-mutuel betting on horses as well as greyhounds. Then there's the Cocopah Gaming Center, a tribal casino south of Yuma on Highway 95, for those who love to fight the slot machines. Because of the large influx of seniors in the winter, these facilities do quite well.

Outdoor sports quite naturally tend toward the warm-weather variety. Several golf courses offer desert play, which should best be completed early in the morning on most summer days. The other major outdoor interest here is fishing in the Colorado River. Great bass fishing is enjoyed here, with catches of bluegill, crappie, and king-size catfish to fill your boat.

Even though Yuma can hardly qualify as a college town, several institutions of higher learning are situated here. Arizona Western, a two-year state college, offers continuing education programs. A branch of Northern Arizona University is also located in Yuma, about as far south as a northern branch can be. Two private colleges complete the roster.

## Real Estate

Prices in Yuma have risen over the past couple years, with the overall cost of living slightly above the national average. Utility costs of 45 percent above average are responsible for this increase in costs. Housing is still a bargain with homes offered at 10 percent less than most other Arizona locations. Comfortable homes in many neighborhoods are often found for under $100,000.

## Medical Care

One major hospital and various care centers attend to the medical needs of Yuma retirees. A major home-care service is available. Because of the large number of seniors here, medical care is said to be excellent.

## When Grandkids Visit

The Colorado River can be a central attraction for kids. A recently developed historical park on the river, Yuma Crossing, shows how Yuma was in the days of the Wild West, before the railroad arrived. Along with the usual staged gunfights, the children will enjoy the overall Western theme. Another special treat might be fishing from the banks of the Colorado River, one of the few places in the world where you can be in the middle of the desert and pull in a catfish.

## Addresses and Connections

*Chamber of Commerce:* 377 South Main Street, Yuma, AZ 85364
*Newspaper: Yuma Daily Sun,* 2055 Arozoa Avenue, Yuma, AZ 85364
*Senior Center:* Yuma Adult Center, 160 First Avenue, Yuma, AZ 85364
*Airport:* Yuma International Airport
*Bus:* both a city bus and Greyhound serve the area

## Yuma Area Weather

| | In degrees Fahrenheit | | | | | |
| | Jan. | April | July | Oct. | Rain | Snow |
|---|---|---|---|---|---|---|
| DAILY HIGHS | 69 | 86 | 107 | 91 | 2.65" | — |
| DAILY LOWS | 43 | 56 | 80 | 62 | | |

# Colorado

When you think of mountain scenery, you think of Colorado. The state boasts some of the most gorgeous peaks on the continent—several passes climb above 10,000 feet. The highways that cross them are at such high altitudes that some people have trouble breathing. When they do catch their breath, though, the scenic views immediately take it away again.

These magnificent mountains are Colorado's greatest natural resource. Much more than a tourist attraction, they are rich in minerals and teem with wildlife—deer, antelope, elk, black bear, and bighorn sheep. About one-third of the state is forested with ponderosa and lodgepole pine, spruce, Douglas fir, and aspen. The forests are rich in fur-bearing animals, such as muskrat, raccoon, beaver, and fox, plus game birds, such as pheasant, quail, and grouse, which are all protected by carefully regulated hunting laws. Mountain streams are the hideouts of rainbow and German trout, and lakes hold trophy bass and schools of perch.

Even though Colorado is famous for its Rocky Mountain scenery, with its forested slopes and snowcapped peaks, much of the state is in high desert, with equally interesting landscapes. The eastern portion of the state, from Denver to the Kansas state line, is pure Great Plains—sparsely populated and not the type of landscape one normally thinks of when talking about retirement.

On the western side of the Rockies, the Colorado Plateau spreads out into a vast, arid tableland, rising from 4,000 to 8,000 feet above sea level. In places, the region is wildly eroded into a jumble of flat-topped mesas and steep-walled canyons. Deep canyons along the Gunnison and Yampa Rivers are some of the most spectacular in the world. These great differences in elevation cause Colorado's climate to vary widely from one part of the state to another, thus giving newcomers a choice of surroundings. Most areas have certain weather characteristics in common—lots of sunshine, low humidity, and little rainfall.

Colorado has a lot to offer: legendary mining towns, ultramodern cities, farmlands, forests, mountain peaks, and desert dunes. Full-time retirees like the reasonable housing rates, low property taxes, and mild winters in most parts of the state. Others choose to retire in Colorado on a seasonal basis. Many part-timers love the state for its wonderfully

# COLORADO

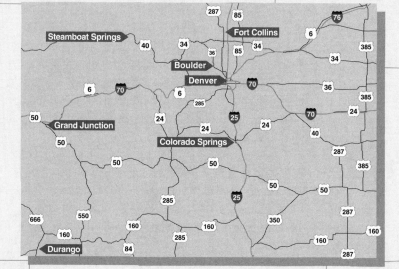

refreshing summers, maintaining homes in high-altitude, picture-postcard locales, then returning to their Phoenix or Yuma homes before snow begins to cover the ground. Others come here for the opposite reason, to enjoy superb skiing and Colorado winter sports.

Yet the state is more than an outdoor paradise. Modern cities and progressive towns are scattered throughout Colorado, places that provide all the amenities of civilized, cultured retirement. University towns, residential communities, and tourist attractions offer delightful lifestyles for retirees, and all are close to Colorado's outdoor wonderlands.

A word about high-altitude living: Those with health problems might want to consult with their doctors before considering a move to towns at high elevations. At high altitudes, oxygen is less dense, and humidity is 50 to 80 percent lower than at sea level. You need to breathe more deeply to draw enough oxygen into your lungs. Sudden changes in environment from low to high altitudes can produce symptoms of nausea, rapid heartbeat, fatigue, and other problems. Usually, your body adjusts to lower oxygen supplies and dryness in the air after two or three days. Many people, like me, experience no altitude symptoms other than initial drowsiness at altitudes above 11,000 feet. That's no problem; I simply take an extra nap every day until my body adjusts. When my body adjusts, I still take an extra nap. I'm retired—I nap when I want to.

# History

Early native peoples known as the Basket Makers or Cliff Dwellers—probably related to the Anasazi of Arizona—established a sophisticated civilization that flourished in what is now Colorado from about A.D. 100 to 1300. Possibly a great drought, lasting from 1276 to 1299, may have forced them to abandon their dwellings high in the canyon walls. It's all very mysterious; another possible scenario is that they were chased away by invading tribes coming down from the area that comprises present-day Alaska. Their multistoried apartment buildings are well preserved in Mesa Verde National Park and in the Yucca House and Hovenweep national monuments.

By the 1700s, when Spanish and French explorers visited the area, the native tribes had long been replaced by nomadic, sometimes fierce,

## Colorado Tax Profile

Sales tax:
5% to 7.5%; food and drugs exempt

State income tax:
5% of federal taxable income; federal income tax not deductible

Property taxes:
average 1.4% of purchase price

Intangibles tax:
none

Social Security tax:
half of benefits taxable for higher incomes

Pension taxes:
excludes first $20,000; double deduction for taxpayers older than 65

Gasoline tax:
22¢ per gallon

Plains tribes—the Cheyenne, Arapaho, Comanche, and Kiowa. The Ute mostly controlled the mountain regions where many retirees are now settling.

In 1803 the United States acquired the eastern part of Colorado from France as part of the Louisiana Purchase. The rest belonged to Spain and became part of Mexico when Spain relinquished claim to its western possessions. Then, in 1848 Mexico decided (at gunpoint) that it might not be a bad idea to hand over the rest of Colorado to the United States via the Treaty of Guadalupe-Hidalgo.

Early adventurers who explored the Colorado territory included Kit Carson, John C. Fremont, and Zebulon Pike. These "mountain men"— fur traders and hunters—established early settlements and forts as they followed the existing Indian trails that usually paralleled the courses of the rivers. Today, Colorado's major highways and interstates cover these same trails.

The big development boom began in 1859; the gold and silver strikes opened the floodgates. Colorado became the destination of thousands of fortune seekers and immigrants. "Pikes Peak or Bust" became a national slogan. The final connection was forged in 1870 when a railroad linked Denver with the Union Pacific. Modern development was under way and hasn't slacked off a bit since.

# Boulder

A growing trend is toward college-town retirement. Even if they haven't the slightest interest in continuing education, retirees often find that a university influences a community, serving as an exciting source of entertainment and cultural stimulation. Many of these social and cultural activities wouldn't exist without the school's presence.

Boulder is one of the better examples of university retirement locations. This wonderfully cosmopolitan city of 96,000 inhabitants is the home of the University of Colorado. The university, students, and faculty influence the city's environment in many pleasant ways, carrying the institution's intellectual excitement into the community as a whole.

The school's influence is most obvious in the downtown area, as you stroll along the renovated pedestrian mall known as Pearl Street. This vibrant historic-preservation district is the focal point of the city, its traditional heart and soul. Mimes, jugglers, and musicians mingle with the crowds, adding a touch of magic to the scene, something you'd expect to find in San Francisco or Paris rather than Colorado. All generations mix here, as a place to meet for coffee, read a newspaper or magazine, or perhaps browse in a book store or boutique. Pearl Street offers a great selection of good restaurants, art galleries, and specialty shops, of a variety and quality seldom seen in downtown areas of other cities. It is the site of continuous activities, both formal and spontaneous—art festivals, musical performances, birthday celebrations—a place for people-watching and relaxing. In short, downtown Boulder is a friendly, enjoyable place to visit.

The University of Colorado encourages retirees to enroll in classes for credit or as auditors. But for those who don't feel up to total immersion in the university's curriculum, an extraordinary senior center gives classes in everything from papermaking to computers. It even offers sailboat instruction on Boulder Reservoir and day trips to archaeological sites and theaters in Denver. Coupled with an active volunteer program, this is one of the better senior centers we've seen. (Boulder Senior Services comes under the aegis of Boulder Housing and Human Services, in case you need to look it up.)

Boulder's immediate surroundings are as beautiful as you could imagine. It's about 27 miles northwest of Denver, with the Flatiron Mountains and snow-covered peaks looming in the background and Rocky Mountain National Park just minutes away.

Boulder's winters look bad statistically—that is, if you consider snow bad—because Boulder catches even more snow than Denver. December and February receive the heaviest blankets of the white stuff, but like Denver, daily temperatures climb high enough to get rid of it quickly. It doesn't hang around for long. Most days of the year can be spent enjoying walking, biking, or other outdoor activities. Summer makes amends by providing gloriously sunny and comfortable days.

The cost of living here is about 18 percent above the national average, mostly because of the high cost of housing, which is 55 percent above average. The last few years have seen a spectacular rise in the selling price of homes, with a large increase over the last couple of years.

## Recreation and Culture

The Boulder area offers plenty of opportunity for outdoor recreation. You'll find three public and one private golf courses and forty-four tennis courts. If you don't know how to play, Boulder Senior Services sponsors golf and tennis lessons. You can even take classes in canoeing. Lessons aren't necessary to utilize the 150 miles of hiking trails in Boulder's immediate vicinity. Ski buffs will be happy to learn there's a choice of ten ski areas within 110 miles. Indoor sports fans will be delighted to discover that there are thirty-seven gambling casinos within 46 miles of Boulder.

When football or basketball season rolls around, Boulder, like any college town, comes alive with enthusiasm. Even nonfans are drawn into the gaiety when pep rallies and celebrations charge the air with excitement. The best part is, tickets to college sporting events are usually very affordable, sometimes free.

Among the outstanding cultural events generated by the university is its Shakespeare festival, one of the top three in the country. There's also a nationally praised Bach Festival and the Colorado Dance Festival. Every summer the Chautauqua Auditorium sponsors a popular film series as well as dance, music, and dramatic presentations. The list of festivals, musical productions, expositions, and plays is far too long to be presented here. It seems there's not a day in the year without two or more interesting activities going on.

## Real Estate

The average sales price of a three-bedroom home in early 2000 was almost $262,000. Town homes and condos had an average sales price of $132,000. Homes selling for more than $500,000 are common here, as are homes selling for less than $120,000. Rentals are correspondingly high, with two-bedroom apartments running from $650 to $1,300. Partly this is due to student and faculty pressures on the rental market.

## Medical Care

The largest health care center is Boulder Community Hospital, with a full staff of physicians and 265 beds. With Denver just a half-hour drive away, the total hospital and doctor situation is excellent for retirement. The County Health Department operates a Wellness Program for people fifty-five and older, conducted at the Boulder Senior Services facilities. Registered nurses perform screening tests for blood sugar, cholesterol, and blood pressure.

## When Grandkids Visit

One option is to visit the Fiske Planetarium on the University of Colorado campus. You'll enjoy an armchair trip around the galaxy via the Star Show. The Friday evening show is followed by free stargazing through telescopes at the university's observatory. A self-guided tour of the Colorado Scale Model Solar Systems gives the grandkids (and you) a sense of where planets are in relation to one another.

## Addresses and Connections

*Chamber of Commerce:* 2440 Pearl Street, Boulder, CO 80302

*Senior Services:* 909 Arapahoe Avenue, Boulder, CO 80302

*Newspapers: Daily Camera,* 1048 Pearl Street, Boulder, CO 80302; *Colorado Daily,* 839 Pearl Street, Boulder, CO 80302

*Airport:* fifty minutes from the Denver International Airport; hourly shuttles

*Bus:* city bus with discounts for senior citizens; intercity connections to Denver

## Boulder Area Weather

| | In degrees Fahrenheit | | | | | |
|---|---|---|---|---|---|---|
| | Jan. | April | July | Oct. | Rain | Snow |
| DAILY HIGHS | 43 | 56 | 86 | 67 | 17" | 90" |
| DAILY LOWS | 18 | 30 | 57 | 39 | | |

## Boulder Area Cost of Living

| (percentage of national average) | | | | |
|---------|---------|---------|-----------|-----------|
| Overall | Housing | Medical | Groceries | Utilities |
| 118% | 155% | 108% | 117% | 86% |

# Colorado Springs

In 1870, Gen. William Jackson Palmer, founder of Colorado Springs, had this to say about his new home: "Could one live in constant view of these grand mountains without being elevated by them into a lofty plane of thought and purpose?"

Pikes Peak dominates the view from every part of Colorado Springs, towering 14,110 feet high, presenting an ever-changing picture depending on the angle of the sun, the clouds, and the amount of snow. The altitude of the city is a bit higher than Denver, at 6,035 feet. It would seem only natural that Colorado Springs should receive more snow than Denver, but oddly enough, it receives about 30 percent less.

Although today's Colorado Springs is booming, with high-tech industries bringing in more residents daily, it doesn't look like a boomtown. As it grew over the years, the city matured gracefully. The result is that you'll find a variety of housing options and neighborhoods, ranging from older stately homes to modern planned communities and custom homes built in outlying wooded areas. Today's population of 350,000 makes Colorado Springs a good-size city, yet it's an easy place to drive in, with wide roads and boulevards accommodating traffic and seldom bogging down with gridlock, as so often happens in some cities of this size.

The central section of town is vintage Colorado, with comfortable and affordable residential environs. As you move outward, neighborhoods become newer and more expensive. Most neighborhoods are safe; Colorado Springs ranks high in personal safety, according to annual FBI Crime reports. The Tri-Lakes area, a few minutes' drive north of Colorado Springs, boasts several newer, upscale communities: the towns of Monument and Palmer Lake and the luxury developments of Woodmoor and Glen Eagle.

The military plays an important role in Colorado Springs's economy. The North American Air Defense Command is headquartered in nearby Cheyenne Mountain. The Fort Carson Army Base, Peterson Air Force

Base, and the U.S. Space Command are all located in or around Colorado Springs. As if this weren't enough, the Air Force Academy is situated on the north side of the city. Many military families choose to retire here because of their experience with the town while stationed at one of the military installations.

The Air Force Academy joins an amazing number of institutions of higher education in Colorado Springs. Besides Colorado State University, you'll find branch campuses here of four or five other universities, two junior colleges, and several private colleges. This spacious academic environment can't help but have a beneficial impact on the community. Colorado State University, for example, presents plays, lectures, concerts, and book signings to the public, sometimes free, sometimes for a modest admission charge.

The cost of living is just slightly above the national average but nevertheless is fifteen points below Denver's. This is due in part to exceptionally low utility costs, more than 30 percent below average. This becomes important when heating a home during the winter season.

## Recreation and Culture

Most retirees who decide to move to Colorado Springs will have some golf clubs tucked away in the moving van. The quality of the courses are famous far and wide. This is where the annual World Senior Tournament is held, as well as the Ladies' and Men's Invitationals and the Ladies' U.S. Open. Golfers can select from seven public and eleven private courses.

Because of the great skiing available, some sports fanatics golf in the morning and ski that afternoon. Colorado is famous for hunting, fishing, and river rafting. Colorado Springs is in the middle of it all.

For continuing education, Pikes Peak Community College offers a program of unlimited courses for $11 for those older than sixty. The University of Colorado gives senior citizens 50 percent off tuition for those auditing classes.

Near the Colorado College campus is the Fine Arts Center, with a 450-seat theater hosting performing arts series, classic film festivals, and lectures. This is where the American College Players put on Broadway plays and musicals during the summer, while the Civic Music Theater performs year-round. The Fine Arts Center also houses the Taylor Collection of Native American and Hispanic Art and an art school. During July and August, the Colorado Opera Festival is held at Pikes

Peak Center, and the Broadmoor International Center presents theatrical events and concerts.

## Real Estate

Real estate is lower than Denver but is still 12 percent over national averages, with prices reflecting a rising market. Median selling prices are almost $152,000. Prices vary widely, with the less-expensive places in the center of town, sometimes selling for around $115,000. On the north side of Colorado Springs, prices tend to be higher. Several gated communities have prices starting even higher. Because of rapid population growth and a slow rate of new construction, waiting lists are sometimes necessary for apartments. Since heating costs are usually included in the rent, apartment living can be more economical than rents would indicate.

## Medical Care

Colorado Springs is a healthy place to be sick because of the abundant medical facilities here. Memorial Hospital has a burn unit and specializes in intensive coronary care and cancer treatment. Other medical facilities are Penrose Community Hospital, St. Francis Hospital, and Cedar Springs Hospital, with a total of 1,000 beds. Colorado Springs is the home of the oldest Visiting Nurses Association in the state. Of interest to veterans are the military hospitals at the Air Force Academy and the Army hospital at Fort Carson.

## When Grandkids Visit

An hour or two could be well spent at the Garden of the Gods. Hike the trails through this 940-acre park, where fantastic natural sculptures have been eroded from red sandstone bluffs. Among other items there is a balancing rock and one formation that resembles "kissing camels." For real camels, there's the Cheyenne Mountain Zoo, on the other side of town, with more than 500 animals on display.

## Addresses and Connections

*Chamber of Commerce:* P.O. Drawer B, Colorado Springs, CO 80901

*Senior Services:* 1514 North Hancock Avenue, Colorado Springs, CO 80903

*Newspaper: The Gazette,* 30 South Prospect Street, Colorado Springs, CO 80903

*Airport:* Colorado Springs Airport provides major airline service

*Bus:* there's a good local system and an intercity bus, TNM&O, that connects with Greyhound

## Colorado Springs Area Weather

| | In degrees Fahrenheit | | | | | |
| | Jan. | April | July | Oct. | Rain | Snow |
|---|---|---|---|---|---|---|
| DAILY HIGHS | 41 | 60 | 85 | 65 | 15" | 43" |
| DAILY LOWS | 16 | 33 | 54 | 37 | | |

## Colorado Springs Area Cost of Living

| (percentage of national average) | | | | |
| Overall | Housing | Medical | Groceries | Utilities |
|---|---|---|---|---|
| 99% | 112% | 120% | 97% | 79% |

# Denver

Back in 1858, a few flakes of gold were discovered in the waters of Cherry Creek, where it emptied into the South Platte River. This unleashed the famous "Pikes Peak or Bust" gold rush that almost overnight transformed the little mining camp into the city of Denver. More gold and silver were discovered in nearby mountains, and Denver became the natural place to spend mining profits. From the beginning, Denver became Colorado's showplace of culture, a place for elegant mansions and glittering entertainment. With the finest restaurants, stores, and theaters between San Francisco and St. Louis, it is not surprising that it acquired the title "Queen City of the Plains."

The largest city within a radius of 600 miles (an area almost the size of Europe), Denver has a population of around a half million and a metropolitan population of close to two million. As the center of commerce for this large area, Denver maintains its "Queen City" title with its large infrastructure of culture, arts, and commerce, much larger than most towns of this size. Its restaurants, theaters, and department stores are geared for customers coming from the entire area.

This is a clean city, with pleasant, tree-shaded residential areas and loads of inexpensive apartment buildings. Most homes are built of brick, especially older ones. According to a common story, an early-day mayor owned a brick factory, so he passed laws that all homes must be constructed of brick. Maybe it's not true, but the brick construction does add a special touch to Denver's architectural flavor.

Many economical neighborhoods offer bargain housing, but some low-cost districts might cause retirees to feel uncomfortable. These neighborhoods are the ones that push Denver down on the personal safety charts. Much crime in these areas is gang related and rarely involves seniors, but why bother? Understand, crime rates here aren't horrible but I'd recommend checking out a neighborhood closely before making any decisions. Good places to look for safe housing possibilities are the outlying areas such as Aurora. Just about anywhere on Denver's perimeter is safe. From there, it's a quick shot downtown for shopping, theater, or cultural events.

Denver is also called the "Mile-High City," and indeed you will be precisely 1 mile high if you stand on the west steps of the state capitol. Actually, compared with other Southwest locations discussed in this book, Denver's mile-high status is no big deal, being almost 2,000 feet lower than places like Santa Fe or Flagstaff. Of course, the altitude affects the weather, and Denver's weather is interesting from the perspective of a retiree. At first glance it would seem to be a horrible place to winter, what with a yearly snowfall of 60 inches. It seems as if every winter, TV newscasts feature Denver's airport buried under drifting snow. But that's only part of the story. Yes, it can snow a foot or more overnight, but within a couple of days, if not the next day, it's all gone, and you'll be basking in sixty-five degree sunshine. The sun shines on Denver about 300 days a year, more hours of sunshine than places like Miami and San Diego. Even the coldest months average forty-seven degrees every afternoon. Snow doesn't have a chance to stick around. Furthermore, the dryness of the air fools you into thinking it is far warmer than it really is.

## Recreation and Culture

Denver golf courses are open for play year-round, and there have been as many as thirty playing days in January. The city operates seven golf courses and often sponsors tournaments between courses. Ten more golf courses, eight of them open to the public, are scattered around the metropolitan area. Both horse and greyhound racing tracks operate part of the year, with the doggies running from June 16 through February 10.

If you like to visit museums and art galleries, you'll have a ball here.

Denver boasts six art museums, sixteen historical museums, four natural history museums, and twenty-nine art galleries. That's in addition to many outdoor parks and displays that are essentially open-air museums. Denver also maintains a sort of museum with a herd of forty buffalo in a natural setting 20 miles west of the city. These are the direct descendants of the last wild herd left in North America.

Theatergoers have a wide choice, with four dinner theaters and several other conventional houses. The Denver Center for the Performing Arts hosts professional touring, cabaret, and resident theater presentations. Denver has its own opera, with in-the-round and proscenium-staged productions featuring international artists.

About thirty gambling casinos are within an easy drive of Denver, notably in Central City, Blackhawk, Cripple Creek, and Georgetown. The casinos provide buses that will take you to the gambling joints and refund your bus fare. Sounds generous, but not to worry, they'll get it all back before you leave.

## Real Estate

A few years ago, Denver was the most depressed big-city market we found anywhere in the country. The reasons were twofold: First, the oil shale boom had inflated new construction; second, the savings-and-loan industry (or racket?) had been disbursing construction loans and financing homes, apartments, and office buildings for anyone who asked. Then, when the petroleum companies suddenly pulled out of the shale exploration business and fired most of their employees, the boom turned into a disheartening bust.

However, the market made a remarkable turnaround. Today homes sell for 25 percent above the national average. This is partly responsible for an overall cost of living that's 10 percent higher than the national average. Utility costs are much lower than average, which helps keep down living costs. Home and condo prices and rents vary widely, depending on what part of the city or suburb you choose.

## Medical Care

Saint Joseph Hospital offers Med Search, a free physician referral service. This helps newcomers find a conveniently located specialist or general practitioner to meet their needs. Numerous top-rated hospitals and clinics guarantee quality medical care for the entire region.

## When Grandkids Visit

The Denver Zoo might be just the place to take the little ones. The zoo's exhibit is nicely laid out, with spacious, natural habitats for the animals. The newest exhibit is a rain forest display called Tropical Discovery, which attracts thousands of people who are interested in tropical habitats.

## Addresses and Connections

*Chamber of Commerce:* 1445 Market Street, Denver, CO 80202

*Senior Services:* 135 California Street, #300, Denver, CO 80202

*Newspapers: Rocky Mountain News,* 400 West Colfax, Denver, CO 80204; *Denver Post,* 1560 Broadway, Denver, CO 80202

*Airport:* Denver International Airport, thirty minutes from the city, with bus connections

*Bus:* city and Greyhound

## Denver Area Weather

| | In degrees Fahrenheit | | | | | |
|---|---|---|---|---|---|---|
| | Jan. | April | July | Oct. | Rain | Snow |
| DAILY HIGHS | 43 | 61 | 88 | 67 | 15" | 60" |
| DAILY LOWS | 16 | 34 | 59 | 37 | | |

## Denver Area Cost of Living

| (percentage of national average) | | | | |
|---|---|---|---|---|
| Overall | Housing | Medical | Groceries | Utilities |
| 108% | 126% | 123% | 105% | 88% |

# Durango

Tucked away in a horseshoe of the San Juan Mountains in the south-western corner of the state, Durango has been the gateway to south-western Colorado's natural riches for more than one hundred years. Native tribes and fur traders, miners and prospectors, ranchers and railroad engineers alike passed through Durango on their way to seek their fortunes. Many found that Durango itself was the treasure they sought. Two million acres of national forest surrounds the city today, providing countless places for outdoor recreation.

Although the town is relatively young (it was established little more than a century ago), the Four Corners region where it's located boasts evidence of ancient glories. Two thousand years ago, this was home to a mysterious aboriginal culture known as the ancestral Puebloans (the Ancient Ones). For some unknown reason the Puebloans abandoned their sophisticated, several-storied buildings and left the area to the next wave of inhabitants, the Ute, who arrived a couple of centuries later. They were there to welcome the Spanish, who explored the region in the 1500s.

The town of Durango got its start in 1880, as a depot and roundhouse location for the railroad, and grew rapidly into a town of 2,000 residents just a year later. Before long the fledgling town boasted twenty saloons and 134 businesses. Today the population is 15,000 and still growing. Retirees make up a good percentage of the inhabitants; almost 30 percent are sixty-two or older. The business community and residents recognize the treasure of those original buildings constructed by Durango's pioneers that are still in use today. Parts of the downtown area have been named by the Colorado Historical Society as a National Historic District, bestowing Durango with Victorian splendor and elegance.

Residents like the town because it's a pleasant and peaceful community, with a below-average crime rate and above-average quality of living. One recent retiree put it this way: "The difference between Durango and tourist places like Telluride and Aspen is that we have a real town, with permanent people, employed in all kinds of trades and professions, yet we enjoy the ambience and excitement of a resort town."

A 6,500-foot elevation ensures a four-season climate with bountiful snowfall, yet not so high an altitude that temperatures don't rise above freezing every winter day. With 85 percent solar exposure, snow removal is seldom a problem. You're also guaranteed cool summer evenings without the need for air-conditioning.

Because Durango sits all by itself in the Four Corners area, by necessity it has become a self-contained little city. As Will Rogers once said, "Durango's out of the way and glad of it." All the shopping needs are met by commercial development in and around Durango. Turn-of-the-twentieth-century hotels and commercial buildings abound in the business district, and an unusual number of good restaurants serve a variety of cuisines. The tourist business encourages upscale establishments, to the benefit of year-round residents.

Durango is also gaining recognition as an artist's colony. In addition to several well-known painters, half a dozen authors make this their home, as well as a number of essayists, freelancers, and poets. Three galleries here are nationally recognized for quality Native American arts, Navajo weavings, jewelry, paintings, and sculpture.

## Recreation and Culture

Skiing at Purgatory Ski Resort, 26 miles away, is reputed to be among the best in the country. Nine lifts and 250 inches of snow account for the resort's impressive increase in ski-hours. Purgatory Resort now has a high-speed quad. Although the resort has record snowfall, it also has record blue-sky days, which makes for great downhill fun. It's not too late to learn to ski, and Purgatory has a beginner's lift especially for those who are brave enough to give it a try.

Three eighteen-hole golf courses, ten tennis courts, and five walking trails in Durango encourage outdoor recreation. A growing sport, one that mature adults find enjoyable, is mountain biking. I'm assuming that the biking is down the mountain, not up, or else it wouldn't be quite as enjoyable.

The Animas River flows through town, offering excellent trout fishing, rafting, kayaking, and other recreational activities. This is the third most rafted river in the state. You have your choice of a guided raft trip or a do-it-yourself journey (or fiasco, depending on your experience in rafting). A guided trip is an excellent way to learn fishing skills. Fishing at several stocked trout lakes in the area provides a more restful adventure.

Hunting for big and small game is an attraction that draws tourists and brings local residents out during the seasons. Camping is also popular here, with more than 900 campsites within a 40-mile radius.

Durango is also a progressive college town. Fort Lewis College, a four-year, fully accredited institution, offers continuing education classes for local retirees. It also adds a vibrant dimension to the local lifestyle, with cultural and artistic programs. A $5 million Community Concert Hall is the latest cultural addition to Durango. The theater's 600 seats are placed in a unique three-level arrangement, with the closest seat only 5 feet from the stage and the farthest only 60 feet.

For those interested in archaeology, within an hour's drive of Durango are Mesa Verde Park, Crow Canyon Archaeological Center, Chimney Rock, the Anasazi Heritage Museum, and the Ute Mountain Ute Tribal Park.

Casino gambling, ever increasing in the Southwest, is available near Durango. The Sky Ute Casino is 25 miles from town, and the Ute Mountain Casino about 50 miles away. Slot machines, keno, bingo, and poker games operate well into the wee hours of the morning to relieve you of your money.

## Real Estate

The cost of living here is slightly below the national average, despite higher real estate prices than in some other Colorado locations. The reason for this is a smaller inventory of lower-cost "starter" homes than elsewhere. Contractors prefer to build more upscale places since they sell well. The average price for a three-bedroom home is $140,000, with starting prices around $80,000 and upper prices around $385,000. Condos start at $60,000 and reach $150,000 at the higher end of the scale. Homes with acreage and fantastic views start in the $150,000 range.

## Medical Care

Mercy Medical Center is the largest "rural" hospital in the state. It has 105 beds and is the regional referral center for specialized care throughout a six-county region. It has more than eighty physicians on staff. There's also skilled nursing care at Four Corners Health Care Center, with 156 beds and outpatient services for therapy.

## When Grandkids Visit

Try the Durango & Silverton Narrow Gauge Railroad, an authentic steam-powered train ride through the valleys and beside the peaks of the scenic San Juan Mountains. In continuous operation since 1882, this railroad line carried food and provisions to miners around the turn of the twentieth century and returned loaded with silver ore for the mills in Durango. If you can't get reservations on the train, only 36 miles from Durango are the most famous and best preserved cliff dwellings of the ancient Anasazi Indians at Mesa Verde National Park. By the way, *Conde Nast Traveler* awarded Mesa Verde the prestigious first place for historic destinations. The Vatican came in second.

## Addresses and Connections

*Chamber of Commerce:* 111 South Camino Del Rio, Durango, CO 81302

*Senior Services:* 2424 Main Avenue, Durango, CO 81301

*Newspaper: Durango Herald,* 1275 Main Avenue, Durango, CO 81301

*Airport:* La Plata Field has several commuter connections

*Bus:* the "Durango Lift" takes you around town, and the TNM&O bus service has connections with Greyhound

## Durango Area Weather

| | In degrees Fahrenheit | | | | | |
| | Jan. | April | July | Oct. | Rain | Snow |
|---|---|---|---|---|---|---|
| DAILY HIGHS | 41 | 62 | 85 | 66 | 19" | 68" |
| DAILY LOWS | 10 | 29 | 50 | 31 | | |

# Fort Collins

This is another town that receives favorable reviews in national publications as a desirable place to live, work, and retire. A scenic place with 90,000 residents and friendly neighborhoods, Fort Collins views the panorama of the nearby Rocky Mountains. The Cache la Poudre River, which runs along the upper edge of the city, is famous for white-water rafting, fishing, and just plain scenic enjoyment. The upper stretches of the river are protected by the federal Wild and Scenic Rivers Act. The river received its name back in 1836 when a party of French trappers cached an excess cargo of gunpowder on the banks of the river in preparation for a trip into the mountains. The French word for gunpowder is *poudre*—thus the name Cache la Poudre.

The city of Fort Collins seems to put special emphasis on services for seniors. There's an impressive list of activities, from senior employment and training to senior games and line dancing classes. Trips to Breckenridge Ski Area and to concerts in Boulder are other examples of city-sponsored activities, with door-to-door transportation provided at an additional fee of $2.00.

As with other Colorado retirement locations, the cost of living in Fort Collins is slightly above average. One item, however, is very favorable: utility costs. They run almost a third less than the national average. This is important in an area where winter heating bills will figure importantly into the family budget.

## Recreation and Culture

Skiing at world-class resorts is a matter of a few hours' drive from Fort Collins. The runs at Loveland Pass, an hour west of Denver, offer free skiing for those older than seventy. One woman I interviewed in Colorado Springs moved here when she was seventy-eight to take advantage of the great skiing.

River rafting on the wild and scenic Cache la Poudre River can be unlike anything you've ever tried. Although you might get doused with spray and rock and roll as you ride the waves, it's a sport that doesn't require strength or skill, at least not if you go rafting with a guide who will do all the work. If you prefer, you can go with a guide who has the passengers do the work. It's fairly safe, too, because you will be wearing a helmet and a life jacket.

Hunting and fishing are, of course, excellent anywhere in Colorado. The Poudre Canyon can be fished throughout its length. On the Cache la Poudre River, beginning 9 miles northwest of Fort Collins, Colorado's famous "Trout Route" begins. Fishing enthusiasts don't want to miss this. For those who like their outdoor recreation a bit less adventuresome, six public golf courses and plenty of tennis courts provide traditional exercise.

Fort Collins is home to Colorado State, the second-largest university in Colorado, with more than 25,000 students, faculty, and staff. Front Range Community College has an additional 3,500 students. The school gives 10 percent discounts off tuition for those older than sixty, 20 percent if you're older than seventy, and a full 30 percent for those students older than eighty. You can be sure that the student population makes a difference in the community. One way this manifests itself is in the quality and variety of inexpensive restaurants. When you put a large body of students and retirees into the restaurant-shopping area, you'll find better and more imaginative cooks.

## Real Estate

Although Fort Collins was established back in the mid-1800s, more than 65 percent of its homes have been built since 1970. This points out the fast-growing nature of Fort Collins and its relatively modern-looking appearance. The average selling price for a single-family home is much higher than in Denver, reflecting the overall high quality of the city. With a median sales price nearing $153,000, lower-priced neighborhoods are often in the above-$100,000 bracket. Some acceptable low-cost neighborhoods have homes for considerably less. Condos sell for about $60,000 to $85,000. The large college-student population places pressures on rentals, so apartments aren't as plentiful as elsewhere.

## Medical Care

Even though Denver is less than an hour away by Interstate 25, medical care in Fort Collins is more than adequate. The Poudre Valley Hospital acts as the regional medical hub of northern Colorado. The facility boasts 235 beds, eleven surgical suites, and twelve intensive- and coronary-care unit beds. The hospital has a Geriatric Assessment Program that offers medical, nutritional, and daily living assistance for at-risk hospitalized senior citizens.

## When Grandkids Visit

An exciting white-water rafting trip down the Poudre River will get your blood racing as waves crash over the side of the raft and you paddle for dear life. If that sounds too daring, then think about going to City Park, where you can rent a paddleboat on the lake. The grandkids can paddle. It isn't as exciting as a river trip, but who the heck needs racing blood, anyway? There's also a slow-moving miniature train to ride and tame geese to feed.

## Addresses and Connections

*Chamber of Commerce:* 420 South Howes Street, Suite 101, Fort Collins, CO 80522

*Senior Services:* 1200 Raintree Drive, Fort Collins, CO 80526

*Newspaper: Fort Collins Coloradoan,* 1212 Riverside Avenue, Fort Collins, CO 80524

*Airport:* local airport offers eight commuter flights to Denver International

*Bus:* local bus service, Greyhound/Trailways, Senior Alternatives in Transportation (for in-town service), hourly bus/van service to Denver International Airport

## Fort Collins Area Weather

| | Jan. | April | July | Oct. | Rain | Snow |
|---|---|---|---|---|---|---|
| | In degrees Fahrenheit | | | | | |
| DAILY HIGHS | 43 | 61 | 88 | 67 | 15" | 60" |
| DAILY LOWS | 16 | 34 | 59 | 37 | | |

## Fort Collins Area Cost of Living

| Overall | Housing | Medical | Groceries | Utilities |
|---|---|---|---|---|
| (percentage of national average) | | | | |
| 104% | 113% | 111% | 109% | 80% |

# Grand Junction

Grand Junction is another example of an economic disaster that turned out to be a bonanza for retirees and illustrates how an influx of retirees helped turn the disaster into a success story. During the late 1970s, encouraged and subsidized by the government, oil companies began experimenting with the enormous oil shale deposits of Colorado and Wyoming. Thousands of workers flocked here to help develop this potentially valuable natural resource. Grand Junction participated in this welcome economic boom. New houses and apartments went up like mushrooms after a rainstorm.

Suddenly, the bubble burst. Slumping oil prices had made it too expensive to squeeze petroleum from the shale. One Sunday afternoon, Exxon announced that it was closing its $5 billion Colony Oil Shale Project. Grand Junction remembers this date as Black Sunday. Almost 8,000 workers lost their jobs. As quickly as they came, they began leaving. Knowing they hadn't even a prayer to make payments, many simply walked away from their homes. They couldn't even give the properties away because they owed more money on the mortgages than the market value. The few buyers who were in the market simply waited for foreclosure and then bought from the banks at bargain prices. As in Bisbee and Ajo, Arizona, the workers who lost their jobs suffered, both financially and emotionally.

The surviving businesses realized that the solution to the problem lay in attracting an industry with a stable financial base, something not subject to boom or bust, like petroleum. Economic incentives, such as free land for new and expanding industries, were offered. At the same time, local officials began concentrating on a special business, one that's clean, doesn't pollute the air, and brings in an obvious source of steady income: the retirement industry. Other nearby towns, such as Parachute, Palisade, Fruita, and Clifton, joined in the movement to attract retirees.

Their efforts were successful. Gradually, the economy recovered, due in large measure to retiree money. Surplus homes were eventually purchased, and the population began rising once more.

Grand Junction would be a great retirement destination regardless of housing bargains. It's just a nice place to live. This is the largest city in western Colorado, located in a broad valley in high plateau country west of the Rocky Mountains. Its name came from its location near the junction of the Colorado and Gunnison Rivers (the Colorado was originally called the Grand River). Grand Junction is the center of an urban area of some 103,000 people, although the town itself has a comfortable population of 42,000. Shopping malls, an active senior citizens' center, and excellent health care are among the attractions. A 4,500-foot altitude and low rainfall combine to ensure four pleasant seasons, with an abundance of sunshine and mild winters. Golf and tennis are year-round sports, adding to Grand Junction's desirability for retirement.

For some reason, the city ranks 149 out of 220 cities in personal safety. This is puzzling, since everyone I've spoken with in Grand Junction swears that the town is safe. Sometimes these statistics can become off-balance because of the way crimes are reported. Unlike some towns of similar size, *all* crimes are reported to the FBI, no matter how minor. The local police chief points out that this skews the crime-rate numbers unfavorably upward.

## Recreation and Culture

With mild weather, golf is a practical, almost year-round sport. Four eighteen-hole courses and one nine-hole layout afford plenty of opportunities to whack the balls. Two clubs plus courts in public parks allow tennis players their exercise. White-water rafting and fishing on the Gunnison and Colorado Rivers are popular and convenient pastimes. Grand Junction is forty-five minutes from Powderhorn Ski Resort on Grand Mesa and less than three hours from most major Colorado ski resorts. A series of trails for walking and biking follow the Colorado River for those who don't care to brave the slopes.

Mesa State College, a four-year institution, offers a variety of continuing education courses of interest to seniors. Grand Junction also has a symphony orchestra that presents concerts from October through April.

## Real Estate

After an initial bottoming out, the real estate market came back dramatically. In fact, both the cost of living and sales prices of homes are slightly above the national average today. According to a local real estate broker, about 50 percent of today's buyers are retirees from out of state. Although the bargain-basement housing market is history, homes are still plentiful, and some inexpensive places are always available. Exceptional bargains can be found in the small towns and neighborhoods outside Grand Junction's city limits. Starter homes sell for between $89,000 and $128,000, with 20 percent of those on the market advertised at $110,000 or less. Another 20 percent of the housing inventory on the market sells between $200,000 and $300,000. Most buyers want to live in their own houses rather than to use them for rentals; for that reason, rentals are scarce.

## Battlement Mesa

During the oil boom period, Exxon, one of the larger companies, was forced to enter the construction business to provide housing for its employees. It developed a flat mountaintop, called Battlement Mesa, into a spiffy housing development. The company constructed 684 residences, complete with a multimillion-dollar recreation center. When employees left, Battlement Mesa became an upscale retirement community.

## Medical Care

Grand Junction has three major hospitals: St. Mary's Hospital, with 325 beds and in the process of enlarging; Community Hospital, with seventy-eight beds; Hilltop Rehab Center; and Veterans Administration Medical Center. The veterans facility is the only one between Denver and Salt Lake City. Forty family practitioner physicians and 115 specialists serve the area.

## When Grandkids Visit

Because this was a heavy-duty dinosaur playground several million years ago, you might want to take the kids to Dinosaur Valley, a museum with dinosaur bones and fossils typical of that era. Seeing animated models of those prehistoric cuddly creatures ought to bring some open-mouthed attention from the grandkiddies.

## Addresses and Connections

*Chamber of Commerce:* 360 Grand Avenue, Grand Pass, CO 81501

*Senior Services:* 550 Ouray Avenue, Grand Junction, CO 81501

*Newspaper: Daily Sentinel,* P.O. Box 668, Grand Junction, CO 81502

*Airport:* there are commuter airline connections to major regional hubs

*Bus:* the newly lauched Arandy Vally Transit System offers transportation from Fruita to Palisade as well as much of the city; there's an on-demand shuttle for seniors, called Mesability Pickup, and regular Greyhound service

## Grand Junction Area Weather

| | In degrees Fahrenheit | | | | | |
| --- | --- | --- | --- | --- | --- | --- |
| | Jan. | April | July | Oct. | Rain | Snow |
| DAILY HIGHS | 36 | 65 | 94 | 69 | 8" | 25" |
| DAILY LOWS | 15 | 38 | 64 | 41 | | |

## Grand Junction Area Cost of Living

| (percentage of national average) | | | | |
| --- | --- | --- | --- | --- |
| Overall | Housing | Medical | Groceries | Utilities |
| 102% | 107% | 104% | 104% | 85% |

# Steamboat Springs

You say you love winter? You can't wait until ski lifts start running? Maybe Steamboat Springs is your town. Snuggled in a high valley at 6,700 feet, the town's alpine climate features low humidity, warm summer days, and cool, crisp nights. It also features winter snow, from 170 to 450 inches. Most of that is on the slopes, thank goodness.

This is a charming, upscale place for those who enjoy delightful summers and abundant outdoor winter sports. While its winter "champagne powder" skiing brings winter athletes from around the country, Steamboat Springs enjoys wonderful summer weather, just what you might expect from its Rocky Mountain setting. Even in July and August, temperatures rarely climb out of the eighties and every evening drop into the fifties. Like Durango, residents appreciate Steamboat Springs for its hometown feeling. One retiree said, "There are so many genuine people who live and work here and raise their families here. That's hard to find in a tourist-dominated ski town."

The town's name came from a mineral spring that made a chugging noise that sounded like a steamboat to the early fur trappers who passed through the area. More than 150 mineral springs are found nearby, supplying medicinal waters for modern-day residents' hot tubs and baths at the public swimming pool.

Abundant wild game and rivers teeming with fish encouraged settlers, and the development of the town as a ski resort brought Steamboat Springs to its present population of about 7,000 inhabitants. Its early development is evident in the well-preserved Victorian homes and substantial brick buildings that date to the late 1800s. Folks who've moved here recently say they appreciate the change from the hectic lifestyle of big cities.

Although the town sits on U.S. Highway 40, a major east-west route, Steamboat Springs is somewhat isolated, being 157 miles from Denver. However, express shuttles to the Denver airport, plus frequent shuttle flights from the local Yampa Valley Regional Airport, keep residents in touch with big-city civilization (for those who need that sort of thing).

## Recreation and Culture

Of course, the major recreational drawing card here is skiing. Steamboat Springs bills itself as "Ski Town USA" and has produced more Olympic skiers than any other U.S. town. With twenty lifts, 141 trails, and a 3,668-foot vertical rise to 10,500 feet, this area is recognized as one of the best in the country. The season lasts from Thanksgiving to Easter each year. Snowmobiling, sleigh rides, and backcountry skiing are also enjoyed.

Summer outdoor sports feature golfing at one nine-hole and two eighteen-hole courses, including a Robert Trent Jones Jr. championship course, and tennis at two public facilities. River rafting, hiking, camping, and soaking in natural hot springs are other outdoor fun things to do here.

Colorado Mountain College/Alpine Campus, a two-year school, offers extensive continuing education classes. The Steamboat Springs Arts

Council coordinates a number of cultural groups, including several dance groups, drama and music ensembles, the Ballet Northwest, the Mountain Madrigal Singers, and a writers' group.

## Real Estate

This is not a place to look for bargain real estate; it's an upscale area, and property offerings show this. This higher-priced real estate pulls the overall cost of living up as well. Condos are big here, and practical, because they can be turned into rentals anytime you're someplace else. The average condo sold in 1999 for more than $100,000. The median sales price for a three-bedroom home was closer to $177,000, with $123,000 in more ordinary neighborhoods. In the exclusive Mt. Werner area, the average selling price of a home approaches $400,000.

## Medical Care

The new Yampa Valley Medical Center serves the community with twenty-four-hour emergency care. The Northwest Colorado Visiting Nurse Association provides home health care for handicapped persons and the terminally ill. There are a couple of small clinics, plus several doctors who are accepting new patients.

## When Grandkids Visit

Check out Fish Creek Falls, where water plunges 280 feet in a spectacular display. This is a place for picnicking and exploring hiking trails. Inner tubing on the Yampa River might appeal more to the grandkids than to more mature folks.

## Addresses and Connections

*Chamber of Commerce:* P.O. Box 774408, Steamboat Springs, CO 80477

*Senior Services:* 1255 Lincoln, Steamboat Springs, CO 80477

*Newspapers: Steamboat Pilot,* P.O. Box 774827, Steamboat Springs, CO 80477; daily free paper: *Steamboat Today,* P.O. Box 774827, Steamboat Springs, CO 80477

*Airport:* Yampa Valley Regional Airport, with year-round service by commuter airlines and express service to Denver International Airport

*Bus:* local service is provided by Steamboat Springs Transit, and Greyhound will get you to Denver and Salt Lake City

## Steamboat Springs Area Weather

| | In degrees Fahrenheit | | | | Rain | Snow |
|---|---|---|---|---|---|---|
| | Jan. | April | July | Oct. | | |
| DAILY HIGHS | 30 | 52 | 82 | 60 | 26" | 60" |
| DAILY LOWS | 1 | 24 | 41 | 24 | | |

# NEVADA

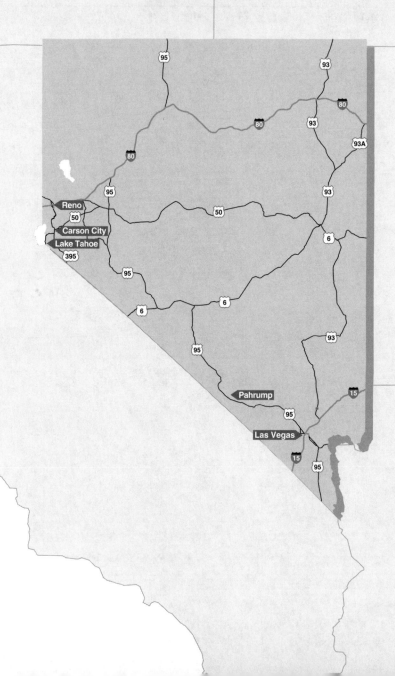

# NEVADA

Because a high mountain range, the Sierra Nevada, extends along the California-Nevada border, cutting off rain-bearing winds from the Pacific Ocean, Nevada is the driest of the Southwestern states. Extensive deserts cover most of the land, with most residents choosing to live in or near one of Nevada's major towns. In fact, more than half of them live in the vicinity of Las Vegas or Reno. Including both rain and melted snow, the average precipitation is only 9 inches in northern Nevada, around Elko, while the southern part, around Las Vegas, receives about 4 inches. Most rain falls in the spring, at which time barren deserts become a riot of color, with the blossoms of cactus, sagebrush, and wild iris embellishing the landscape.

Of all the Western states, Nevada most represents the Old West. Sparsely settled, yet growing with new arrivals daily, Nevada feels like a frontier, a place of new beginnings. Something about Nevada's wide-open spaces stimulates a spirit of adventure and a go-for-broke attitude. It's a place where string ties, jeans, and snakeskin boots feel like natural apparel, a place where you might even be tempted to wear a Stetson hat, confident you won't look downright foolish.

Perhaps a holdover from an era of frontier gambling and gold rushes, a definite atmosphere of excitement hovers over Nevada. Gambling casinos are everywhere, and slot machines are strategically located in gasoline stations, drug stores, and supermarkets. Sometimes you'll even find them in rest rooms; the gambling syndicates don't want to miss a bet. This is a state where lucky gamblers made a stake and lucky miners made fortunes. (Nobody talks about the unlucky stiffs.) This is evident today: Prospecting for precious metals is a popular hobby in Nevada. There's always that chance that the next rock you crack open with a hammer will expose a gleaming streak of gold. (I've broken open many a rock myself in Nevada.)

Nevada is the country's fastest-growing state, by the way, with a 6 percent increase in population every year. And there's plenty of room to grow, since 87 percent of the land is public property, owned by the federal government. Newcomers aren't strangers here, because their neighbors come from all over North America. In Nevada casinos, you'll notice that blackjack dealers, bartenders, and security guards wear name tags that tell you where they came from. According to my figures, only 386 Nevada residents are native Nevadans—the rest come from somewhere else. (I can vouch for the accuracy of this figure, since I made it up myself.)

Gambling fever is a good reason for not retiring in Nevada, especially if you're a compulsive gambler. Sometimes people are surprised to discover they are compulsive. After a lifetime of not being exposed to gambling, the overpowering temptation of large casinos—packed with slot machines, roulette wheels, and card games—hooks them, but good. Today, however, most areas in the country are infected by legal gambling, either by state governments running lotteries and numbers games or by legalized casinos. By the way, Nevada casinos set the odds so they can rake off 10 to 20 percent for overhead and profit. But state lotteries stiff you for 40 to 60 percent, maybe even more.

Should you suspect that you or your spouse have a tendency to go overboard on gambling and could succumb to the irresistible fever of chance, please forget Nevada. Go around it, fly over it, or head in the opposite direction. The round-the-clock excitement is just too much for some folks. They end up throwing their household money on the tables in increasing amounts in a desperate attempt to recoup their losses. The sad thing is, when they do hit a lucky streak and win a bundle of money, the fever won't let them quit. They'll play until they are broke again.

On the other hand, many retirees handle gambling quite well, taking advantage of all the freebies and bargains the clubs offer to lure customers inside. Some never put even a nickel in the machines but have a great time anyway. Buffet tables, laden with salads, entrees, and desserts, offer unlimited visits for $3.00 or $4.00. Prime rib dinners can cost as little as $5.50. Lounge entertainment, with music, dancers, and comedians, is free, although you're encouraged to buy a drink. Some casinos even present free circus acts, complete with animals, high-wire performers, and clowns.

One reason many people give for retiring to Nevada retirement is that the state collects no income tax. Of course, this is an advantage only if your income is substantial and your tax liabilities will be large. Be aware, however, that money earned in another state, rental income—on property in your home state, for example—can be taxed in that state. You'll probably have to fill out a state income tax form to take care of this. At one time, some states were taxing pensions or annuities that came from former employers based in states where you used to live. Recent federal laws now prohibit this; however, you may have to pay taxes to the state in which you reside—depending upon the tax laws of the particular state. Your tax accountant can help you with your decisions.

# History

In 1833 Joseph Walker's expedition followed the Humboldt River in search of new fur-trapping country. The group found several different tribes inhabiting the area, mostly peaceful, nomadic hunters and seed gatherers, such as the Shoshone and the Paiute. The Washoe tribe lived in the west near Lake Tahoe. Today, about 14,000 Native Americans live in Nevada, more than half of them on reservations. The largest reservations are Pyramid Lake, in Washoe County; Walker River, east of Carson City; and Western Shoshone, on the Nevada-Idaho border.

The first road across Nevada followed the Humboldt Trail blazed by Joseph Walker and became part of the gold rush–era California Trail. It followed the Humboldt River, which provided water for wagon trains as the settlers crossed this dry region. Today this trail is called Interstate 80.

Nevada's early history was largely the story of its mining discoveries, booms, and busts. The discovery of the Comstock Lode and other deposits in 1859 started a twenty-year boom, followed by a twenty-year depression in the industry. Then, around 1900, another boom boosted Nevada, with silver and gold strikes at Tonopah and Goldfield and the development of copper mining at Ely. Between the two world wars, another decline in mining activity depressed the economy.

Although minerals and mining play an important part in Nevada's present-day economy, a new, nonmining economy has finally emerged, largely due to the state's fabulous year-round gambling industry. Casino gambling started this economy rolling, and it seems to be continuing with great success even though gambling casinos are no longer the monopoly of Nevada.

# Las Vegas

Once mainly a glittering entertainment focal point for Los Angeles high-rollers, Las Vegas is gaining a national reputation as much more than a gambling center. Today it's a virtual boomtown and is the fastest-

## Nevada Tax Profile

Sales tax:
**6.5% to 7%; food and drugs exempt**

State income tax:
**none**

Property taxes:
**about 1% of appraised value; a typical $100,000 home pays about $1,000**

Intangibles tax:
**none**

Social Security tax:
**none**

Pension taxes:
**none**

Gasoline tax:
**23.5¢**

growing city in the nation. Thousands of new residents arrive each year, many of them retirees, and they're spreading the city farther out into the desert every day. Today's population is around 390,000 and growing.

Because of this vigorous growth, retirees easily find part-time work if they so desire, and oftentimes more than just minimum-wage jobs. Casinos, restaurants, and other tourist businesses need part-time help, but incoming industries and businesses siphon new residents from the labor pool, offering them full-time jobs. High-tech firms also figure big in the employment picture, opening part-time and consultant positions to skilled Silicon Valley–type retirees. The Las Vegas area leads the nation in job creation, which equals a pleasant employment climate. As in Reno, casinos tend to give special consideration to hiring senior citizens; the percentage of older employees is impressive—well, except for the cocktail waitresses, who tend to be young, peachy-cheeked, and bosomy. Clearly, this is age discrimination, but you probably wouldn't care to run around half naked, delivering booze to a bunch of gamblers in the first place, would you?

Many retirees who normally might have chosen Phoenix are trying Las Vegas instead. Heading their list of reasons are the casino excitement, absence of state income taxes, and proximity to southern California. (Las Vegas is a five-hour drive to Los Angeles, compared to Phoenix's seven to eight hours.) There's talk of a privately financed supertrain that will link

Las Vegas and southern California, moving millions of visitors at a fantastic 250 miles per hour. Las Vegas wants to get 'em there fast, fleece 'em fast, and send 'em home fast.

Other taxes in the state are low, because about 50 percent of all state tax revenues come from the resort, tourism, and casino industries. Because of this bountiful source of income, Nevada doesn't depend on corporate income or personal income taxes, and its property taxes are among the lowest in the West.

Those questioned about their choice of Las Vegas as a retirement destination usually include weather as a factor. Make no mistake, summers in Las Vegas are hot—commonly above one hundred degrees—yet those who retire here maintain that they love it that way. (Everything is air-conditioned, so what do they know about hot weather?) Winters are delightful, except for a few windy days now and then and an occasional flash flood that takes out a casino or two. (Somebody keeps forgetting that building casinos in dry river beds is a bad idea, even if the land is bargain priced.)

Because of low humidity and the absence of freezing weather, mobile homes are quite practical and a source of lower-cost housing. Inexpensive evaporative coolers do a fine job during the hot months. Mobile home parks present a wide choice of options, from inexpensive to superluxurious. During the winter, RV parks fill with cold-weather fugitives, who, as expected, depart for cooler climes come the summer. Nevertheless, retirees in Las Vegas form a steady, year-round population as opposed to the floating, second-home group found along the Colorado River and in southern Arizona.

Las Vegas has several active senior citizens' groups as well as the usual volunteer organizations like RSVP. Local newspapers run regular features covering news and activities of interest to retirees. Because this is a city, senior citizens' centers aren't intimate as you might expect in a small town, but they certainly offer a wide range of activities to keep active people busy and happy.

## Recreation and Culture

As in most heavily populated tourist towns, golf, tennis, and swimming facilities are bigger than in real-life, nontouristy places. Golf in Las Vegas is too big a subject to cover here. Suffice it to say that courses are famous, numerous, and challenging. Tennis players will find many municipal courts scattered about town, which are augmented by countless courts at resorts and casinos. Fishing and boating on Lake Powell and Lake Mead bring a water wonderland to one of the driest deserts in North America.

Las Vegas casinos promote some of the most spectacular sporting events of the year. Championship prizefights, bowling invitationals, golf tournaments, and the World Series of Poker are held in Vegas, not to mention off-road racing, rodeos, and softball championships.

Las Vegas nightlife is legendary, with Hollywood headline stars appearing with hopeful newcomers in all sorts of revues, musicals, and concerts. Some presentations are expensive, but other shows have a two-drink minimum instead of a cover charge. Lounge shows, with up-and-coming (as well as never-going-anywhere) entertainers are both enjoyable and inexpensive, since buying a drink is all that's expected.

Several Las Vegas cultural centers present concerts, plays, and dance programs. Free concerts by the Nevada String Quartet are regularly given in the Flamingo Library auditorium. The University of Nevada stages classical and contemporary theater throughout the year, as well as symphony and ballet, directed by internationally known artists. And unlike in many cities, where lack of library funding is a perennial issue, Las Vegas retirees have a huge new city library to meet their literary needs.

## Real Estate

As you might suspect, housing activity keeps up with the influx of newcomers. In fact, it has more than kept up. From its inception, Las Vegas has tended to overbuild; optimistic developers keep supply ahead of demand, thus keeping housing costs under control. Two- and three-bedroom homes can be found at prices that would seem like bargains in other parts of the country, where they would cost twice as much. Apartments are plentiful, with high vacancy rates. In short, Las Vegas housing isn't inexpensive, but neither is it prohibitive. Most neighborhoods report median sales prices of $136,000, up about $10,000 from a couple of years ago. Many homes sell for less than $100,000.

## Medical Care

Surprisingly, Las Vegas's level of medical care is only adequate instead of superb, as is the case in Phoenix and Los Angeles. Las Vegas has a few good-size hospitals, but from personal experience with them, I'd travel to Phoenix or Los Angeles if I had a serious problem. My observation is that the quality of doctors and hospitals in Las Vegas leaves much to be desired. Friends who live there tend to agree with me. You'll need to check it out for yourself.

## When Grandkids Visit

There aren't many places to take them that don't involve a hefty entrance fee. That's the way it is in tourist towns. However, Red Rock Canyon is one place, and it's the next best desert trip to a long drive to Death Valley. The 13-mile scenic road takes you by the 3,000-foot-high Red Rock Escarpment, and you stand a chance of seeing wild burros and possibly even bighorn sheep. Another idea is to visit the Circus Circus casino, where kids are allowed in to watch high-wire gymnastics and circus acts. There's also a large video arcade where you can leave the kiddies with a pocketful of quarters and let them shoot down space invaders while you make a surreptitious visit to a blackjack table.

## Addresses and Connections

*Chamber of Commerce:* 2301 East Sahara Avenue, Las Vegas, NV 89104

*Senior Services:* 450 East Bonanza Road, Las Vegas, NV 89106

*Newspaper: Review-Journal and Sun,* 1111 West Bonanza Road, Las Vegas, NV 89106

*Airport:* McCarran International

*Bus/Train:* Citizens Area Transit buses serve the area (and give senior discounts), and Greyhound and Amtrak provide out-of-area transport

## Las Vegas Area Weather

| | In degrees Fahrenheit | | | | | |
|---|---|---|---|---|---|---|
| | Jan. | April | July | Oct. | Rain | Snow |
| DAILY HIGHS | 56 | 77 | 105 | 82 | 4" | 1" |
| DAILY LOWS | 33 | 50 | 76 | 54 | | |

## Las Vegas Area Cost of Living

| (percentage of national average) | | | | |
|---|---|---|---|---|
| Overall | Housing | Medical | Groceries | Utilities |
| 107% | 97% | 125% | 115% | 87% |

# Pahrump

A fast-growing star among Nevada's retirement communities is the town of Pahrump, located 63 miles west of Las Vegas and about the same distance east from Death Valley. The setting is pure desert, as Pahrump sprawls in a long valley with the Spring Mountain range on one side and the Nopah Mountains on the other. One couple I interviewed in Pahrump said, "We love the desert. As often as we can, we drive our Jeep into the hills and prospect for gold. We haven't found any yet, don't really expect to, but that's not the point. Most of the fun is just getting out there in the wild, surrounded by desert plants and mysterious animal tracks."

When I first visited Pahrump several years ago, it consisted of little more than a couple of small taverns, a handful of stores, and some cotton farms. Today it has grown into a small city. Complete with a senior citizens' center, a library, a medical facility, a bowling alley, and a community center (with swimming pool), Pahrump has moved from the category of crossroads settlement to a viable retirement community. In fact, about 40 percent of the residents are retired. The town has grown at an astounding 15 percent per year for the last several years to its present size of 30,000.

The major drawing cards in this valley are sunshine, mild weather, low-cost land, and friendly neighbors. Pahrump ranks just below Yuma, Arizona, as one of the places with the most sunny days in the United States. Its low humidity makes even the hottest days feel bearable, if not comfortable. The mountains surrounding Pahrump act as effective barriers to moisture-laden storms that drift in from the Pacific Ocean. You can count on very few overcast or rainy days. The average rainfall is only 4 inches, and the relative humidity is about 29 percent, making this one of the driest localities in the nation. Yet water supplies are not a problem, because Pahrump sits on the third-largest underground supply of water in the United States.

People who live in Pahrump commonly spend a great deal of time arguing over where the name of the town came from. According to some resident experts, *Pahrump* is a Paiute word that means "water rock." Since water rocks are rare hereabouts, other experts insist that the Paiute chief who sold land to the original settlers, when asked about a deed and title insurance, nervously cleared his throat with a "pahrump" sound. Other residents ridicule this theory, maintaining that the Native American simply belched in an effort to change the subject, and that's where Pahrump got its name.

Travelers are often unaware they've entered the town of Pahrump, because its inhabitants are scattered over an area of 25 square miles. A feeling of spaciousness is enhanced by homes sitting on large parcels of land, mostly one acre in size—sometimes ten to twenty acres—and as far off the main highway as possible. Since desert land is inexpensive, folks see no need to crowd themselves next to the neighbors. Pahrump also lacks a compact, traditional downtown center so characteristic of other communities its size. Like residential homes, businesses tend to locate on large pieces of land, spaced apart from competitors. There's never a problem finding a parking space here! Several small shopping centers host a collection of stores grouped about a supermarket, but with plenty of open space between the complex and other businesses. Since everyone drives a car here, sidewalks are absent, adding to the rural feeling of Western desert living.

## Recreation and Culture

As you might expect, fishing, boating, and waterskiing aren't all that great around Pahrump. Snow skiing isn't too popular, either. But outdoor sports enthusiasts will enjoy two golf courses, and rock hounds and amateur prospectors have a ball with all that open country to explore.

Although cultural activities are understandably limited in a desert community, the Oasis Writers' Guild is quite active, as well as the Visual and Performing Arts Council, which always has great events planned. The Community College of Southern Nevada offers evening courses at Pahrump Valley High School.

Several small casinos provide gaming excitement for those who enjoy exercising by way of pulling slot machine handles or tossing ivory cubes across a green felt table. Since these places are small and tourists relatively scarce, the bulk of the patrons are Pahrump residents, so the sterile, impersonal air of Vegas casinos is absent here. These places serve as gathering centers for friends and neighbors, sometimes for a social evening of dancing and entertainment by local bands. I might mention that the one and only time I hit a jackpot in a Pahrump casino, the bartender immediately hung an OUT OF ORDER sign on the machine.

The Pahrump Valley Harvest Festival and Fair had its beginnings more than thirty years ago. It has grown from an unofficial weekend of relaxation for farmers after the harvest into a three-day event that attracts more than 20,000 people from the surrounding desert towns and villages. A highlight of the celebration is a deep-pit barbecue and 6,000 pounds of beef to feed the throngs. A rodeo, stock car races, and dancing under the stars are also on the program.

## Real Estate

The town of Pahrump straddles the dividing line of Nye and Clark Counties. You know when you cross into Nye County, because the architectural styles change. At one time, Nye County had no strict building codes, so homeowners built any way they pleased. It made for some interesting and innovative buildings. However, this is changing, as Nye County is adding building inspectors to enforce Nevada state building codes.

Because desert land is so plentiful, acreage is inexpensive. Large tracts in town are becoming scarce nowadays, as owners are tempted to break them into acre-size parcels and get more money. The price of a typical three-bedroom home ranges from $75,000 to $270,000. Rentals used to be scarce, but lately they've become plentiful, with prices starting at $450 for a town house or apartment. Mobile homes are big here and are a great option for low-cost housing on your own acreage. Many residents start off with an inexpensive mobile while they construct their more substantial home.

## Medical Care

One drawback about living in a small town far from a metropolitan center is that you'll have a long way to go to get to a full-service medical facility. However, two small clinics take care of emergencies, and a twenty-four-hour emergency center will soon be available. Doctors here are accepting new patients.

Home Health Services of Nevada (HHSN), a nonprofit home health agency, has been in Pahrump for more than twenty years now. According to the local manager, "The cost for HHSN to visit a patient in the home for a month is less than for a patient to stay in the hospital for two days." While this care isn't free, most patients are covered by Medicare, Medicaid, or private insurance companies.

## When Grandkids Visit

Be sure to take them to Death Valley, about an hour's drive away and one of the nation's natural wonders. Pahrump also has a historical museum that's good for a short visit. Cathedral Canyon, 14 miles to the southeast, is another place, with hiking paths and unusual displays of sculpture. For things to do in town, there's the Valley Fun Park, with go-cart rides, a bungee jump, and a miniature golf course. (Who knows, you might be entitled to a senior citizen's discount on the bungee jump.)

## Addresses and Connections

*Chamber of Commerce:* (on Highway 160) P.O. Box 42, Pahrump, NV 89041

*Senior Services:* 1300 West Basin, Pahrump, NV 89041

*Newspapers: Gazette,* Pahrump, NV 89041; *Pahrump Valley Times,* 2160 Calvada Boulevard, Pahrump, NV 89048

*Airport:* the nearest is Las Vegas, but there's no shuttle service

*Bus:* none; you'll need an automobile here

## Pahrump Area Weather

|  | In degrees Fahrenheit | | | | | |
|---|---|---|---|---|---|---|
|  | Jan. | April | July | Oct. | Rain | Snow |
| DAILY HIGHS | 56 | 77 | 103 | 81 | 4" | 1" |
| DAILY LOWS | 32 | 59 | 75 | 54 | | |

# Reno

In the past, Las Vegas and Lake Tahoe were formal but glitzy places, while Reno tended to be informal and relaxed. Las Vegas was the Eastern-style glamour girl, adorned with mink and diamond bracelets; Reno was pure Western, a cowboy with a string tie and Stetson hat. Time was, neckties and cocktail dresses were as out of place in Reno casinos as pigs in church. Western wear and work clothes were more Reno's style. Within the past few years, however, the town has changed somewhat, as large Las Vegas– and Lake Tahoe–style casinos cropped up all over the place. Nowadays neckties and cocktail dresses attract no attention in Reno's nightlife emporiums. (Not unless both are worn at the same time, of course.) But some older establishments, especially in the downtown center, still cater to the blue-jeans-and-work-shirt hometown crowd.

Reno is a much older town than Las Vegas and in many respects has managed to preserve its Old West atmosphere. People are proud of the town's rowdy gold- and silver-mining past, and they love Reno's picturesque setting, with its backdrop of snow-fringed peaks looming in the distance. Originally, Reno's major business was supplying the booming mining camps that flourished nearby. About the time the mines played out, a new industry arose in the form of quickie divorces. Reno divorces were considered the only practical way to go for an uncomplicated marriage dissolution. As other states liberalized their divorce laws, legalized gambling became the leading industry. Ironically, Reno has become a quick marriage center, with wedding chapels scattered around town like fast-food restaurants. Today, marriages in Reno outnumber divorces by ten to one.

Like Las Vegas, Reno has undergone a building boom, with the city expanding outward at a rapid pace. Including the adjoining city of Sparks, the population is nearing 200,000, which makes Reno a good-size city. Yet residents here are proud of Reno's self-bestowed title of "The Biggest Little City in the World." This hometown feeling was deliberately cultivated when gambling was first legalized, during the depression days of the 1930s. Harold Smith, founder of Harold's Club, decided to go after local money instead of depending on tourists. He instituted the practice of giving free drinks and double odds on craps tables. He cashed paychecks without charge and tried to make people feel at home. Harold's Club also started the practice of preferential hiring of local people and senior citizens. That policy remains in force today, with retirees doing everything from dealing blackjack to making change.

Because of the large number of retirees, services for senior citizens are plentiful. Retiree clubs and organizations are unusually active. Programs such as Meals on Wheels and Care and Share are active, as well as several city, county, and state programs. The local senior center operates a senior citizens' employment service and law center, providing free assistance with wills, leases, and things of that nature.

Some retirees choose Reno for its casino excitement and other amenities, but everybody likes its extraordinary climate. The 4,440-foot altitude and very low humidity keep the weather pleasant year-round. For those who cannot stand hot summer weather, Reno is perfect. Expect to enjoy about 300 sunny days in Reno. Even though July and

August midday temperatures usually approach ninety degrees by midafternoon, you will sleep under an electric blanket every night of the year; the thermometer almost always drops into the forties. Even in the middle of winter, the daily high temperatures are about the same as summer nighttime lows.

A light jacket or sweater feels warm in this dry climate, even when the temperature is below freezing. I am always surprised to walk outside wearing a short-sleeved shirt and feeling perfectly comfortable, then notice a thermometer announcing that it is thirty-eight degrees. Air-conditioning is unknown in residential properties, and low electricity rates keep winter heating bills within a reasonable range.

Reno's cost of living is considerably higher than that of Las Vegas, a fact that puzzles me. One might think that it should be the other way around, given Las Vegas's glamorous reputation. Living costs here are 12 percent above the national average. Housing costs are also higher. Utility rates, however, are low, helping to equalize living expenses.

Reno's gambling excitement attracts people from around the country, and as you might expect, a percentage are predictably unstable. As they lose their money, they turn to crime to recoup their loses. Therefore, like all gambling centers, Reno has more than its share of crime. But the majority of the transgressions are crimes like shoplifting and car break-ins. Retirees report that they feel perfectly safe in their residential neighborhoods.

## Recreation and Culture

Reno's weather encourages a variety of outdoor activities. Skiing at nearby Sierra Nevada resorts is a matter of less than an hour's drive. This same country is wonderful for warm-weather fun. There are lakes and streams for fishing and camping, and the hiking trails are seemingly unlimited. Rock hounds, gold panners, and amateur prospectors enjoy the marvels of Nevada's mineralized districts, some less than an hour's drive from the city. Reno is also famous for annual events such as the National Air Races, the Reno Rodeo, and balloon races. Because of an appreciable Basque influence in western Nevada, a Basque Festival is celebrated here every year. By the way, don't pass up the opportunity to dine at a Basque restaurant around Reno; the food is served family style and is hearty and always delicious.

## Real Estate

Although Las Vegas construction imitates the style of southern California—stucco ranch houses with tile roofs—Reno prefers old-fashioned houses built of honest red brick. The older neighborhoods are comprised of solidly built, no-nonsense homes—a settled, mature city. The area has been undergoing a tremendous expansion, both in growth of business and in the number of new homes under construction. The desert around the city seems to be sprouting subdivisions. Economical homes start at around $95,000, with the median price closer to $132,000. Condos and apartments have seen some of the housing boom but have barely kept up with demand, and as a result are slightly higher priced than average for a city the size of Reno. Thirteen apartment complexes specialize in assisted housing for the elderly, handicapped, and disabled, plus there are three large full-service retirement facilities.

## Medical Care

Reno is the medical center for the western Nevada–eastern California area. Washoe Medical Center has an important cardiac rehabilitation facility and is where other hospitals send patients when serious problems arise. St. Mary's and four other hospitals serve the Reno area.

## When Grandkids Visit

If they're old enough to appreciate a museum of antique, classic automobiles, take them to the National Automobile Museum. Its display of 200 cars makes an interesting tour.

## Addresses and Connections

*Chamber of Commerce:* 4590 South Virginia Street, Reno, NV 89502
*Senior Services:* Sutro and Nineth, Reno, NV 89502
*Newspaper: Reno Gazette-Journal,* 955 Kuenzli Street, Reno, NV 89502
*Airport:* Reno Airport, with connections to major airlines
*Bus/Train:* city buses; Greyhound and Amtrak serve the area

## Reno Area Weather

| | Jan. | April | July | Oct. | Rain | Snow |
|---|---|---|---|---|---|---|
| | In degrees Fahrenheit | | | | | |
| DAILY HIGHS | 45 | 63 | 91 | 70 | 8" | 24" |
| DAILY LOWS | 20 | 29 | 48 | 31 | | |

## Reno Area Cost of Living

| (percentage of national average) | | | | |
|---|---|---|---|---|
| Overall | Housing | Medical | Groceries | Utilities |
| 110% | 117% | 123% | 109% | 95% |

# Lake Tahoe

A short drive from Carson City—up the mountainside along a wide, four-lane highway—a bustling, fast-growing community clusters around one of the country's most famous lakes. Many consider the Lake Tahoe area a prime place for retirement, despite its drawbacks of heavy tourism and crowded streets. What most people refer to as "Lake Tahoe," however, is actually a sprawling collection of small cities that group near the lake and sometimes straddle the line between Nevada and California. A majority of retirees live on the California side; all of the gambling is on the Nevada side. Also on the Nevada side are some residents who have enough income that California state income taxes could hurt.

Well known for luxurious hotels and gambling casinos, Lake Tahoe is also celebrated for its beauty; it sits next to one of the most gorgeous lakes in the world. After a while you become numb trying to take in all of its delights. Mark Twain had this to say about Lake Tahoe, in his book *Roughing It:*

> Three months of camp life on Lake Tahoe would restore an Egyptian mummy to his pristine vigor and give him an appetite like an alligator. I do not mean the oldest and driest mummies, of course, but the fresher ones. The air up there in the clouds is very pure and fine, bracing, and delicious. And why shouldn't it be? It is the same the angels breathe. Lake Tahoe must surely be the fairest picture the whole earth affords.

Snow is an important part of Tahoe's winter. If there isn't at least a 6-foot pack on the ski slopes, skiers feel cheated. From anywhere in town it is a matter of minutes to a ski lift, a joy to those who enjoy the sport. The snow typically falls in isolated, heavy storms that dump up to 3 feet in one night; then the weather turns sunny for days or weeks until the next snow. From my perspective, the best thing about Lake Tahoe snow is that it takes only a twenty-minute drive to be out of it. You can be skiing at Incline

Village in the morning and wandering through Carson City in shirtsleeves that same evening.

Why would people consider retiring here? "Living here is like being on permanent vacation," says a friend of ours who owns a lakefront cottage near North Shore. Like many residents, he bought his home several years ago, in anticipation of retirement. He rented out his place by the day or week at premium rates to regular visitors—vacationers, skiers, and gamblers—and by the time he was ready to retire, a good portion of his retirement home had been paid off. The deductions and depreciation as a rental also helped ease his tax burdens. Long-term rentals, however, are usually available at rates one would expect to pay in most California urban areas. That can be expensive and worth it only if you cannot consider living anywhere else because you love Lake Tahoe so much. Many people living here feel just this way.

## Recreation and Culture

Outdoor recreation is superb, since Tahoe sits smack in the middle of a national forest wonderland, with high lakes, rivers, and streams, not to mention Lake Tahoe itself. It goes without saying that skiing around the lake and in places like Squaw Valley is world famous. Golf courses are plentiful, and most are open to the public.

Since the Lake Tahoe economy is basically tourist oriented, many normal cultural and entertainment activities are lacking. For example, to the best of my knowledge, there are no senior citizens' centers other than three nutrition programs. But the lack of organized recreation is more than made up by the top-notch talent presented by the casinos. Hollywood entertainers regularly appear at the gambling emporiums, often at a fraction of the entrance fees you'd expect in a noncompetitive economy.

In addition, the area is served by Lake Tahoe Community College, which offers various courses for seniors, from computer to exercise classes.

## Real Estate

The cost of living here is clearly higher than in nearby Reno or Carson City. With tourist dollars floating around freely, you can expect that prices will float with them. Housing is expensive as well. But for many, a higher cost of living is a reasonable trade-off for the quality of the surroundings and the excitement of the lake area. Affordable housing can be found, but you certainly won't have a lake view. The sudden boom of Silicon Valley millionaires in the San Francisco area has had an affect on Tahoe; everyone wants to have a weekend getaway by the lake.

## Medical Care

One major hospital, Tahoe Forest, serves the medical needs of the Lake Tahoe area. The facility is equipped to handle most cases, and there is quick transportation to either the University of California Hospital at Davis, near Sacramento, or the Washoe Medical Center in Reno.

## When Grandkids Visit

Consider the Ponderosa Ranch in Incline Village, on the Nevada side of the lake. If they've watched reruns of the *Bonanza* television show, they'll enjoy this theme park, which features the original Cartwright ranch setting. The park includes a museum, a petting farm, a mystery mine, and a saloon (thank God).

## Addresses and Connections

*Chamber of Commerce:* Crystal Bay Chamber, 969 Tahoe Boulevard, Incline Village, NV 89451

*Senior Services:* 885 Highway 50, Zephyr Cove; or write P.O. Box 1771, Zephyr Cove, NV 89448

*Newspaper:* none, but see the Reno and Carson City papers

*Airport:* Tahoe Airport, with connections to major airlines

*Bus:* a local bus serves South Lake Tahoe, while shuttles get you to and from the airport; Greyhound passes through the area as well

## Lake Tahoe Area Weather

| | In degrees Fahrenheit | | | | | |
| --- | --- | --- | --- | --- | --- | --- |
| | Jan. | April | July | Oct. | Rain | Snow |
| DAILY HIGHS | 42 | 61 | 86 | 67 | 18" | 60" |
| DAILY LOWS | 16 | 24 | 49 | 34 | | |

# Carson City

Carson City is the state capital and is Nevada's fifth-largest city, even though it has a population of less than 50,000. The downtown area's old buildings give you a feeling for Carson City's historic past and rich Western heritage. The old State Legislature and Courthouse probably look much the same as they did back in the days when Mark Twain worked in nearby Virginia City.

The altitude here is 4,697 feet, approximately the same as Reno's. Carson City shares Reno's cool, dry climate. As has been the experience of larger Nevada towns, Carson City has seen a population explosion. But here the expansion is outward, spreading into the desert rather than upward, with tall casinos. Tourist demand for large, luxurious casinos hasn't hit Carson City as it has Reno and Las Vegas, so the funky old downtown has changed little over the years. This is one of the city's charms: a comfortable, slow-paced, nontouristy atmosphere. Subdivisions fan away from the city, with both upscale and moderate construction. All neighborhoods enjoy views of nearby mountains, and the clear air seems to magnify their majestic presence.

The senior citizens' center here is exceptionally active, providing a long list of services, from health programs to Social Security counseling. Volunteering is an important part of the center's structure, with more than 200 volunteers working on various projects.

Don't expect much help from the chamber of commerce here. In response to my request for retirement information for this book, the chamber sent a pamphlet with an order blank for a packet of information, at $12.50 plus tax.

FBI statistics aren't available for Carson City, but presumably they would be similar to Reno's crime rates; that is, they would fall into a middle range. I would suspect that since Carson City is a much smaller place, with less concentration on gambling, crime rates might even be somewhat lower here.

## Recreation and Culture

Carson City's location, in the desert yet close to the mountains, gives easy access to year-round sports and recreation opportunities. Within a thirty- to ninety-minute drive, there's an impressive concentration of world-class ski resorts. Trout fishing in mountain streams or alpine lakes is the best imaginable, with rare golden trout lurking in the higher altitudes. Big-game hunting includes elk, antelope, deer, and bighorn sheep in the mountains and deserts (hopefully shot with cameras, not rifles). Both amateur and professional golfers will appreciate Carson City's championship golf layouts. Eagle Valley offers two challenging eighteen-hole courses.

Despite what some may believe, cultural events in Carson City do not involve cards, dice, and roulette wheels—not always, at least. The Brewery Arts Center supports a variety of visual and performing arts. The center also houses the Nevada Artists Association Gallery, and a broad range of arts and crafts classes are available. There's also the Carson City Chamber Orchestra, the Carson City Community Band, and the Carson Chamber Singers, all of which present musical, theatrical, and dance productions at the Brewery Arts Center, the Carson Community Center, or Western Nevada Community College. The college has a variety of community service classes that may be of interest to retirees.

An interesting side trip, and a possible place for retirement, is nearby Virginia City. Known as the "Queen of the Comstock," this is probably one of the best-preserved ghost towns in the West. At one time Virginia City had 30,000 residents, a hundred saloons, banks, theaters, and elegant hotels, the likes of which couldn't be matched between Denver and San Francisco. Today the population is not much more than 1,000. This is where Mark Twain and Brett Harte got their start as writers, working on the old *Territorial Enterprise.* Many buildings from those boom days are still inhabitable, and many have been refurbished and used as residences, bed-and-breakfasts, and shops. Virginia City has a special place in my heart, because that's where my grandfather worked deep within the Comstock Lode and where he died back around 1910.

## Real Estate

Carson's City's cost of living is about the same as Reno's but is still about 11 percent above the national average. Utilities used to be low but for some reason have climbed to above average. Median sales prices of homes are almost $150,000.

The housing market reflects the growing interest in Carson Valley. New homes, with all amenities, are selling from $100,000 to $149,000, depending on size and location. Since Carson City is expanding at such a rate, many choose to look in Gardnerville or Minden, which are centered on smaller downtown areas but offer adequate shopping and amenities. Older homes in Carson City, closer to downtown, sell for below average, but you'll need to investigate the neighborhood and condition of the home carefully.

## Medical Care

Carson City is not far from the large-scale medical facilities of Reno and has its own 116-bed hospital. The Carson-Tahoe Hospital offers nutritional counseling, wellness programs, and hospice services. The hospital recently completed an $8.5 million expansion and remodeling project.

## When Grandkids Visit

Tour the Nevada State Railroad Museum. On display are more than twenty-six pieces of equipment that once were used on the Virginia and Truckee Railroad. This line carried silver ore from the famous Comstock Lode mines in Virginia City for years. If you time it right, you and the grandkids can catch a ride on the train pulled by a working steam engine.

## Addresses and Connections

*Chamber of Commerce:* 1900 South Carson Street, Suite 100, Carson City, NV 89701

*Senior Services:* 901 Beverly Drive, Carson City, NV 89706

*Newspaper: Nevada Appeal,* 200 Bath Street, Carson City, NV 89703

*Airport:* Reno Tahoe International; local general aviation airport

*Bus:* Greyhound service and airport shuttle to Reno; no city bus service

## Carson City Area Weather

| | In degrees Fahrenheit | | | | | |
| | Jan. | April | July | Oct. | Rain | Snow |
|---|---|---|---|---|---|---|
| DAILY HIGHS | 45 | 63 | 91 | 70 | 7.5" | 24.4" |
| DAILY LOWS | 20 | 29 | 48 | 31 | | |

## Carson City Area Cost of Living

| (percentage of national average) | | | | |
| Overall | Housing | Medical | Groceries | Utilities |
|---|---|---|---|---|
| 111% | 111% | 122% | 117% | 104% |

# Ghost Towns and Prospecting

Two favorite pastimes for Nevada retirees are exploring historic relics of Nevada's past and visiting nearby mines that once supported the towns. Ghost towns are fun places to search for old purple-glass bottles and other treasures discarded by yesterday's miners. It's not difficult to go one step further and try your hand at prospecting for valuable minerals. Not only is this fun, but it's healthy outdoor recreation that doesn't require special athletic skills or investment. Because the desert and mountain terrain is usually free of vegetation, prospecting is relatively easy. Classes in mineralogy are available through Reno's adult education program to prepare you for some serious rock hunting and prospecting.

Don't think prospecting for valuable minerals is just a dreamy fantasy. It's still possible to strike it rich (not probable, just remotely possible). Most Western silver mines were abandoned back in the 1930s when silver dropped to 25 cents an ounce, and gold mines were closed during World War II on orders of the federal government. After the war, mining activity never regained its momentum, and gold and silver mines were left to revert to nature. With today's higher gold and silver prices, prospects once passed over because of low values could now be valuable. A case in point: My brother, an amateur prospector on a weekend outing, stumbled across a lead-silver outcropping in Death Valley that turned out to be the state's largest silver producer for the sixteen years it yielded ore.

Some ghost towns are marked by shells of buildings, roofless and disintegrating with time. Others are found only by studying maps and looking for old dumps and traces of foundations. The dumps, incidentally, are the best places to find old bottles and artifacts.

Not all ghost towns wasted away to true "ghost" status. Many held on to a percentage of their population, partly because residents couldn't sell their real estate and partly because these old towns are fascinating places to live. Today, some mining towns are making a comeback, and it turns out these are great places for retirement for a certain type of retiree. Ghost towns appeal to those fascinated by history who don't mind living in a rustic, isolated area with few neighbors or community facilities. If you've read this far, maybe the notion of ghost town retirement is an appropriate one to pursue. Frankly, it's not something my wife or I would consider, but those who do retire in ghost towns love every minute of it.

Places like Ely (pop. 4,800), Tonopah (pop. 2,700), and Goldfield (pop. 3,600) never died out completely and will never completely make it back to their former glory. Other places, even smaller, such as Austin (pop. 400) and Eureka (pop. 800), are worthwhile to investigate, if only out of curiosity. But I can't emphasize too strongly that you must be specially suited for living in a place that time has left behind. This is not a situation in which you can invest impulsively and expect to sell out quickly and move on if you find out you've made a mistake. The reason for so many vacant houses is that it's neither a seller's market nor a buyer's market.

# NEW MEXICO

The state of New Mexico is shaped like a rectangle, bounded on the north by Colorado and on the south by Mexico and Texas, with Arizona bordering the west and Oklahoma and the Texas panhandle on the east. At New Mexico's northwest corner you'll find the only point in the nation where four states meet: New Mexico, Colorado, Arizona, and Utah. This is the famous "Four Corners" area. New Mexico is a state big on land—the nation's fifth largest (after Alaska, Texas, California, and Montana). Yet, with only about 1.5 million residents, it's lightly populated (fewer people live in the entire state than in the metropolitan area of Denver), so there's plenty of room for newcomers. With its scenic deserts, lush forests, and high mountain ranges, New Mexico clearly lives up to its nickname: the Land of Enchantment.

The state has a partly dry to dry climate, not particularly different from other arid Southwestern regions. A combination of low humidity, high altitude, and abundant sunshine makes this a pleasant and healthy place to live. Summer days are hot, but nights in New Mexico are always cool. Many localities commonly find that temperatures can register ninety degrees on a sunny day and fall to fifty degrees in the evening. Although daytime air-conditioning may be popular in some areas, most of the time you'll sleep under blankets at night. Precipitation (including snow) varies from 8 inches a year in some places to as much as 24 inches in some mountainous areas. Yearly snowfall ranges from 0 to 300 inches near Ruidoso.

About a third of New Mexico's population consider themselves to be Hispanic and are very proud of their heritage. Their ancestors were the early Spanish explorers and colonists, the first Europeans in this area. These Spanish settlers were farming and creating towns and villages in New Mexico a full generation before the Pilgrims ever set foot on Plymouth Rock. By the way, New Mexican Hispanics dislike being called "Mexican-Americans." It's considered very rude. After all, their forefathers were living here more than three centuries before there even was a Mexico. People here converse in an archaic form of Spanish, the cultured manner of speaking that was in vogue back in the sixteenth and seventeenth centuries. Some words in the local vocabulary wouldn't be

# NEW MEXICO

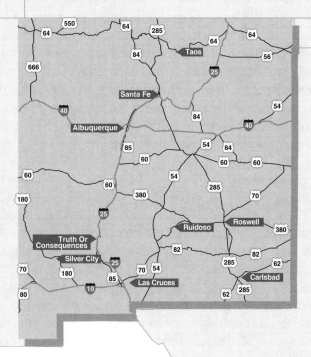

understood in Mexico. The New Mexican Hispanics have been isolated so long that their customs, cooking, and world views are also unique. And, although New Mexico shares a border with Mexico, no highways, railroads, or connections with Mexico exist along the desolate southern frontier other than one minor border crossing at Columbus. Historically, Mexican immigration has bypassed New Mexico, moving into California, Arizona, and Texas instead.

New Mexico's tax burden is the lowest of any of the Southwestern states mentioned in this book. The state ranks fifteenth lowest overall in taxes and almost at the bottom in property taxes. However, New Mexico does tax retirement income. As for state income taxes for residents, New Mexico is a mixed bag. For those with low income levels (less than $15,000 a year), New Mexico's income taxes are lower than most other popular retirement states. For those earning more than $95,000 a year, tax rates are higher.

# History

Like many Southwestern areas, ancient Pueblo Indian ruins and cliff dwellings show that the region was inhabited long before Europeans explored America. Many were abandoned a couple of centuries before Spanish conquistadores explored what is now New Mexico as early as 1536. Inexplicably, some ancient towns remained populated—remnants of the early civilization—even when the Spanish arrived.

One example of this is Acoma, the so-called Sky City, in Cibola County. Continuously inhabited for unknown centuries, the village sits atop a sheer cliff that rises 357 feet above the plain. Multiroomed, three-story adobe buildings impressed early explorers, including Francisco Coronado, who thought he had found one of the legendary Seven Golden Cities of Cibola when he discovered the site in 1540.

The first Spanish settlers moved into New Mexico in 1598 and twelve years later established a political capital and governorship in Santa Fe. Native Americans living in the area were peaceful farmers when the Spanish first encountered them, raising crops and engaging in trade. Even the Apache tribes, later to gain fame as warriors, lived along river bottoms in small villages, tranquilly growing corn, beans, and pumpkins. However, as so often happened when white settlers moved into Native American territory, squabbles broke out over who owned the land. Fighting escalated over the years and didn't cease until almost 300 years later, when the last Apache war chief, Geronimo, signed a peace treaty with the U.S. government in 1886.

Isolated from the Spanish vice royalty in distant Mexico City, the territory developed slowly and quite independently from other colonial possessions. Thus the New Mexican cultural fabric gradually separated itself from the traditions of Spain and Mexico and became "Hispanic." In 1821, after Mexico won independence from Spain, the province came under Mexican rule, but this meant little to the people—Mexico was too far away.

About this time, Americans started entering the territory by way of the Santa Fe Trail, which Capt. William Becknell had traced across the Great Plains from Missouri in 1821. Then, in 1846, during the Mexican War, Gen. Stephen Watts Kearney seized the province for the United States. The change of government wasn't supposed to have had much of an impact on the Hispanic residents, since the Treaty of Guadalupe-Hidalgo guaranteed their lands, their language, and their customs and granted full citizenship in the United States of America. Later, many of the treaty's provisions were ignored or overturned. Yet, because New Mexico was predominantly Hispanic and the people were politically astute, they escaped many of the injustices wrought against the original landowners in California.

In 1862, during the American Civil War, the Confederate flag flew over Santa Fe for a time, when the city was occupied by troops from Texas. Rebel forces were driven back into Texas later that year. The Apaches and Navajos took full advantage of this conflict between white soldiers, declaring war on the enemy. In 1864 Union troops defeated the Navajo warriors, forcing them to accept confinement within a reservation. It took another twenty years for government troops to defeat the Apaches.

From that time until after World War II, New Mexico developed rather slowly. The Hispanics were left pretty much to their old, traditional, laid-back ways. Then suddenly, between 1950 and 1960, the population of New Mexico increased by more than a third. During the next ten years (1960–1970) the state's population increased by another 6.8 percent. Another decade of growth in the 1980s increased the state's population by another 20 percent, nearly three times the national growth rate. (More recent data are unavailable.)

## New Mexico Tax Profile

Sales tax:
**5% to 7.27%**

State income tax:
**graduated from 1.8% to 8.5% over $41,600; federal income tax not deductible**

Property taxes:
**about 0.7%**

Intangibles tax:
**none**

Social Security tax:
**none**

Pension taxes:
**up to $8,000 excluded, depending on income level**

Gasoline tax:
**16¢ per gallon, plus local taxes**

# Albuquerque

High in the middle New Mexico desert, on the east bank of the Rio Grande, is Albuquerque. A combination of high altitude (5,000 feet), dry air, and mild temperatures provides exactly what many people are looking for in a retirement spot. Summer temperatures rarely get out of the nineties, and winter almost never sees zero degree readings. With low humidity, the weather seems even milder than statistics might indicate. In July, the hottest month, the average daytime temperature goes into the nineties, but you'll almost always be wearing a sweater at night.

For most residents, good weather is what Albuquerque retirement is all about. Rainfall is a scant 8 inches a year, which means lots of brilliant, sunny weather. The best part is that the winter months of December and January are the sunniest. It's a four-season year, with about 11 inches of snow expected every winter. The snow doesn't stick around for long, though, because winter days usually hit fifty degrees by noon. Muggy days and long rainy spells are just about unknown in Albuquerque. Summers can become quite dry, however, causing the mighty Rio Grande to dwindle to a muddy trickle. Once, when Will Rogers was giving a talk in Albuquerque, he cajoled: "Why, you folks ought to be out there right now irrigating that river to keep it from blowing away!"

The city has taken pains to preserve its historic sector. Preservation was possible partly because the coming of the railroad in 1880 moved the "downtown" district away from the original plaza, thus sparing it from development. Today the area, now known as Old Town, offers interesting restaurants and shops and maintains the historic flavor of the Old West. Venerable adobe buildings and museums cluster around the Duke of Albuquerque's village.

The downtown section is clean, modern, and prosperous; everything seems polished and tastefully designed. A pedestrian mall completes the picture of a pleasant city center. The rest of the metropolitan area is also pleasant, with a mixture of Western ranch-style homes and pueblo-adobe buildings, with huge shade trees in the older areas of town.

The metropolitan hub of New Mexico, Albuquerque is also a high-technology center of the Southwest. As such, it attracts people from all over the country to work and live here. Almost any direction from the city leads to interesting day trips of historical, cultural, and scenic marvels. The snowcapped 10,000-foot Sandia Mountains tower on the east, and a chain of extinct volcanoes are to the west. The Turquoise Trail (Highway 22) to the north takes you through the old mining towns of Golden, Madrid, and Cerillos. To the south on the Mission Trail (Highway 14) are the pueblos of Gran Quivira, Abo, and Quarai. Several Zuñi pueblos are within easy visiting distance; Mescalero and Jicarilla Apache and Navajo reservations are not far away.

There's no getting around the fact that Albuquerque is a big city; more than a half million live within the city limits, and several large developments and communities encircle the city. As you might expect from a big city, the crime rates here aren't low, but neither are they particularly out-of-hand. The city ranks slightly below average in personal safety according to FBI statistics.

People looking for retirement have the choice of numerous neighborhoods, so many that I can give you only a sample.

In the city proper, one recommendation would be around the campus of the University of New Mexico in the southern part of the city (east of downtown). This neighborhood is typical of the pleasant, livable areas in and around Albuquerque. Mature trees shade the streets, and most homes are of tasteful brick-and-frame construction. A similar neighborhood, known as Taylor Ranch, is in the northwestern sector of the city. Those with deep pockets looking for an upscale community—one built around twenty-seven holes of golf—visit, as an example, Tanoan, a gated community with luxury homes and prices to match.

## Rio Rancho

An Alternative to Albuquerque living, the residential community of Rio Rancho is about twenty minutes from downtown Albuquerque. It's the home of Intel's large plant that employs 5,500 people, most of whom live in Rio Rancho. A wonderfully diverse area, Rio Rancho has safe, secure neighborhoods; quality homes; clean streets; and all conveniences. Everything looks neat and new here because Rio Rancho is practically new. It recently celebrated its twentieth birthday as a city. From a start-up development twenty-five years ago, Rio Rancho is now New Mexico's fourth largest city. About 50,000 people live on ranch land that twenty-five years ago supported fewer than 200 cows. Rio Rancho is one of the fastest-growing communities in the country. It's a great place for retirees, but it's basically a multigenerational community.

With a twenty-seven-hole golf course and a panorama of the Sandia Mountains in the distance, Rio Rancho is a blend of Southwest desert and middle-class suburb. When you encounter a 25-mile-an-hour speed limit in Rio Rancho, even in a rural area with nothing but empty fields about, don't even think of going 26. They are serious about law enforement.

## Recreation and Culture

Skiers have the choice of eleven downhill complexes within striking distance of Albuquerque. Sandia Peak (15 miles northeast of Albuquerque) has lifts that rise above 10,000 feet. Hunting, fishing, prospecting, and rock hunting are all great outdoor pastimes. But all outdoor activities don't require going into the wilderness. Horse-racing fans will find seven tracks within driving distance of Albuquerque, with the season starting in January at the Downs at Santa Fe.

The University of New Mexico contributes to the rich cultural offerings of the city. There's a full calendar of lectures, concerts, drama, and sporting events. The school offers numerous classes of interest to senior citizens.

## Real Estate

In Albuquerque, more than 70 percent of the dwellings are single-family homes. Housing prices are about 5 percent above the national average. Average homes run from $75,000 to $90,000. More upscale areas run upwards of $140,000, and houses in exclusive neighborhoods start at $200,000. Mobile home park and apartment rents are moderate.

Newly constructed Rio Rancho homes are being offered from $95,000 to $118,000. Homes ten years and older sell for even less, often below $50,000. We've seen virtual dream homes listed here for $120,000.

A particularly beautiful residential area is out of town, near the Sandia Peak Tramway, the longest continuous aerial tramway in the world. The houses are constructed with nature in mind, each designed to fit in with the gnarled juniper trees, rocks, and boulders, looking as if they grew naturally rather than being built by humans. There's also a great view of the city. Prices aren't cheap, starting at $350,000, but the homes are worth it. Condos or town houses can be bought for $90,000 and up.

## Medical Care

High-quality health care is available from major medical centers in Albuquerque, including urgent care centers and top-notch hospitals. The nearest urgent care center to Rio Rancho is St. Joseph's, located fifteen minutes away.

## When Grandkids Visit

The Rio Grande Zoological Park has an astounding number of animals for your enjoyment. You'll find 300 species represented by 1,300 animals, including New Mexican natives, African gorillas, Indian tigers, polar bears, and even sea lions.

## Addresses and Connections

*Chambers of Commerce:* Albuquerque: P.O. Box 25100, Albuquerque, NM 87125; Rio Rancho: 1781 Rancho Drive, Rio Rancho, NM 87124

*Senior Services:* Meadowlark Senior Services, 4330 Meadowlark Lane SE, Rio Rancho, NM 87124

*Newspapers: Albuquerque Journal,* 7777 Jefferson Street NE, Albuquerque, NM 87109; weekly: *Rio Rancho Observer,* 1594 Sara Road, Suite D, Rio Rancho, NM 87124

*Airport:* Albuquerque City Airport, with major airline connections

*Bus/Train:* a city bus system, Greyhound, and Amtrak all serve the Albuquerque area

## Albuquerque Area Weather

| | In degrees Fahrenheit | | | | | |
| | Jan. | April | July | Oct. | Rain | Snow |
|---|---|---|---|---|---|---|
| DAILY HIGHS | 47 | 70 | 93 | 72 | 8" | 12" |
| DAILY LOWS | 22 | 40 | 65 | 43 | | |

## Albuquerque Area Cost of Living

| (percentage of national average) | | | | |
| Overall | Housing | Medical | Groceries | Utilities |
|---|---|---|---|---|
| 101% | 103% | 100% | 103% | 96% |

# Carlsbad

Tucked away in the southeastern corner of New Mexico, on the banks of the slow-moving Pecos River, Carlsbad sits at an altitude of 3,200 feet and enjoys a mild, four-season climate. It's a pleasant city of 27,000 inhabitants who swear by Carlsbad's peaceful, quiet location. They unanimously endorse the weather as well. With only 12 inches of rain a year, the residents enjoy an average 340 days of sunshine, warm days, and cool nights, which add up to a comfortable climate for retirement living.

The local chamber of commerce actively solicits retirees and works hard to bring its story to the retiring public. The retirement attraction program has been very successful, bringing many new households of retirees into the community in recent years. However, local boosters also concentrate on bringing in light industry, particularly high-tech companies. This means mixed, multigeneration neighborhoods rather than predominantly retirement groupings.

For its size, Carlsbad has impressive services for retirees, with two senior centers and the active Senior Recreation Center. Three retirement communities offer services from independent living through full care.

The city has no bus service, but taxis give seniors a discount. A major problem for some retirees is Carlsbad's isolation from the nearest cities, El Paso and Albuquerque. If you don't need access to major shopping and big-city amenities, that may not be a problem. Carlsbad is self-contained for shopping and commerce.

## Recreation and Culture

The Pecos River runs through town and forms a nearby lake for boating and fishing year-round. According to local anglers, "Catfish is king in Carlsbad." The slow-moving river waters, warm and rife with protected holes, brush piles, and undercut banks, make the river a natural haven for channel catfish. Other fish that thrive in the river and nearby lakes are white and black bass, crappie, and walleye. Anglers occasionally hook trout in the colder waters in winter. Hunters go after deer, squirrel, and game birds, often not far from the city limits.

Two eighteen-hole golf courses and a lighted nine-hole, par-three course are open year-round for play. A seniors annual golf pass is available at a nice discount. The local country club, with its eighteen-hole course, charges a $50 initiation fee and $95 a month for a family membership. A lighted tennis complex offers nine courts plus three handball/racquetball layouts.

The Carlsbad Community Theater presents four quality dramatic presentations each year. Two colleges, College of the Southwest/Carlsbad, a four-year institution, and New Mexico State University/Carlsbad, a two-year branch school, offer many community interest classes. The schools give Carlsbad a sort of university-town flavor.

Carlsbad Museum has an exhibition of Native American crafts, pottery, and jewelry; the Hollebeke Collection of historical artifacts; a display of minerals; and Tarahumara tribal artifacts from Northern Mexico.

## Real Estate

With low housing costs (the chamber of commerce says apartment rents average $412 month) and taxes ranking at the bottom of the scale, Carlsbad could be a possibility for those who want economical retirement and who don't need a big city nearby.

The average selling price of a home in early 2000 was almost 11 percent below national averages, with prices starting at $87,000 and the higher end just below $150,000. Some perfectly livable houses in town sell for around $70,000 and up. For places with acreage, suitable for keeping horses, you'll find something from $100,000 to $200,000.

## Medical Care

Carlsbad has a good-size medical center (144 beds) that offers all services except invasive cardiology and neurosurgery. Patients that require assistance in these two areas are flown by helicopter to Lubbock, Texas. Otherwise, all other medical services are available, and area doctors are accepting new patients.

## When Grandkids Visit

Don't miss the opportunity to visit world-famous Carlsbad Caverns. One of the largest caves in the world, you have a choice of several tours. One trail descends the equivalent of seventy-nine stories below the main cavern level. Don't panic, you don't have to climb back up; an elevator whisks you to the top.

## Addresses and Connections

*Chamber of Commerce:* P.O. Box 910, Carlsbad, NM 88221

*Senior Services:* 1112 North Mesa, Carlsbad, NM 88220

*Newspaper: Carlsbad Current-Argus,* 620 South Main, Carlsbad, NM 88220

*Airport:* commuter airline service, with twenty-six flights a week to Albuquerque and Dallas

*Bus:* no city bus, but Greyhound does serve the area

## Carlsbad Area Weather

| | Jan. | April | July | Oct. | Rain | Snow |
|---|---|---|---|---|---|---|
| | In degrees Fahrenheit | | | | | |
| DAILY HIGHS | 58 | 80 | 96 | 79 | 12" | 4" |
| DAILY LOWS | 28 | 47 | 67 | 48 | | |

## Carlsbad Area Cost of Living

| Overall | Housing | Medical | Groceries | Utilities |
|---|---|---|---|---|
| (percentage of national average) | | | | |
| 95% | 100% | 94% | 101% | 78% |

# Roswell

Some 75 miles north of Carlsbad, Roswell is another popular New Mexico retirement location. Once described by Will Rogers as "the prettiest little town in the west," local residents insist that Roswell is also one of the best little town in the West.

Originating near Roswell, the famous Chisum Trail became famous in the annals of Western folklore as cowboys drove herds of wild and rangy longhorm cattle to the railhead at Las Cruces. At first a crossroads where several springs provided cattle herds with water. Roswell began to grow slowly. Today a bustling city of 50,000 inhabitants, the city of Roswell consistently receives high ratings for retirement. *Kiplinger's* magazine recently featured Roswell in its list of "Great Places To Retire."

## Recreation and Culture

Since the sun shines just about every day in New Mexico, a wealth of outdoor activities are enjoyed by retirees. You have your choice of fishing, boating, or sailing on one of several nearby lakes, or camping, hiking, or horseback riding in closeby state and national parks. In town, there's swimming, golf, or tennis, and afterward, dinner at the country club.

For a small city, Roswell offers many cultural happenings. For more than thirty-eight seasons, the troupe of talented performers with Roswell Community Little Theater has staged excellent dramatic productions for the community. The community's Symphony Orchestra has held performances for more than thirty-nine seasons.

The Roswell Museum and Art Center has several galleries that focus on Southwestern art, history, and technology. A special wing of the museum has been set aside as a re-creation of rocket pioneer Dr. Robert H. Goddard's workshop. Roswell is home to Eastern New Mexico University–Roswell, which offers a variety of courses for both the young and old, both credit and noncredit.

## Real Estate

Roswell's median sales price of real estate is $134,000, with many neighborhoods of quality housing at economical prices. Many three-bedroom homes are priced in the $60,000 to $97,000 range.

## Medical Care

The 162-bed medical center in Roswell recently completed more than $25 million in renovations. This backs up Eastern New Mexico Medical Center's claim to be the largest, most comprehensive, and technically advanced medical center in southeast New Mexico.

## When Grandkids Visit

In July 1947 a UFO crashed near Roswell, New Mexico. According to reports, the bodies of several aliens were found near the ship. In other reports, one or more of the aliens survived for a period of time. You'll learn all about it when you take the grandkids to Roswell's International UFO Museum and Research Center.

## Addresses and Connections

*Chamber of Commerce:* P.O. Drawer 70, Roswell, NM 88202

*Newspaper:* Weekly: *Roswell Daily Record,* 2301 North Main Street, Roswell, NM 88201

*Airport:* Roswell Airport, Mesa Airlines, commuter connection

*Bus:* TNM&O intercity bus service: Pecos Trails Transit provides service within Roswell

## Roswell Area Weather

| | In degrees Fahrenheit | | | | | |
| | Jan. | April | July | Oct. | Rain | Snow |
|---|---|---|---|---|---|---|
| DAILY HIGHS | 55 | 77 | 94 | 76 | 13" | 6" |
| DAILY LOWS | 27 | 47 | 69 | 48 | | |

## Roswell Area Cost of Living

| (percentage of national average) | | | | |
| Overall | Housing | Medical | Groceries | Utilities |
|---|---|---|---|---|
| 96% | 100% | 93% | 108% | 78% |

# Las Cruces

In Spanish, *Las Cruces* means "the crosses." The town's name derives from a group of crosses marking the graves of victims of an Apache attack, back in 1830. The entire area is steeped in history. This was the home of the earliest human inhabitants known on the continent—the Clovis and Folsom cultures—and nearby cliff dwellings are among the oldest structures found in the United States. The Spanish settled the valley before the Pilgrims landed on Plymouth Rock. Famous outlaws, lawmen, and gunfighters contributed to the valley's history. Billy the Kid was tried for murder here, sentenced to hang, and then escaped. Later he was cornered and shot just outside Las Cruces by the county sheriff, Pat Garrett.

Today, Las Cruces consistently earns high ratings as a retirement location and a quality place to live from publications like *Money* magazine. Although Las Cruces is the largest town in southern New Mexico, its population is less than 67,000. It's a city, but not a metropolis. For big-city shopping and special needs, El Paso is only 45 miles away via fast-moving Interstate 10. However, as one local booster put it, "Don't move here if you expect Las Cruces to stay small and quiet. We're the second-fastest-growing city in America!"

Nestled in the fertile Mesilla Valley, which draws irrigation water from the Rio Grande, Las Cruces is the center of a prosperous farming district, producing cotton, pecans, and chili peppers. Because it sits on a large natural underground water reservoir, the town isn't troubled by water shortages, as are some desert cities.

Architecture here reflects the region's multicultural history by blending Native American, Spanish, and modern into a distinctive Las Cruces style. Newer neighborhoods clearly suggest a Santa Fe "pueblo" influence. Quiet, earthen tones predominate yet manage to avoid a regimented, stiff adherence to style. Contrasting pastels and bright colors intersperse with muted browns and tans so characteristic of Santa Fe.

Mountains surround Las Cruces, rising to above 9,000 feet to block most northern winter winds. This results in a mild, low-humidity winter. Summers are warm, not hot, with a high of ninety-four degrees in July and August; residents are proud of the area's high number of sunny days. The combination of high altitude (4,000 feet) and low humidity guarantees that the temperature will drop as soon as the sun sets. Instead of air conditioners, most residents rely on inexpensive evaporative coolers (swamp coolers). Even during the coldest winter months, afternoon temperatures usually climb into the sixties, enabling you to spend time outdoors year-round.

## Recreation and Culture

Mild weather permits fishing every month of the year in nearby Elephant Butte and Caballo Reservoirs, with trophy-size striped bass upwards of fifty pounds lurking in the depths. Las Cruces has two public golf courses and a private country club. Eighteen lighted tennis courts make for comfortable play on warm summer evenings. For horse racing, Sunland Park Racetrack, about 30 miles to the south.

For those many sports fans addicted to duck racing, you'll have to travel to Deming, some 50 miles distant. However, if ostrich races, camel races, or pig races are among your favorite spectator sports (or participant sports, for that matter), you'll have to travel to Alamogordo, 70 miles east. (I'm not making this up.)

New Mexico State University exerts a considerable influence on the city's cultural life. The school brings the community together by inviting participation in activities and by sponsoring a theater ensemble and a symphony orchestra. Its cultural and entertainment events are a definite plus. Seniors are welcome to take regular courses or occasional classes at the Weekend College. A new program just for seniors offers mini-courses on subjects that range from local history to opera appreciation. A community college with 3,600 students completes the continuing education opportunities, offering more than one hundred unusual courses, many specifically designed for retiree participation.

For a city its size, Las Cruces has a large selection of cultural activities. The Doña Ana Lyric Opera stages several full-scale musicals each year, including classical operas as well as lighter Broadway productions. The Las Cruces Chamber Ballet offers an annual *Nutcracker Suite* program at Christmastime as well as full-scale ballet productions in the spring. Old and foreign movies are presented by the Mesilla Valley Film Society, with senior discounts.

## Real Estate

Las Cruces ranks about average in the national cost of living in most categories except housing, which is about 11 percent above the norm. When visiting here, we looked at a display of exceptionally imaginative homes of elegant, Old West style. They were set on low-maintenance landscaped lots that incorporated local shrubs and cacti. My wife and I guessed the price at $250,000 and were surprised to learn the asking price was a little more than $100,000. A buyers' market prevailed in Las Cruces at the time of our last visit.

Low-end, three-bedroom homes in an acceptable neighborhood sell for $70,000 and high end at $475,000. The median price is a little less than $140,000. An average three-bedroom home rents for $750 and a two-bedroom apartment for $600. According to local real estate people, good home rentals are scarce, although apartments are easy to find. Mobile homes for sale are also heavily advertised, at seemingly bargain prices.

## Medical Care

Medical care here is exceptional, with one of the best-equipped hospitals in the state, the 286-bed Memorial Medical Center. Las Cruces is the medical hub of a five-county region. Even larger medical facilities in nearby El Paso are just a short drive down the interstate. As in many localities in the United States, some doctors are reluctant to accept new Medicare patients. Most will take on new patients if the first few visits are paid in cash, with Medicare reimbursement going to the patient.

## When Grandkids Visit

Drive down to El Paso and cross the Rio Grande into Mexico for a cultural experience in another nation. It's less than an hour's drive. There, in Ciudad Juárez, the kiddies can load up on curios such as green-and-purple penguins, imitation leather goods, and stuffed and varnished frogs. Meanwhile, you can shop for tax-free rum or onyx chess sets.

## Addresses and Connections

*Chamber of Commerce:* 750 West Picacho, Las Cruces, NM 88005
*Senior Services:* 975 South Mesquite Street, Las Cruces, NM 88001
*Newspaper: Las Cruces Sun News,* 256 West Las Cruces Avenue, Las Cruces, NM 88001
*Airport:* Las Cruces International Airport, served by Mesa Airlines; El Paso International Airport is a forty-five-minute drive
*Bus:* local bus system gives seniors 50 percent discounts, and Greyhound serves the town

## Las Cruces Area Weather

|  | In degrees Fahrenheit | | | | | |
|---|---|---|---|---|---|---|
|  | Jan. | April | July | Oct. | Rain | Snow |
| DAILY HIGHS | 59 | 79 | 96 | 76 | 9" | 3" |
| DAILY LOWS | 27 | 42 | 63 | 44 | | |

## Las Cruces Area Cost of Living

| (percentage of national average) | | | | |
|---|---|---|---|---|
| Overall | Housing | Medical | Groceries | Utilities |
| 101% | 111% | 96% | 101% | 97% |

# Santa Fe

Fifty-nine miles northeast of Albuquerque, the city of Santa Fe sits like an antique jewel in the picturesque Sangre de Cristo Mountains. This is high-desert country, at an altitude of 7,000 feet, which means cool summers and crisp (but dry) winters. An awesome sense of history pervades the streets and byways of Santa Fe, the oldest capital city in the United States. It has been an important seat of government for more than 375 years. When the Pilgrims set foot on Plymouth Rock, Santa Fe had already been a bustling commercial center for several years. The oldest private home in the United States is here. A prized landmark is the Palace of the Governors, the oldest public building in the country. The palace became General Kearney's headquarters in 1846, when his troops captured Santa Fe during the war with Mexico. Incidentally, this was the first foreign capital ever captured by U.S. armed forces.

Santa Fe, with a population of 67,000, is a city steeped in history and culture, and its residents work hard to keep it that way. Strict building codes insist that all new construction be of adobe or adobe-looking material; all exteriors must be earth tones. This preserves the distinctive Spanish pueblo style for which Santa Fe is famous. Occasionally, one sees a home that was built in the days before zoning codes, and the blue or white building sticks out like a proverbial sore thumb. At first the shades of sand, brown, and tan can seem a bit somber, but after a while, one grows to appreciate the way they complement the setting.

Art affects the everyday life of Santa Fe residents, with literally thousands of working artists and more than 150 galleries exhibiting their treasures. The old plaza in the heart of the city is often lined with street artisans displaying jewelry, paintings, leather goods, and all kinds of quality artwork. Local Native Americans bring intricate silver-and-turquoise jewelry to sell in the plaza.

Santa Fe is about tied with Albuquerque for percentage of sunshine; around 300 days each year are guaranteed to be at least partly sunny. Santa Fe gets more rain, about 8 inches a year, and there's three times as much snow, about 32 inches annually. This keeps Santa Fe greener. A friend who retired in Santa Fe said this about her new hometown: "We love knowing that almost every day, when we get out of bed, we're going to see incredibly blue skies and brilliant sunshine. That's only the beginning of the day."

You'll find a true four-season year with very pleasant summers. Be prepared to wear a sweater on summer evenings—the temperature typically drops to below fifty degrees at night.

For some reason, the city of Santa Fe isn't covered in the FBI Uniform Crime Report. My feeling is that the crime rate may be a bit higher than average. Many homeowners have installed security systems, and a number of private security companies patrol neighborhoods on a regular basis. It's suggested that you discuss with the police the likelihood of burglary in the particular areas you are considering. My own observation is that, overall, it's a safe place to live.

## Recreation and Culture

A rodeo every summer attracts those who enjoy outdoor sports, and the thoroughbreds race at the nationally famous Santa Fe Downs from May to Labor Day. Two public golf courses and twenty-seven tennis courts allow year-round play because of Santa Fe's mild climate. Whitewater rafting is just an hour away, and there's trout fishing in nearby rivers and lakes.

The Santa Fe Ski Area is only a thirty-minute drive from downtown. Sitting at an elevation of more than 12,000 feet, this is one of the nation's highest ski resorts. With an average of 225 inches of snow a year, the area isn't likely to disappoint you.

The highly regarded Santa Fe Opera company performs in a unique outdoor theater. Fortunately, Santa Fe's weather seldom interferes with the performances. A year-round calendar of events includes concerts by the Orchestra of Santa Fe, the Chorus of Santa Fe, the Desert Chorale, and the Santa Fe Symphony, as well as Native American fiestas, festivals, and celebrations. Numerous theater and drama presentations are given by the New Mexico Repertory Theatre, the British American Theatre Institute, the Armory for the Arts, the Santuario de Guadalupe, the Community Theatre, and the Greer Garson Theater. The Santa Fe Community College offers a wide range of classes designed for seniors, and three private colleges plus the University of New Mexico's Graduate Center provide educational opportunities.

## Real Estate

Santa Fe is one of those places where people who can afford to buy a second house anywhere buy their second homes. That should tell you something about Santa Fe's quality of life. It also tells you something about the cost of living here, the highest in the state, at 23 percent above the national average. A bright spot on the cost-of-living landscape is the cost of utilities, about 15 percent below average. That's more than offset by housing costs, at 42 percent above average, among the highest in the nation. The only place in the state more expensive is nearby Los Alamos, where a preponderance of scientists earning very good money jack up the local housing costs.

The problem is, Santa Fe has such a reputation as a retirement and artist center that outsiders have bid up real estate prices to an unusual level. "It's getting so that we natives can't afford to live here anymore," lamented one hometown resident; yet housing is curiously mixed in price. Generally, it's much more expensive than Albuquerque, particularly for nicer housing. But economical housing can be found for a little more than $100,000 per unit (occasionally). The median price of a city home is $205,000, which tells you that many homes are selling in the half-million-dollar-and-up range. Several high-end developments are under way, at least one with its own private golf course. A few attractive full-care retirement residences are located in Santa Fe; one of them (the Ponce de Leon) is unique in that it doesn't charge endowment or entrance fees. You pay a monthly fee for an apartment, take meals in the dining room if you wish, and receive weekly housekeeping and maid service. Be aware that there could be a waiting list.

Santa Fe is a retirement possibility for people with moderate to affluent means, those with deep interests in art and culture, and those who like cool, crisp, sunny weather. It offers a great ambience for writers or artists who need the company of kindred souls.

## Medical Care

Four hospitals and many private practitioners make Santa Fe an excellent place for health care. The 265-bed St. Vincent Hospital is prepared for almost any contingency, and large-scale facilities at Albuquerque are an hour's drive away.

Four different senior citizens' centers serve the city, with services such as adult protection and health care. An active senior citizens' program, Open Hands, offers services and an opportunity to volunteer for satisfying and worthwhile community projects. The city furnishes transit services to seniors for grocery shopping and doctor and social service agency appointments. The city also offers taxi coupons for 75 percent discounts off the standard fare. The local bus system, with new, clean-burning, natural-gas engines, services main routes that cover most of the city and offers 25 cent fares for senior citizens.

## When Grandkids Visit

Take a drive to one of the nearby pueblos. Eight different Native American villages invite visitors to enjoy a rare opportunity to experience cultures that date back centuries, well before European settlers came here. Each village is unique, with its own art, dances, and ceremonies.

## Addresses and Connections

*Chamber of Commerce:* P.O. Box 1928, Santa Fe, NM 87504

*Senior Services:* 520 Onate Place, Santa Fe, NM 87501

*Newspapers: The New Mexican,* P.O Box 2038, 202 East Marcy Street, Santa Fe, NM 87501; weekly: *Santa Fe Reporter,* P.O. Box 2306, Santa Fe, NM 87504

*Airport:* shuttle to Albuquerque Airport

*Bus/Train:* the vicinity is served by Greyhound, a local bus system, and Amtrak

## Santa Fe Area Weather

| | In degrees Fahrenheit | | | | | |
| | Jan. | April | July | Oct. | Rain | Snow |
|---|---|---|---|---|---|---|
| DAILY HIGHS | 40 | 60 | 82 | 63 | 8" | 32" |
| DAILY LOWS | 19 | 35 | 57 | 39 | | |

## Santa Fe Area Cost of Living

| (percentage of national average) | | | | |
| Overall | Housing | Medical | Groceries | Utilities |
|---|---|---|---|---|
| 113% | 142% | 103% | 103% | 85% |

# Silver City

For a thousand years the area around Silver City has been a source of valuable minerals. Early Native Americans mined outcrops of copper to fashion ornaments and spearheads. In the 1790s Spanish miners worked the copper deposits, loading the ore on the backs of burros and trekking south into Chihuahua for smelting. But Silver City itself wasn't established until returning California 49ers discovered silver ore a few miles north of the present town site. This kicked off a mining boom, with the tent city replaced by substantial brick buildings. When the silver mines gave up the last of their treasures, Silver City would have turned into a typical Western ghost town except that the miners next turned their attention to the enormous copper deposits nearby. Two large companies operate open pit mines to this day, twenty-four hours a day, providing steady employment for thousands of residents.

For years, Silver City was well known to El Paso residents for something other than minerals: pleasant summer weather. Like nearby Ruidoso, this area became popular as a summer getaway location, a haven to escape scorching west Texas and southern New Mexico weather. Silver City's 6,000-foot altitude provides cool, dry weather and beautiful, forested mountain vistas. It seemed only natural that when retirement time rolled around, vacationers would begin thinking about Silver City. Today, west Texas retirees are being joined by others from all over the country who seek quality living in a mild climate at affordable prices. With a population of 12,000, Silver City is large enough to supply most services but still small enough to escape big-city crowding, crime, and pollution.

The town's architectural style clearly reflects the period when Silver City was developed. The downtown sector shows the influence of the town's ranching and mining background; the area is rich in Victorian brick buildings that were so popular in Western boomtowns. In fact, Silver City's historic district boasts the largest concentration of Victorian homes in southern New Mexico.

Silver City is some distance from the nearest interstate, but access to airports and Amtrak is available by Greyhound and shuttle. Traffic along Interstate 10 is almost nonexistent, so it is an easy drive of 110 miles to Las Cruces, the nearest large town; two and a half hours to El Paso; and a little more than three hours to Tucson.

The presence of Western New Mexico University takes Silver City out of the category of an ordinary mining town and protects it from the boom-and-bust nature of mining business cycles. The school brings stability to the community and adds intellectual and cultural diversity. In the process of expanding, the university recently added a nursing curriculum, which is proving very popular.

The university is also responsible in part for inspiring a fast-growing artist colony in Silver City. An astonishing number of galleries, studios, and workshops welcome art lovers, either regularly or by invitation. Dozens of artisans display their works here, and some offer lessons. At the rate the community is growing, it promises to become one of the premier art centers in the state.

A fascinating place a few miles north of Silver City is an even older mining town called Pinos Altos. Not quite a ghost town today, Pinos Altos is worth a visit, possibly as a place to live for those who want the peace and quiet of a village. Pioneer buildings, a famous saloon, and an old opera house are still standing, as well as Fort Cobre, which is now a museum. Here is where the famous Apache chief Mangas Coloradas was captured and murdered by U.S. soldiers in 1863 when he attended a peace conference. Tourism here is light, so local residents aren't overwhelmed by traffic.

Western history buffs might be interested to learn that Silver City is where the famous outlaw Billy the Kid grew up, went to school, committed his first known crime, was arrested for the first time, and made his first of several escapes from jail. By the way, according to local historians, Billy the Kid's first known crime was not killing a man when he was twelve years old, as is commonly believed, but robbing clothes from a Chinese laundry when he was fifteen.

## Recreation and Culture

Western New Mexico University sponsors a variety of cultural and sporting events, as well as numerous learning opportunities, which are available to the general public. According to the school registrar, a considerable number of over-fifty students are always registered here. The university is famous for its collection of prehistoric pottery, ancient jewelry, and centuries-old Mimbres pottery.

Surrounded by the 3.3-million-acre Gila National Forest, Silver City offers outdoor enthusiasts much to do within a short distance from the town. Five fishing lakes offer good catches of bass and crappie, plus rivers and streams teem with trout. Two hours away is Elephant Butte Lake, New Mexico's largest body of water, where fishing for lunker bass can be a memorable experience. Hunters can find one of the few places in the nation where seven species can be stalked in a single season. Skiing is four hours away at Ruidoso. Five tennis courts and an eighteen-hole golf course augment the ten parks and two swimming pools in Silver City.

## Real Estate

Affordable real estate is one of the attractions that draw retirees here. In nearby Tyrone, Phelps Dodge decided to move some of its company housing by marketing the workers' homes as retirement locations. Homes were refurbished and sold starting at $40,000. Now that these are gone, executive housing is on the block—at higher prices, of course.

Silver City neighborhoods are quite comfortable, with most homes priced less than $100,000. For $155,000 you can buy a very nice home on three-quarters of an acre with an impressive view. For exceptionally low-cost housing, several mobile home parks fill the bill.

## Medical Care

Gila Regional Medical Center, one of the newest and most modern multi-service facilities in the state, serves residents in a 100-mile radius. The center boasts a staff of more than 450, including more than forty physicians and dentists. There's a twenty-four-hour emergency room, full-service radiology department, and home health and hospice program. The hospital also has strategically located ambulances to serve the county.

## When Grandkids Visit

Be sure to see the Gila Cliff Dwellings, located about 44 miles up Highway 15. Discover how prehistoric cultures developed and browse through forty-two walled rooms in five caves in this thirteenth-century citadel. Camping facilities are located nearby. Here you can hike through fields of spring wildflowers, follow meandering streams to waterfalls, set up your tent under the stars, or backpack into high mountain meadows. It's all free. Another educational experience is a visit to the Santa Rita copper mine, the oldest active mine in the Southwest.

## Addresses and Connections

*Chamber of Commerce:* 1103 North Hudson Street, Silver City, NM 88061

*Senior Services:* 1016 North Silver Street, Silver City, NM 88061

*Newspaper: Silver City Daily Press,* 300 West Market Street, Silver City, NM 88061

*Airport:* Grant County Airport offers commuter flights on Mesa Airlines

*Bus/Train:* no local bus, but there's Greyhound and a shuttle service to Las Cruces, forty-five minutes away, by Amtrak

## Silver City Area Weather

| | Jan. | April | July | Oct. | Rain | Snow |
|---|---|---|---|---|---|---|
| | | In degrees Fahrenheit | | | | |
| DAILY HIGHS | 48 | 70 | 85 | 71 | 15" | 12" |
| DAILY LOWS | 22 | 40 | 66 | 47 | | |

# Taos

Seventy miles north of Santa Fe, another famous New Mexico artists' colony has been attracting painters, writers, musicians, and artisans for more than a century. Taos sits in a high mesa valley, perched at an altitude of 7,000 feet at the foot of the Sangre de Cristo mountain range. The scenic drive up the Rio Grande Valley is worth the trip even if you have no intention of retiring here. You'll watch the river change from a meandering, flatland stream into a rushing current that cuts a canyon 650 feet below the plain, a not-so-miniature Grand Canyon.

Bustling tourist village, quiet retreat, art colony, ski resort—these are but a few of the many descriptions that fit Taos. Its fifty-five art galleries and numerous art programs emphasize the large number of artists and art lovers in residence. Like its sister city, Santa Fe, Taos is a well-known creative center for painters, writers, weavers, musicians, and artists of all categories. Nationally recognized artists in Taos have made a profound mark on the U.S. art scene. Because of its small population (about 4,100), Taos allows resident artists to form a closely integrated group. The successful and well-known mingle with the unsuccessful and amateur much more freely than they do in large-scale Santa Fe. One resident said, "We permanent residents of Taos achieve social equality that you seldom find elsewhere. Some very wealthy, successful people I know prefer to drive rusty pickups instead of Mercedes and wear blue jeans and boots instead of city dress. I've attended cocktail parties where starving artists, multimillionaires, and local businesspeople mix as if they were at class reunions."

Picturesque adobes; narrow, winding streets; and the ancient Pueblo village on Taos's outskirts provide awesome inspiration for the artistic set. But there are three other parts to the residential equation: winter skiers, summer tourists, and seasonal residents.

Skiing at nearby Ski Valley draws snow enthusiasts beginning at Thanksgiving. Ski Valley averages 321 inches of snow each year, so the season lasts into mid-April. Then, just when ski traffic thins out, camera-toting tourists take up the slack. They come to photograph the village of Taos as well as the nearby 1,000-year-old Taos Pueblo, one of the most photographed sites in the West. World-famous photo opportunities and museums are bonanzas for tourists. However, the one main complaint you'll hear from permanent residents is about tourist traffic and the business community's dependence on tourism for survival. Part-time residents are divided between wealthy folks who can afford a summer home, or perhaps a winter ski home, and those who come to rent a condo for a few months to experience the magic ambience of the area.

The county's ethnic composition may be of interest. New Mexican Hispanics make up 66 percent of the population, with Anglos 27 percent and Native Americans 7 percent. What about Taos as a retirement location? For those who are drawn here by the artistic, intellectual, and historical atmosphere, Taos can be a dream retirement home. However, it's easy to become disappointed, to wonder what the fuss is all about should you not "fit in" or if you should find a small town boring, far removed from large-scale shopping and city conveniences. For example, there is no full-fledged supermarket here. Only two regular grocery stores serve the area, augmented by two organic food stores. It's difficult to comment on crime and personal safety in the Taos area, because FBI statistics aren't available. A surprising number of people in the county live at the below-poverty level (if that means anything), but residents we interviewed expressed no particular concern in this regard.

Well, what about retirement here? In short, a special sort of person will adore Taos; others will enjoy it only as a tourist attraction and move on. Do yourself a favor—at least see Taos and the surrounding countryside; it's very interesting.

## Recreation and Culture

There's prime skiing at Taos Ski Valley, considered one of the premier winter sports areas in the Southwest. The resort is at 9,200 feet and features seventy-two slopes. Another ski resort can be found, with a little more driving, at Angel Fire Mountain; it's not quite as high as Taos, so the season probably doesn't last as long.

Golf nuts needn't worry about neglecting their swing; they can check out the Taos Country Club, with its eighteen holes, 4 miles from Taos Town Plaza. The club also offers three-acre homesites on or near the course.

Cultural interests are served by several museums and the intense focus on artistic endeavors. The Taos Institute of Arts is one example. A branch of the state university system enlarged its campus in Taos recently to handle 1,300 students.

## Real Estate

Property falls into two categories here. The most desirable real estate is surprisingly expensive, partly because Taos is a popular place and partly because the rest of the properties look substandard, probably not the kind of housing most retirees would choose. In the town of Taos, few real estate listings are less than $95,000, with $150,000 and up more common, sometimes for postage-size lots. Homes in nearby Ranchos de Taos have larger lots—and some larger prices as well. Land is also surprisingly expensive. Most of the town's surrounding acreage belongs to the Pueblo Indian Reservation, the U.S. Bureau of Land Management, or the Forest Service, so the supply is finite. According to the local chamber of commerce, land prices more than doubled over the past five years or so. Rentals seem to be plentiful, starting at $450 for a small place near the village's main plaza and going up quickly for larger digs.

Strict deed restrictions insist upon new buildings being of adobe, or at least looking like adobe, to blend in with the very old, the sort of old, and the look-like-old buildings already there. Local residents feel that anything out of place would disturb the charm and quaintness. I suppose they're correct, but it's a bit jarring to see gasoline stations, hardware stores, and plumbing shops disguised as ancient adobes. You'll even see an occasional mobile home, sides plastered with earth tones and wooden vigas protruding at the roofline, trying desperately to fit into the ancient Pueblo style. However, research clearly demonstrates that the ancient Pueblos rarely constructed their mobile homes of adobe brick.

## Medical Care

A new hospital recently opened in Taos, a forty-five-bed acute care facility. Local people say the quality of doctors at the hospital is high, because many physicians have moved here for the good skiing. The hospital states that physicians are always available, so it's okay to get sick during ski season.

## When Grandkids Visit

Be sure to visit the Taos Pueblo, just a couple of miles from the center of Taos Town Plaza. The Native Americans in this incredibly ancient pueblo maintain their village much the same as when Spanish explorers found it four centuries ago. To this day they refuse to accept such amenities as running water and electricity. The site, which has the tallest buildings of any pueblo (some five stories high), is considered to be the oldest continuously occupied town in the United States.

## Addresses and Connections

*Chamber of Commerce:* P.O. Drawer 1, Taos, NM 87571
*Newspaper: The Taos News,* P.O. Drawer U, Taos, NM 87571
*Airport:* there's a shuttle on demand to Albuquerque's airport
*Bus:* shuttle services to Taos Ski Valley, Santa Fe, and Albuquerque

## Taos Area Weather

| | In degrees Fahrenheit | | | | | |
| --- | --- | --- | --- | --- | --- | --- |
| | Jan. | April | July | Oct. | Rain | Snow |
| DAILY HIGHS | 40 | 63 | 86 | 66 | 12" | 35" |
| DAILY LOWS | 9 | 29 | 51 | 32 | | |

# Truth or Consequences

Back in 1950, Ralph Edwards, host of a popular radio program called *Truth or Consequences,* offered to stage a special broadcast from a town that was willing to change its name to "Truth or Consequences." The new Mexico town of Hot Springs accepted the challenge as a way to publicize its wide spot in the road. This explains the town's curious name.

Retirees looking for inexpensive living have discovered Truth or Consequences and found a pleasant community with a comfortable, small-town atmosphere. Since most folks come from somewhere else, local residents welcome newcomers with exceptional friendliness. Realize, however, the emphasis in Truth or Consequences is on "comfortable" rather than "elegant," so don't expect another Santa Fe. The pace here is slow; because there is only one stoplight in town, traffic is easy to manage.

The entire downtown area of Truth or Consequences sits above a system of hot springs. Hot mineral water, which ranges from 80 degrees to a bottom-scorching 115 degrees, can be pumped from wells or pools. It's used for heating as well as for saunas and hot tubs.

## Recreation and Culture

Golf is played year-round at two public golf courses, and tennis buffs have four facilities. A new bowling alley and two city parks with trap shooting, tennis courts, softball fields, and exercise courses complete the recreational roster.

Nearby Elephant Butte is an extension of the retiree neighborhoods here. The lakeside village offers a variety of services, including restaurants, lounges, motels, boat storage, fishing supplies, and sports equipment. Elephant Butte is one of two large lakes formed by damming the Rio Grande and supplies great fishing, which is, truthfully, why most retirees come here.

On the educational front, Western New Mexico University holds extension classes here, and a community college, New Mexico Tech, also offers classes for senior citizens.

## Real Estate

The majority of Truth or Consequences housing is in single-family homes, mostly modestly priced and affordable. According to local real estate people, three-bedroom homes in an economical neighborhood start at $60,000 and go as high as $175,000 in the better areas. Home rentals can be found for as low as $450 and apartments for $350. Mobile homes are a popular form of housing, with numerous parks around town as well as units on privately owned lots.

## Medical Care

The local hospital is a forty-three-bed medical/surgical facility with a full complement of inpatient and outpatient services. For a small town, medical care is above average. The hospital, by the way, does accept Medicare assignments.

## When Grandkids Visit

Take them to the Geronimo Springs Museum for displays of prehistoric Native American pottery and artifacts. There's also a historical exhibit that depicts the valley's mining and ranching industries. In case you're interested, you'll also find mementos of Ralph Edwards's *Truth or Consequences* radio show.

## Addresses and Connections

*Chamber of Commerce:* 201 Foch Street, Truth or Consequences, NM 87901

*Newspaper: The Herald,* 517 Main Street, Truth or Consequences, NM 87901

*Airport:* Albuquerque Airport, an hour and a half drive, or Las Cruces, fifty minutes away

*Bus:* Greyhound, plus local bus transportation for senior citizens only

## Truth or Consequences Area Weather

| | In degrees Fahrenheit | | | | | |
|---|---|---|---|---|---|---|
| | Jan. | April | July | Oct. | Rain | Snow |
| DAILY HIGHS | 54 | 75 | 92 | 75 | 12" | 6" |
| DAILY LOWS | 27 | 44 | 66 | 47 | | |

# Ruidoso

Ruidoso bursts upon travelers as an absolute surprise; it's a setting you don't expect from New Mexico. Almost magically, the landscape changes from hot desert covered with brush and patches of carrizo grass to a gorgeous, winding river canyon graced with tall, majestic evergreens perfuming the air. Cool mountain air and lush vegetation make Californians imagine they're at Lake Tahoe. Easterners might recall Maine forests or Canadian mountain vistas.

Of course, this isn't news to west Texans; they've known for decades that the Ruidoso Upper Canyon is an excellent place to escape blazing Texas summers. The crystal clear river cascading through the tree-shaded canyon makes for a wonderful escape and family fun. Summer cabins sprang up among the large ponderosa pines, all along the small river. By the way, *Ruidoso* in Spanish means "noisy," an apt description of the sound of cascading water.

With the opening of the racetrack at Ruidoso Downs in 1947, people started thinking of Ruidoso as a resort instead of merely a summertime mountain getaway. About thirty-two years ago, the Mescalero Apache tribe, with the help of a Texas oil man, developed a ski run high up on Apache Peak, a part of the Mescalero Reservation. They called it Ski Apache and established Ruidoso's second career as a winter resort. The 12,000-foot ski run immediately attracted the attention of ski buffs from around the country. This is the southernmost place to ski in the Southwest, and because of its exceptionally high location, skiing lasts long after many other areas have closed down, providing some of the best warm-weather powder skiing in the world. Not long ago, *Ski* magazine rated Ruidoso as one of the ten best ski towns in which to live.

Skiing did more than simply bring tourists and increase employment opportunities; it brought visitors and allowed them to observe the area under winter as well as summer conditions. Visitors were pleasantly surprised to discover relatively mild winters here and to learn that fall and spring are delightful seasons as well. This launched Ruidoso upon yet another career as a center for year-round residence and retirement.

Summer cabins were enlarged, and larger homes started springing up for both retirees and working-class families. This continuing growth provides employment for even more new residents and encourages more businesses to open. Today Ruidoso has blossomed into a pleasant town of about 8,500 inhabitants and is still growing. The county population is pushing 16,000. However, the area supports many more shops, stores, restaurants, and businesses of all kinds than you might expect of a town this size. Since Ruidoso draws visitors and tourists all year long, small businesses flourish, and you'll find an astonishing selection of excellent restaurants, serving almost any kind of cuisine imaginable, from French to Chinese, from prime rib to Indian squaw bread. April is an excellent time of the year to investigate Ruidoso as a retirement destination. Not only will you find less traffic and more off-season rates for motels, but you'll also experience Ruidoso's spring, one of its best seasons.

At first, the vast majority of the retirees here came from Texas, but this is changing rapidly. Ruidoso now draws people from across the United States and even from foreign countries. Some expensive homes belong to wealthy Mexican families, who enjoy the novelty of skiing, a sport somewhat rare in sunny Mexico. At least one family is said to have retired here from Canada.

## Recreation and Culture

A combination of tourism and local community spirit keeps recreational opportunites going all year, with art shows, chili cook-offs, parades, golf tournaments, and so forth. Locals say it seems as if there's never a week without something happening.

You can play golf locally at one of the highest courses in the world. Because of the heavy tourist traffic, the area maintains three courses of high-altitude play. One boasts an island fairway and has been listed as one of the top twenty-five golf courses in America. There are also several public and private tennis courts.

Ruidoso Downs has earned a national reputation for its top-rated quarter-horse facilities. The world's richest quarter-horse race, the All American Futurity, boasts a purse averaging $2 million. The track also hosts the Southwest's finest thoroughbreds.

Three hundred miles of trails wind through the region, inviting hiking, horseback riding, and mountain biking, with most trails on U.S. Forest Service land. Rainbow and German trout lurk in streams and small lakes to thrill anglers, and wild game and game birds such as elk, deer, quail, and turkey challenge hunters.

Ruidoso also boasts the largest uphill lift capacity of any ski area in New Mexico. The run has a vertical drop of 1,900 feet and averages more than 180 inches of exceptionally light powder snow annually. The abundance of sunshine and stunning vistas, created by the juxtaposition of alpine slopes and harsh desert landscapes, makes this a popular skiing destination.

The community has plenty of cultural happenings to keep retirees from becoming bored. The Ruidoso Arts Commission is working on ambitious plans to attract jazz, bluegrass, mariachi, and country-western festivals to use its perfect setting for outdoor performances. Ruidoso's spectacular surroundings make perfect subjects for artists; more are moving here all the time. Of intercultural interest, the Mescalero Apache Reservation celebrates the Fourth of July with a Native American Rodeo and ceremonial puberty rites for young Apache maidens. The festivities feature singing, dancing, and traditional food.

A branch of East New Mexico University provides continuing education opportunities for seniors. Small in size, the school offers many courses of interest to senior citizens. One example is a special course, "Computers for Seniors"; another is a class in basic fly tying given by a well-known local fishing guide. For indoor sports fans there's a class called "Resort Town Casino Gaming," which covers the fine art of blackjack, bingo, and video poker. Tuition is drastically reduced for New Mexico residents older than sixty-two.

## Real Estate

The tall forest makes a proper setting for Ruidoso real estate. Most homes are shaded by a thick green canopy and are casually located in a somewhat hodgepodge way. Elegant homes can sit next door to small cottages, log cabins, and, often, a mobile home. The higher end of the housing scale is also at the highest elevation, at the northern edge of town. One example is Alto, a private golf community where prices range between $175,000 and $350,000 and occasionally up to $750,000. Midway down the canyon, three-bedroom houses average $120,000 to $220,000, with mobile homes on individual lots selling for much less.

The most affordable housing is a few miles down the canyon in the community of Ruidoso Downs. Sitting 400 feet lower than Ruidoso proper, Ruidoso Downs demonstrates the dramatic difference altitude can make in the environment. Trees here are plentiful but are of a different species, smaller and tending to spread out rather than grow tall and slender. This doesn't detract from the beauty of the area, however; it's just different. Nice three-bedroom houses can be found for less than $150,000, and perfectly livable mobile homes tucked away on tree-shaded lots are affordably priced.

## Medical Care

Medical facilities here are adequate, with a forty-two-bed hospital, the Lincoln County Medical Center provides full diagnostic lab and X-ray capabilities as well as an intensive-care unit and emergency-room service. The hospital's motto is "Small town hospital, big city care." There's also a nursing home with eighty-five beds and a home health care service.

## When Grandkids Visit

Take a day hike along the Crest Trail, which snakes along the divide between Bonito and Eagle Creek watersheds. A destination for the hike might be the Mon Jeau Fire Lookout. Should your feet rebel against this suggestion, you could tour the fascinating Hubbard Museum of the American West. This museum's collection includes everything of and about horses, from a Russian sleigh to an authentic 1860 stagecoach.

## Addresses and Connections

*Chamber of Commerce:* 720 Sudderth Drive, Ruidoso, NM 88345
*Newspaper: Ruidoso News,* 104 Park Avenue, Ruidoso, NM 88345
*Airport:* shuttle to El Paso Airport
*Bus:* no local bus, but there is Greyhound service

## Ruidoso Area Weather

| | In degrees Fahrenheit | | | | | |
| --- | --- | --- | --- | --- | --- | --- |
| | Jan. | April | July | Oct. | Rain | Snow |
| DAILY HIGHS | 50 | 65 | 81 | 67 | 21" | 44" |
| DAILY LOWS | 17 | 28 | 48 | 31 | | |

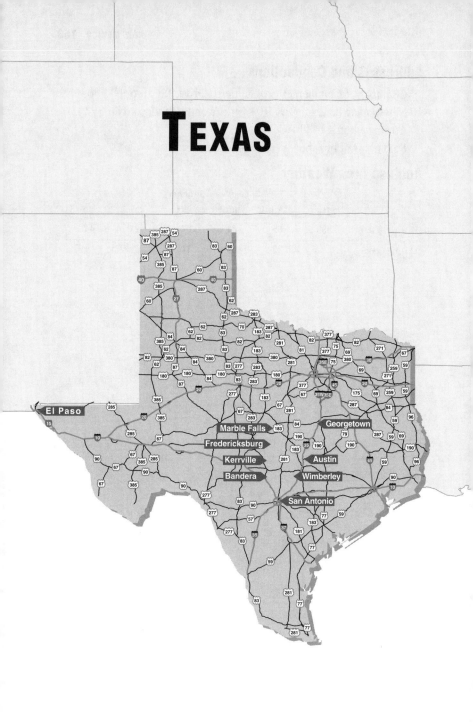

# TEXAS

The largest state in the Union—that is, until Alaska came along and rudely shouldered it aside—Texas is larger than most sovereign nations in the world. In fact, for a brief interlude, it was indeed a sovereign nation, from the time it won independence from Mexico until it joined the United States. Texas covers more territory than the total area of five Midwestern states—Indiana, Illinois, Ohio, Michigan, and Wisconsin.

Texas is also number two in population, recently passing New York as the nation's second most populous state. And the population is growing larger every day, with 300,000 people moving into the state each year, bringing the population to 18.4 million. Before long, Texas may push California out of first place, becoming the most populous in the nation. Ironically, part of the state's growth comes from Californians who are moving to Texas to retire. (Don't feel bad, California; plenty of folks move there from Florida, too.)

Several things make Texas attractive for retirement. For one thing, Texas is the closest Southwest location to Eastern and Midwestern states. Many people, when considering moving away for retirement, hesitate to relocate to Arizona or Nevada; that's too far away from the grandkids and the children who live back East. Texas is a compromise, not so far away that visiting would be out of the question.

The fact that Texas has no state income tax is very attractive for those with the enviable misfortune of making lots of money in retirement. The downside is that Texas sales and real estate taxes are among the highest in the nation. This isn't surprising; the money to run the state has to come from somewhere. If you're among those unfortunate few who make too much money, and your sole motive for moving to Texas is to avoid taxes, you need to sit down with a calculator and figure out whether you'll be saving money or not. After all, if you pay an extra $2,000 a year in property taxes to save $2,000 a year in state income taxes, you're not moving very far ahead financially.

Another consideration is climate. That's not to say that all of Texas has a livable climate, but the places critiqued here all enjoy mild winters and dry, bearable summers. The bonus is cheerful spring and colorful fall seasons. Deliberately excluded are places with world-class blizzards, tornadoes, and baseball-size hail. Few places east of the Sierra Nevada are exempt from the above, but it's my understanding that they occur less in the places described in this chapter than in the open plains area, with its cold winters and hot summers. Quick temperature changes, which are common in this region, can cause tornadoes and hailstorms.

Since this is a book about retirement in the Southwest, don't expect to see places in east Texas mentioned. Of course you'll find some delightful towns and cities in the eastern portion of the state, but they belong in another book. The east Texas region is more closely aligned with the South—culturally and socially—and it has a distinctly "Southern" climate.

Even though this book covers only west Texas, that's still a lot of ground. As it is, hundreds of cities, towns, and crossroads in the western and northwestern sectors of the state that I haven't been able to cover may feel insulted. Indeed, there's no disputing that people retire in these communities and no doubt live happily ever after. No law says a town has to be recommended by some retirement writer for it to be a good place to live, now does it?

Apologizing in advance for possible hurt feelings, I'm going to forge ahead with my listing of west Texas places for retirement, using three criteria. First, this chapter includes only those places where a significant number of people retire, particularly those coming from other states. Second, these locations have access to a quality shopping area within a reasonable driving distance. Third, each has some special charm or appeal over and above the average west Texas plains town. Meaning no disrespect to Texas, but were it not for automobile license plates, the average Texas town could be the average Kansas, Iowa, or Oklahoma town—not much different from thousands of communities around the United States.

A sad fact of modern-day life is that, throughout the country, commerce and shopping have shifted to the outskirts, to strip malls, abandoning the downtown to secondhand stores, gift shops, and antiques dealers. Out on wide stretches of multilane highway—accessible only by automobile—multiacre parking lots accommodate shoppers at Wal-Mart, Piggly Wiggly, and rows of predictable, name-brand, fast-food drive-ins of colorful red-and-yellow plastic construction. Each strip mall looks exactly alike. Of course, this sameness doesn't mean they're unsuitable places for retirement, but it does make it difficult to recommend one over another. And it raises this question: Why bother to change your retirement residence if a town is a near duplicate of your hometown?

## Texas Tax Profile

Sales tax:
**6.25% to 8.25%; food and drugs exempt**

State income tax:
**none**

Property taxes:
**about 2.3%**

Intangibles tax:
**none**

Social Security taxes:
**none**

Pension tax:
**none**

Gasoline tax:
**20¢ per gallon**

With this in mind, you'll notice that only two parts of west Texas will be discussed as possible retirement locations. One is the west Texas Hill Country between and around the cities of San Antonio and Austin. The hills, with their extra rainfall and lush surroundings, seem curiously out of place in west Texas, and this unique setting encourages out-of-state folks to retire here. The other is at the state's extreme western tip, around the city of El Paso. This is chosen partly because of the large number of retirees living there, both civilian and military, and partly because El Paso has a certain Southwest desert charm.

# History

The name Texas comes from a Caddo Indian word meaning "friends" or "allies." Spanish explorers pronounced the word *tejas* and gave this name to the area (in archaic Spanish, the letters *x* and *j* were interchangeable). Texas belonged to Spain for 300 years; its riches remained undeveloped, and its population was limited to a few missions and military outposts. When Mexico became an independent country in 1821, one of the government's priorities was to develop Texas. To populate the vast area, Mexican authorities encouraged new settlers from the United States to move here and become Mexican citizens, to speak Spanish, and to become Catholic. Immediately, a large influx of Anglo-American set-tlers—mostly Protestants from southern states—began developing homesteads, farms, and villages. They became Mexican citizens but retained their own culture and brought with them African slaves. This wasn't exactly what Mexican officials had in mind. With the Mexican government located so far away in Mexico City, the settlers had to deal with the Mexican army instead of regular political processes. This led to a revolution and the eventual defeat of the Mexican forces.

After the successful war of independence against Mexico, Texans raised the Lone Star flag over the Republic of Texas in 1836. The flag flew for nine years, until 1845, when Texas accepted annexation by the United States and was admitted to the Union as the twenty-eighth state. Elated at being U.S. citizens once more, residents discarded their Mexican sombreros in favor of ten-gallon hats and started wearing pointy-toed, high-heeled boots and wide belts with Lone Star Beer buckles enameled in red, white, and blue.

## Texas Hill Country

The picture most of us have of west Texas is flat or rolling stretches of eternity, sparsely covered with prairie grass or low brush that extends to meet the distant horizon. Sometimes wheat replaces grass; occasionally a lethargic steer can be seen munching cactus. Nothing moves except the up-and-down rocking of oil pumps or perhaps a distant windmill. Texas flatlands do indeed flow pretty much undisturbed by mountains, except for the extreme western portion, where the Rocky Mountains march southward through Big Bend National Park.

This bleak picture is more or less accurate, with a notable exception: the Texas Hill Country. A geological formation known as the Balcones Fault has pushed the land a thousand feet above the surrounding plains, creating a mini mountain range. This not only changes the geography of Texas but also profoundly affects the state's climate. Moisture-laden breezes from the Gulf of Mexico can't easily lift over the Hill Country, so they release their rain on the southeastern part of the state and leave the western part arid. You can easily see this, for the great Southwestern Desert begins on the other side of the Texas Hill Country.

This special part of Texas is a wonderland of limestone-cropped hills—not quite large enough to be called mountains—mostly wooded and intersected by a half dozen clear rivers, spring-fed creeks, and lakes. Perhaps about fifty small, friendly towns and cities are scattered throughout the lightly populated countryside, many of them holding great retirement potential. Because much of the Texas Hill Country is rocky, with high concentrations of limestone and caliche, the soil isn't suitable for extensive farming operations. Therefore, customarily the land is left in its natural state. Most acreage is covered by juniper thickets, wild cherry, gnarled oak, native pecan, and mountain laurel trees. Along the slow-moving rivers, magnificent cypress and elms shade the banks and provide cover for wild creatures. Cattle and sheep share the wilderness with white-tailed deer, turkey, javelina (wild pigs), and imported Russian boar.

The Texas Hill Country is as different from many people's view of Texas as it can possibly be. Long considered one of the better living areas in the state, the region has been enjoying nationwide attention through retirement publications. One thing that makes it so different from other parts of west Texas is its year-round rainfall. The Hill Country receives more than 30 inches of rain each year, several times that of many Southwest locations. This accounts for its green, sometimes lush, vegetation. The rain falls every month of the year, helping to keep things fresh looking.

The Hill Country's southeastern edge starts near the city of San Antonio and fans out northeast to include the state capital of Austin, then west for about 150 miles. The area immediately west of Austin has a picturesque chain of lakes formed by damming the Colorado River as it stair-steps downstream. Lakes and rivers throughout this area provide abundant fishing and boat recreation and also create a pleasant background for retirement living.

This area was settled beginning in the 1840s by German immigrants, who brought their customs, language, and architecture with them. An interesting bit of history: During the Civil War, the German settlers remained staunchly loyal to the Union, refusing to pledge allegiance to the Confederacy. They abhorred the notion of slavery and rebellion. One group of sixty-five volunteers tried to join with Union forces in the east, but they were waylaid and slaughtered by Confederate troops as they crossed the Nueces River. A monument to the victims is in the town of Comfort, the only tribute to pro-Union sympathizers to be found in Texas, probably the only such monument in the entire South.

Those settlers who came to Texas later on ignored the Hill Country; they preferred to farm the more level, richer agricultural lands so plentiful in other parts of the state. Therefore, the Hill Country developed at a more leisurely pace. This permitted German settlers to maintain their old-country customs well into the twentieth century. To this day some residents speak German, obviously quite proud of their heritage.

# Fredericksburg

With its setting of scenic hills covered with junipers and low-growing oak trees, Fredericksburg is the Texas Hill Country's most famous pioneer town. More than a century and a half ago, in 1846, a group of German immigrants reached the banks of the Pedernales River and decided this was where they would settle. The group's leader was a German nobleman, Baron Ottfried Hans von Meuseboch (who later became plain John Meuseboch once the town was established). The settlers decided to name the village after Prince Frederick of Prussia and set about constructing homes similar in style to those they had left behind. Abundant limestone made quality construction both possible and practical.

The newcomers were not alone. At night, in the hills surrounding the town, campfires cast ominous glows. Comanche warriors were carefully observing the activity below. To quiet their children's concern, pioneer women explained away the flickering lights as the cooking fires of Easter rabbits, who were simply boiling Easter eggs. But through the leadership of John Meusebach, a peace treaty was signed with the Comanches in 1847, one of the few such pacts that was never broken. The town celebrates this treaty signing with the Fredericksburg Easter Fires. On Easter eve, campfires glow on the hills around the town.

Sturdily constructed pioneer churches, shops, and homes have weathered the passage of time quite well. Many are in everyday use after more than a century, looking as if they're good for another hundred years.

Residents today recognize this treasure and, determined to preserve their heritage, have put it to full advantage as a tourist attraction. An old-fashioned horse-and-carriage ride and period-style restaurants along Main Street help foster this old-time German-village ambience. Fredericksburg attracts tourists from all over the nation, many of whom give serious thought to retirement here.

One tradition in town is the tolling of bells when a church member dies, one peal for each of the years the person had lived on this earth. Church bells ring before weddings and after funerals and, of course, on Sunday mornings as a call to worship.

Fredericksburg's population today is more than 8,000, and the area supports a thriving business community aside from tourism. The town is conveniently located ninety minutes' drive from either Austin or San Antonio for big-city shopping or airline transportation. Regularly scheduled buses pass through town on their way from Kerrville to Austin. The cost of living here is about average. Utility costs, however, are unusually low, partly because the city operates both electricity and water utilities and is said to do a great job of recycling profits into improving the system.

## Recreation and Culture

An interesting concept in outdoor recreation started here in 1976, something called Volksport, which has gained popularity around the nation. Volksport is best categorized as noncompetitive sporting events such as walking, biking, and swimming. Group events are conducted over predetermined routes or courses, and awards are given for completion of the event rather than how speedily you covered the course. You only compete against yourself. Older people find this an excellent way to join in the sociability of healthful exercise without pushing their capabilities or feeling overwhelmed by competition. "I didn't start biking until I was fifty," said one lady, "and I never would have started if it hadn't been for Volksport."

The town has facilities for competitive sports as well. The Lady Bird Johnson Municipal Golf Course is a popular eighteen-hole layout, and you'll find tennis courts throughout the area. The Hill Country area claims to have eleven of the top fifty golf courses in Texas (this is counting several courses in Austin and San Antonio).

Austin Community College has a satellite campus here, but most courses are for credit and are part of degree programs. The school expects to be adding continuing education classes for seniors. For the moment, the local school district offers some interesting adult education classes. Some residents participate by teaching their specialties and sharing their knowledge. "My husband and I just finished taking a computer class," said one retiree, "and before that we enjoyed studying early Fredericksburg history."

## Real Estate

Fredericksburg has many historic homes. Some have been painstakingly restored and put to use as bed-and-breakfasts or other commercial enterprises. Others are used as residences by proud owners. Because of the area's growing popularity, the real estate market has been moving steadily upward. Several well-heeled Hollywood personalities recently purchased estates and game ranches near Fredericksburg, which has helped to inflate prices. Yet, in town it's still possible to find satisfactory three-bedroom homes for less than $80,000. Most properties are selling on average for about $100,000. Really grand places have commanded prices approaching $500,000.

## Medical Care

The privately owned Hill Country Memorial Hospital is the pride of the region. With sixty-one beds and fifty physicians, the facility is beginning its third expansion in only a few years. Also, Gillespie County Emergency Medical Services employs a paid and volunteer staff for twenty-four-hour medical care and assistance.

## When Grandkids Visit

Treat them to a little history of World War II. The Admiral Nimitz Museum of the Pacific War pays homage to the two million Americans who served along with the admiral in the South Pacific. The museum depicts the four years of fighting and the final surrender of the Japanese military on Nimitz's battleship. Nearby is a four-acre display of tanks, airplanes, and weapons used in Pacific battles. The Nimitz family hotel, built by Nimitz's grandfather in 1850, houses the museum and is staffed by local volunteers. It also includes the George Bush National Museum of the Pacific War.

## Addresses and Connections

*Chamber of Commerce:* 106 North Adams, Fredericksburg, TX 78624

*Senior Services:* The Golden Hub, 1009 North Lincoln, Fredericksburg, TX 78624

*Newspaper:* Weekly: *Fredericksburg Standard Radio Post,* 108 East Main, Fredericksburg, TX 78624

*Airports:* the nearest are in Austin and San Antonio, both a sixty- to ninety-minute drive

*Bus:* no local bus system, but the Kerrville Bus Company travels through Fredericksburg to Austin, with connections to Greyhound

## Fredericksburg Area Weather

| | In degrees Fahrenheit | | | | | |
|---|---|---|---|---|---|---|
| | Jan. | April | July | Oct. | Rain | Snow |
| DAILY HIGHS | 62 | 79 | 92 | 81 | 30" | — |
| DAILY LOWS | 39 | 59 | 72 | 59 | | |

# Kerrville

Not far from Fredericksburg, Kerrville is often considered the "capital" of the Hill Country since it's the largest city in the hills and is centrally located among them. With a population of almost 19,000, Kerrville is also Fredericksburg's major shopping destination. Because the city is close to Interstate 10, many residents find it convenient to commute from here to jobs in San Antonio, about forty-five minutes away. Thus Kerrville fulfills two roles: as a retirement community and as a bedroom community.

Kerrville shares in the Hill Country's panoramic views and is further blessed by the Guadalupe River, which flows gently through the heart of town. Kerrville's location at 1,600 to 1,800 feet above sea level (the Hill Country's highest) contributes to its mild climate, providing cooler summers and more clearly defined seasons than in Austin or San Antonio. Local people are happy with July and August days, which are always several degrees cooler here than in the lowland cities. One source of new residents stems from those who customarily visit here for the pleasant summer weather and later decide to move to the Hill Country when embarking on new careers as retirees.

Because of the area's growing population of retirees (almost 30 percent of the town's residents are older than sixty-five), many Kerrville social and business events focus on seniors. The local chamber of commerce really goes all out for retirees and deserves high praise. The chamber's Retirement Marketing Committee organizes events each year to address the needs of retirees. Over the past few years they have hosted a series of Winter Texan Coffees to acquaint the seasonal resident with the community and all that it offers. In 1999 they took their show on the road by touring retirees around the town in trolleys provided by Dietert Senior Center in a program called the Howdy Wagon Tour. Area businesses opened their doors to the retirees, with individual tours and treats.

The crime rate here, as in all Hill Country towns, is low. Kerrville ranks in the top 30 percent of towns for high personal safety, according to the FBI's crime reports.

Kerrville holds a reputation as the Hill Country's preeminent art colony. The picturesque surroundings naturally encourage artistic development and act as a magnet to draw working artists, many of whom display works in local galleries and boutiques. One of Kerrville's galleries, the Cowboy Artists of America Museum, is the nation's only museum whose exhibitions are restricted to Western and cowboy artists. The architectural design of the building is also a work of Southwestern art, combining Moorish and Spanish architecture in a fortressed hacienda style.

## Recreation and Culture

While Fredericksburg has its Volksport, Kerrville's claim to recreational fame is the Kerrville Senior Games. The original intent of the games was to promote active, healthy lifestyles and good fellowship among Kerrville's senior citizens. But the games surprised everyone by becoming a major tourist event in their own right. Planned and executed entirely by Hill Country volunteers, the Senior Games lure close to a thousand participants, some traveling from as far away as Illinois, Montana, and California. Unlike Volksport events, the Senior Games are competitive, with clearly defined winners and losers. However, we get the feeling that winning isn't the important thing. One contestant at this year's games traveled from Houston to compete with his team in the volleyball event. When asked, "How did you do?" he smiled proudly. He replied, "We did great! Well, we lost every game, but we played great!"

For golfers, there's the Scott Schreiner Municipal Course, a public eighteen-hole layout, as well as the Riverhill Country Club, also with eighteen holes. There is a new eighteen-hole public golf course, The Buckhorn, in nearby Comfort. Kerrville's newest master-planned golf community is the Comanche Trace Ranch, featuring an eighteen-hole golf course scheduled to open in November 2000.

The Hill Country Arts Foundation is located just west of Kerrville. A nonprofit organization dedicated to furthering the visual and performing arts, it has enriched the lives of residents for three decades by presenting theater, art instruction, and exhibitions. More than thirty intensive art classes and weekend workshops are presently offered at the foundation's facilities. Topics range from watercolor and ceramics to computer-generated art. The foundation's Point Theatre features a summer outdoor season of musicals, comedies, and dramas.

Another popular cultural offering is the annual Kerrville Folk Festival, held in late spring. Residents and tourists enjoy eighteen days of musical events that include original works performed by artists in an outdoor theater, evening concerts around campfires, and a songwriters' competition.

Kerrville is also fortunate to have a dynamic community education system. The administration is constantly searching for innovative classes and interesting people to teach them. If a retiree comes up with an idea of something he or she would like to learn, the school looks for more students and an instructor. Crafts, languages, dancing, tennis, and cooking are just a few of the subjects covered. A "salons redux" series brings scholars and professionals out of their classrooms to engage in in-depth conversations with the people of the community. The discussions range from classical novelists to philosophy.

## Real Estate

Not much property can be found at giveaway prices anywhere in the Hill Country; it's too desirable for that. Value for your dollar is high. In Kerrville, three-bedroom homes in nice neighborhoods usually sell for $85,000 to $125,000. With persistence and a sharp eye for bargains, you can beat these prices. Average three-bedroom homes rent for $700, two-bedroom apartments from $480 to $900. As in most Hill Country locations, Kerrville has few condos. There are new four-plex rental units designed for seniors called The Meadows. Another seniors' subdivision called The Meridian is also being developed.

## Medical Care

Sid Peterson Memorial Hospital recently completed an $8 million construction/renovation project, which included a new emergency department and a major renovation of the hospital's first floor. More than seventy-five physicians are on the admitting staff. The hospital campus includes a professional building, cardiac rehab center, pulmonary rehab center, and cancer center. A new Ambulatory Care Center will open in the summer of 2000.

The Kerrville VA Hospital provides primary care and specialty services, including transitional nursing and dementia, for veterans.

## When Grandkids Visit

You might consider an inner-tube trip on the lazy sections of the Guadalupe River. You can rent tubes for the day and arrange to be picked up at the end of the journey. You'll find places to dawdle along the way, swimming holes with rope swings to drop you in the middle of the river, and grassy banks for a picnic. No, you won't look foolish floating in an inner tube; you'll have plenty of company, because tubing is a popular sport here. You might look foolish in a swimsuit, though, but that's a different problem.

## Addresses and Connections

*Chamber of Commerce:* 1700 Sidney Baker, Kerrville, TX 78028

*Senior Services:* Dietert Senior Citizens' Center, 617 Jefferson Street, Kerrville, TX 78028

*Newspapers: Kerrville Daily Times,* 429 Jefferson, Kerrville, TX 78028; weekly: *The Mountain Sun,* 301 McFarland, Kerrvile, TX 78028

*Airports:* the nearest airports are in Austin and San Antonio

*Bus:* there's no local bus system; the Kerrville Bus Company offers transportation to Austin, with connections to Greyhound

## Kerrville Area Weather

|  | In degrees Fahrenheit | | | | | |
|---|---|---|---|---|---|---|
|  | Jan. | April | July | Oct. | Rain | Snow |
| DAILY HIGHS | 60 | 78 | 90 | 80 | 30" | — |
| DAILY LOWS | 32 | 51 | 66 | 52 | | |

# Marble Falls

At the northern edge of the Texas Hill Country, the Colorado River feeds a series of seven lakes that work their way southeast through the city of Austin. This water wonderland provides hundreds of miles of waterway, offering every type of lake recreation imaginable. This area, known as the Highland Lakes district, shares the Hill Country's scenic wonders, peaceful surroundings, and pleasant weather. A number of excellent retirement locations are found here.

The largest town on this chain of lakes is Marble Falls, with a population of 5,300 (about 13,000 within a 10-mile radius). Marble Falls takes its name from a former waterfall along the Colorado River said to have been created by a ledge of marble. Early settlers called it Great Falls and dreamed of a manufacturing center that could be powered by the rush of water. Today the falls have been replaced by the waters of man-made Lake Lyndon B. Johnson, and Marble Falls has been spared the ugliness of mills and factories. Instead, tourists and retirees power the town. In fact, the number of over-sixty-five residents is more than double that in the average Texas community.

Some say the marble ledge of the falls was actually granite, maybe the same color as the huge stone monolith called Granite Mountain, which looms on the town's western edge. When Texas officials decided to build a state capitol building in Austin, Granite Mountain's owner convinced the planners to use Texas granite in the construction rather than import-ed limestone. His donation of the granite was a very convincing argu-ment, so the state accepted. The use of convict labor and workers from Scotland stirred the ire of the local labor unions, but work proceeded any-way. When completed, the building was second in size only to the Capitol in Washington, D.C. A visit to the capitol in nearby Austin provides elo-quent testimony to the workmanship of that day. And after one hundred years of continuous quarrying, the mountain still looks virtually intact.

By and large, Marble Falls is a comfortable place with a traditional down-town area. Quaint, old-fashioned Main Street has seven antiques shops that can keep buyers and browsers busy for hours on end. Several historical sites in the downtown area also have been carefully preserved.

Marble Falls is unique among small cities in that it has two assisted-living apartment complexes. Neither of these require a buy-in; that is, you don't have to come up with a large payment to become a resident. You merely get on the waiting list and move in, making monthly pay-ments of about $1,500. This includes three meals and lots of organized activities. If you don't like it, you can always leave without forfeiting an up-front payment.

Most of the Marble Falls area offers modest to expensive housing. Asking prices depend on whether you're sitting on the water's edge or are some blocks away. Almost any neighborhood you look at could be appropriate for retirees. One interesting neighborhood that particularly appeals to retirees (particularly golf nuts) is a lakefront development called

Meadowlakes. This is a gated community on the western edge of Marble Falls. As you might imagine, homes around the golf course are more expensive. Although Meadowlakes appears to be part of Marble Falls, in fact it isn't. To maintain autonomy from the rest of the area, Meadowlakes formally incorporated to form its own little town within a town.

Like all Hill Country and Highland Lakes communities, crime is low and personal safety is high. Burnet County (site of Marble Falls) reported 40 percent fewer crimes than the national average. Many residents told me that they seldom lock their doors. However, most also refused to give me their addresses so I could go and check. The cost of living is also similar to surrounding towns, which is to say, low.

## Recreation and Culture

Outdoor recreation, of course, centers on the lakes. Bass fishing, boating, and sailing bring people from all over the region and encourage them to retire here when the workdays become permanent vacation days. White-tailed deer and wild turkey are said to be plentiful for hunters.

Seven beautiful, all-weather golf courses are within a 20-mile radius. Three of them are Robert Trent Jones layouts at Horseshoe Bay; however, the golf and tennis courts here are restricted to residents and guests of Horseshoe Bay Resort. The eighteen-hole course at Meadowlakes and a nine-hole course at Blue Lake are open to public play for a fee.

The Highland Arts Council is the umbrella organization for six arts councils in the lake area. Most have permanent galleries, which are kept open by volunteer members. Workshops, classes, and demonstrations are given at the Marble Falls location on Main Street. The population hereabouts just isn't large enough at present to support a community college. Although a few adult education courses are taught at the high school, the nearest place for continuing education classes is in Austin.

I've never been quite sure whether a chili cook-off qualifies as a cultural event or as a dangerous contact sport, but in any event, Marble Falls is home to Howdy Roo, the fourth-oldest chili cook-off in the state.

## Real Estate

According to local real estate professionals, the market in and around Marble Falls is vigorous, with homes selling for just a few percentage points short of the asking price. Three-bedroom houses, away from the lakeshore, can be found for less than $100,000. Being on the water raises prices another $20,000 to $30,000, although some homes have been going for much higher. Meadowlakes homes tend to be pricey, just as you would expect from a gated golfcourse community. Beautiful homes here range from $80,000 to $120,000, but on the golf course the prices climb to $150,000 to $180,000. Waterfront homes add $50,000 for the privilege. All property isn't high-priced in Marble Falls, however. Some rather modestly priced neighborhoods feature houses starting at $50,000.

## Buchanan Dam

Around both Lake LBJ and Lake Buchanan you'll find several small communities appropriate for retirement. Buchanan is the largest and highest lake in terms of altitude. The resort and retirement community of Buchanan Dam takes its name from the construction site that created Buchanan Lake. The population here is about 3,800, with many retirees. Buchanan Dam is known for arts and crafts, having the oldest co-op gallery in the nation. Open year-round, the gallery exhibits paintings, weavings, and a variety of crafts. The Highland Lakes Golf Course at nearby Inks Lake State Park is open to the public.

Other nearby locales are Granite Shoals, Sunrise Beach, and Kingsland. Roads encircle the lake, giving access to homes, RV parks, and rental properties.

## Horseshoe Bay

Another popular upscale retirement locale is Horseshoe Bay, about 7 miles from Marble Falls. Situated on 8,500 acres, Horseshoe Bay features three eighteen-hole golf courses, twenty tennis courts, a marina, and its own 6,000-foot airstrip. It isn't a gated community, but it does have its own police and fire departments as well as an emergency medical service to take care of the 1,500 full-time residents. Because this is the most luxurious of the upscale communities around here, real estate is priced accordingly. Older condominiums, away from the golf courses, start at $50,000. Conventional housing starts at $100,000 and goes up to $8 million. Homes on the golf course range from $250,000 to $300,000; on the water, count on $400,000 and up. Other upscale resort-retirement locations in the area are Blue Lake and Deer Haven.

## Medical Care

The hospital that serves the lake district is in Burnet, about 19 miles north of Marble Falls and 13 miles east of Buchanan Dam. The Highland

Lakes Medical Center provides urgent care twenty-four hours a day and supports a full medical staff. In Marble Falls itself the volunteer emergency medical service operates an ambulance and in emergencies offers medical procedures. The area is served by two helicopters that can rush patients to either Austin or San Antonio. In Marble Falls, the new Hoerster Clinic has two full-time physicians on duty. An office of Revis Home Care is also located in Marble Falls.

## When Grandkids Visit

An interesting side trip would be to Longhorn Cavern. Always a comfortable sixty-four degrees, the cave offers a level and easy walk through a natural wonder. It takes about an hour and a half to walk the 1¼-mile circuit. Fossil remains found here indicate a variety of beasts of prey that used the cave as a dining room. Arrowheads show that native tribes lived here, at least temporarily. According to legend, the famous Texas outlaw Sam Bass used the cavern as a hideout, and it was a Confederate stronghold during the Civil War.

## Addresses and Connections

*Chamber of Commerce:* 801 Highway 281, Marble Falls, TX 78654
*Senior Services:* 1200 Seventh Street, Marble Falls, TX 78654
*Newspapers: The Highlander,* 206 Main Street, Marble Falls, TX 78654; *The Picayune,* 905 West Third, Marble Falls, TX 78654
*Airports:* shuttles are available to Austin and San Antonio airports
*Bus:* there's no city bus service, but Burnet County community buses link several towns, with connections to Austin

## Marble Falls Area Weather

| | In degrees Fahrenheit | | | | | |
| | Jan. | April | July | Oct. | Rain | Snow |
| --- | --- | --- | --- | --- | --- | --- |
| DAILY HIGHS | 59 | 79 | 96 | 81 | 30" | — |
| DAILY LOWS | 40 | 59 | 73 | 59 | | |

# Wimberley

This is another Hill Country town that's been basking in the warm light of national publicity as a new "discovery" in retirement destinations. Its photogenic qualities make wonderful color layouts for magazines. This is where the clear, cool waters of Cypress Creek join the warmer waters of the slow-moving Blanco River, a place where large trees and old homes of native stone hark back to another era. Wimberley was a popular getaway during World War II, when rich folks from Houston and San Antonio didn't have enough gasoline to travel to their second homes in the Blue Ridge Mountains. So they built summer homes—or "camp houses," as they called them—in Wimberley. When they retired, these summer places became permanent homes, thus starting a retirement trend. As a result, Houston transplants are well represented here. Wimberley is properly called a village, because it has never been incorporated, and people here like it that way.

The town is attracting new residents, however. One resident observed, "Wimberley used to be thought of as a place for retirement, but in the last five years more and more families with youngsters are moving in. The second-largest group coming here nowadays are artists. This makes a nice mixture of neighbors."

Wimberley also presents many genuinely old, wonderfully preserved buildings for your amazement. The oldest are the Wimberley Mill, built in 1856, and the Winters-Wimberley House, possibly built at the same time as the mill. Many buildings here are of native stone. A walking tour of the historic area leads you to a dozen homes built from the mid-1800s to the 1920s.

The main drawback here is that Wimberley hasn't been a well-kept secret with tourists. They've known about it for many years. Often characterized as a "quaint little village," Wimberley clearly lives up to the reputation, and people from all around come to see for themselves. So many come, in fact, that traffic clogs the main drag. I would characterize Wimberley as a busy quaint little town. It isn't all that small, either—the population is a little less than 9,000. This is a shopper's paradise for the arts-and-crafts crowd, with art galleries, crafts and gift shops, and antiques stores. A couple of fairly nice restaurants feed the crowds, and an old-fashioned ice cream parlor supplies walking-around goodies.

Located between Austin and San Antonio, just 15 miles off Interstate 35, Wimberley sits about 500 feet lower in altitude than other towns in the Hill Country. This doesn't seem to affect the weather. The nearest small city is San Marcos, 12 miles away; that's where most heavy-duty shopping is done. San Marcos is exceptionally popular with some shoppers because it's the nearest place to purchase wine or liquor. (Some local restaurants do serve wine and cocktails by the glass, but you must buy a "membership" card for $3.00 before they'll serve you.) Another reason for San Marcos's popularity with shoppers is it's the location of one of the largest and best-designed factory outlet centers. By the way, San Marcos is a nice-looking little city. For a time I considered covering it as a retirement recommendation even though it isn't really in Texas Hill Country proper.

Wimberley sits at an altitude of 1,100 feet—twice as high as Austin—and therefore enjoys slightly cooler summers and more rain. Like other towns in this part of the country, snow is a rarity. In the past two years approximately 200 families have moved in, with 65 percent of the newcomers retirees. A summer community tradition, from Memorial Day through Labor Day, is an outdoor movie theater. Residents come to watch the latest flicks under the stars. Most bring a lawn chair or blanket, as seating is limited.

Although there is no Greyhound bus service, the county sponsors a service called CARTS, which takes disabled and senior citizens to medical appointments, and even into Austin for shopping and special medical needs.

## Recreation and Culture

Popular with Hill Country residents are rafting and inner tubing on the many rivers that traverse the region. Unfortunately, this is not to be in Wimberley. For some reason the state has set property lines in the middle of the Blanco River, which means the entire river is privately owned. Therefore you aren't allowed access to the river without a property owner's permission. Bummer.

The Wimberley Players, a small theater group, has produced plays of professional quality for more than a decade. The season usually consists of four productions. The group uses the Greenhouse Theatre at Woodcreek Resort, which seats seventy-seven.

For continuing education, people drive to San Marcos, the site of Southwest Texas State University. The school's music department gives concerts in Wimberley several times a year. Other local events are an annual Crawfish Boil and the Lions' Club Market Day, which is held every Saturday from April to December, with 400 booths offering everything from arts and crafts to antiques. Many vendors offer goodies from the backs of their trucks or auto trunks.

## Real Estate

Prices in and around Wimberley are less than the national average but are considerably higher than in San Antonio and Austin. This seems to be the case in many Hill Country communities. However, this isn't a fair comparison of costs, because few neighborhoods in Austin or San Antonio are remotely similar in quality to those in the Hill Country. Homeowners choose among properties on rivers and hills, on city-size lots, or on acreages with homes. Prices range from $79,000 to as much as you can pay.

A few minutes north of Wimberley is Woodcreek, a planned community with an eighteen-hole golf course, tennis courts, clubhouse, and other amenities. Homes here start at around $90,000. A new section of Woodcreek is under development, which means another eighteen-hole golf course to go along with it. Unlike many planned communities, Woodcreek has no formal social planning structure.

Occasionally a few rentals can be found in Woodcreek, mostly two- or three-bedroom town houses. Otherwise, rentals in Wimberley are almost impossible to find, since there are no apartment buildings, just single-family homes. However, there are twenty-nine motels with overnight accommodations and reportedly ninety bed-and-breakfast rooms with accommodations ranging from one place with an indoor swimming pool to a log cabin with indoor plumbing. You'll have a place to stay while looking over the area.

## Medical Care

The Family Clinic, a branch of the Texas Medical Center in San Marcos, operates with family-practice doctors on duty daily. Wimberley has no hospital of its own, but trained volunteer ambulance teams rush emergency cases to the hospital in nearby San Marcos. They have two ambulances available, one of them a mobile intensive-care unit. In San Marcos, there's the Central Texas Medical Center's 109-bed hospital. For exceptional cases a helicopter can whisk patients to Austin. Wimberley does have a 120-bed nursing home and a small assisted-living facility.

## When Grandkids Visit

You might want to visit the 7-A Pioneer Town, about 1½ miles from the senior center on Ranch Road 12. This is a replica of an early-day Texas village, complete with the obligatory shoot-outs with blank cartridges and a ride on a genuine steam-powered train.

## Addresses and Connections

*Chamber of Commerce:* Ranch Road 12, P.O. Box 12, Wimberley, TX 78676

*Senior Services:* Ranch Road 12, P.O. Box 678, Wimberley, TX 78676

*Newspaper: Wimberley View,* Ranch Road 12, Wimberley, TX 78676

*Airports:* you must use either Austin or San Antonio

*Bus:* there is no local bus or taxi service

## Wimberley Area Weather

|  | In degrees Fahrenheit | | | | | |
|---|---|---|---|---|---|---|
|  | Jan. | April | July | Oct. | Rain | Snow |
| DAILY HIGHS | 53 | 79 | 97 | 81 | 37" | — |
| DAILY LOWS | 40 | 58 | 75 | 59 | | |

## Wimberley/San Marcos Area Cost of Living

| (percentage of national average) | | | | |
|---|---|---|---|---|
| Overall | Housing | Medical | Groceries | Utilities |
| 92% | 96% | 83% | 79% | 82% |

# Austin

Eighty miles north of San Antonio on Interstate 35 is Austin, the state capital. Austin's population of 470,000 makes it about half the size of San Antonio, giving residents more elbow room. This also makes it more practical to live closer to the middle of town. Downtown Austin centers on an ornate state capitol building with extensive grounds and parklike landscaping. The capitol is worth a visit just to see the marvelous workmanship in rose-colored granite. If you read the section on Marble Falls, you'll learn where the granite came from.

Not as level as most Texas cities, Austin sits on the fringe of the Texas Hill Country, surrounded by a circle of low hills. Unlike San Antonio, which developed from a haphazard grouping of trails converging at a river crossing, Austin began as a carefully planned city designed to be the state's capital. The downtown section is laid out in an easy-to-follow grid and includes an interesting mixture of modern buildings and older ones, resulting in an easy informality.

## Recreation and Culture

Almost twenty golf courses are open to the public, plus there are another fifteen private clubs in the Austin area. The mild climate permits fairway use throughout the year. Because Austin has more than fifteen tennis facilities, totaling about 200 courts, *Tennis* magazine recently named it one of the ten best tennis cities in the country.

The Highland Lakes are gathering places for sailors, sailboarders, boaters, and, of course, anglers. Austin also has a 30-mile network of hike-and-bike trails that wander through quiet meadows, past restaurants, and across bridges.

The Dallas Cowboys hold a summer training camp here at St. Edwards University. More than 100,000 Cowboys fans turn out to watch practice sessions and collect autographs.

Austin is home to the University of Texas, with its exceptional libraries, museum, sports activities, and cultural facilities, including a world-class concert hall for the performing arts and an 18,000-seat sports arena. The LBJ Library is also located on the university campus. The university and Austin Community College offer many continuing education and personal development courses of interest to senior citizens.

Austin is becoming widely known as a country-music center, second only to Nashville. Not only country-western music but also jazz and reggae can be heard in the clubs around the city, particularly on Sixth Street, the renovated nineteenth-century historic district. The city is also proud of its reputation as a cultural center in arts other than music. Museums, theaters, and art galleries are well attended throughout the city. Symphony, ballet, and lyric opera complement the cultural offerings. Zilker Hillside Theatre stages popular summer music and drama programs.

## Real Estate

Real estate costs here are similar to San Antonio's, with many pleasant-looking neighborhoods on the fringes of the city. For a time repossessions dropped prices to a giveaway level, with new four-bedroom homes going for as low as $57,000. These distress sales forced conventional sellers to drop their prices to be competitive. However, this depressed market recovered to the point where housing costs are 10 percent below the national average. In 2000 sales averaged between $108,000 and $135,000.

Austin is unique in that it has many retirement communities, at least eight newer ones, most along the north and northwestern edge of the city. They offer retirees a variety of living conditions from luxurious to economical. The services range from full care, with personal care apartments and nursing care units, to ordinary apartment-type living.

Hidden Hills appears to be one of the most expensive communities in the area. Although not a retirement community per se, its location on Lake Travis and its eighteen-hole golf course designed by Arnold Palmer have attracted many retirees. Two-bedroom cottages start at $150,000, and some homes are priced at more than $1 million. For this you get high security with guarded gates and in-home security systems linked to the guard station.

Several other luxury retirement developments are connected with the chain of lakes along the Colorado River. One of the better-known places is The Island, located on Lake Travis. Monthly fees start at $1,300 for an apartment, maid service, and some meals. Costs climb to almost $3,000 for the larger units. Many other developments, not necessarily just for retirees, are sprinkled around Austin's western edge. Tennis and golf are often the central focus.

For something a little less expensive, consider Camlu Apartments. The retirement development offers two-bedroom units beginning at less than $1,000 a month, including utilities, daily meals, weekly maid service, and shopping transportation.

## Medical Care

Medical services are more than adequate, with a dozen hospitals and numerous specialists in attendance. Breckenridge Hospital, a teaching hospital, has the only trauma center in the area. The Seton Medical Center, home of the Central Texas Heart Institute, is also located here. The emergency medical service is said to be one of the best in the nation, with loads of equipment, including helicopters.

## When Grandkids Visit

Consider taking them on a half-day train ride with a genuine, 143-ton steam engine. The 1920s-era passenger coaches roll across some of the finest scenery found in the Lone Star State. The round-trip starts at nearby Cedar Park and goes to Burnet.

## Addresses and Connections

*Chamber of Commerce:* 210 East Second Avenue, Austin, TX 78767

*Senior Services:* 405 East Fifteenth Street, Austin, TX 78701

*Newspaper: Austin American Statesman,* 166 East Riverside Drive, Austin, TX 78767

*Airport:* Mueller Field, scheduled to be replaced by a new facility at the old Breckenridge Air Force Base

*Bus:* there's a city bus system and Greyhound, with connections to Kerrville and other Texas Hill Country towns

## Austin Area Weather

| | In degrees Fahrenheit | | | | | |
| | Jan. | April | July | Oct. | Rain | Snow |
|---|---|---|---|---|---|---|
| DAILY HIGHS | 59 | 79 | 95 | 81 | 32" | 1" |
| DAILY LOWS | 39 | 58 | 74 | 59 | | |

## Austin Area Cost of Living

| (percentage of national average) | | | | |
| Overall | Housing | Medical | Groceries | Utilities |
|---|---|---|---|---|
| 92% | 90% | 83% | 79% | 82% |

# Georgetown

Another pioneer town—founded July 4, 1848, by George Washington Glasscock—sits on the banks of the San Gabriel River, not far from Austin. In its early days, Georgetown was a wild and woolly frontier town, a watering place on the famous Chisholm Trail, where cowboys herded longhorn cattle through the center of town.

Georgetown is proud of its history and is a showcase for its Victorian architecture. The centerpiece is the old, historic Courthouse Square, with antiques stores and boutiques. Residents take great care in the restoration and preservation of this historic town, with 180 homes and commercial structures designated as having historical significance. Some are now in use as restaurants and bed-and-breakfasts.

Although sometimes billed as the "Gateway to the Hill Country," Georgetown's altitude is only 750 feet—not much higher than Austin's—so it can't technically be considered part of the Hill Country. That doesn't distract from its charm, however. The population here is a little more than 28,000. Since it's only 27 miles from Austin on the interstate, it's within easy commuting distance from the city. This makes it convenient for those who desire some of Austin's conveniences, things like shopping, college sports events, and continuing education opportunities. As far as personal safety goes, Georgetown ranks in the top 25 percent, according to FBI statistics.

## Sun City Texas at Georgetown

As an indication of faith in Georgetown's future as a retirement location, the Del Webb Corporation developed one of its famous Sun City communities near here. Sun City Texas's 5,300-acre planned community features two scenic creeks meandering through fields of Texas wildflowers and stands of native pecans, walnuts, and majestic live oaks. Del Webb's first Texas venture is an active retirement community designed for those age fifty-five and older.

As envisioned, 10,500 homes will be built, and four eighteen-hole golf courses are planned. Other recreational facilities will include swimming pools, tennis courts, and extensive hiking and biking trails.

When asked why Georgetown, Ken Hull, Del Webb's Sun City Texas's general manager, replied: "Georgetown has an interesting blend of the old and new. It's the archetypical Texas town where people know their neighbors and often greet visitors with a 'howdy' on the streets."

## Recreation and Culture

For swimming, boating, fishing, hiking, and camping, Lake Georgetown is about 5 miles from town. This 1,310-acre bass fishing hole, with limestone bluffs and large herds of deer, has plenty of campsites and places for picnics, plus a crystal-clear swimming area. To the east of Georgetown is Granger Lake, with four state parks; to the west, the stair-stepped lakes on the Colorado River provide even more water recreation. The town of Georgetown has two country clubs, three golf courses, thirty-eight tennis courts, a racquet club, and three swimming pools.

Southwestern University, a small liberal arts institution, is located in Georgetown. The oldest active university in Texas, it has more of an Ivy League atmosphere than any other school in the state. Although the school limits enrollment to only 1,200 students, the institution has considerable impact on Georgetown's cultural climate. The drama and music departments are particularly active, providing the community with many enjoyable performances throughout the year.

A popular event, open to the public without charge, is the annual Brown Symposium, which explores topics as diverse as the cosmology of black holes in space, symphonies of famous composers, and Thailand traditional dances. Nobel prize winners and intellectual celebrities such as Isaac Asimov and Alex Haley have participated in the symposium.

## Real Estate

Because Georgetown is on the interstate and easily accessible to Austin, it has become a bedroom community for those who work in the city. Real estate prices quite naturally are somewhat higher than in the true Hill Country towns. Prices here for an average home start at about $100,000, with mediam selling prices at $122,000. Homes can be found for less by judicious shoppers.

## Medical Care

Besides excellent area medical facilities, a number of major regional providers are nearby. The Georgetown Healthcare System has sixty-six beds and more than thirty active admitting physicians. Scott & White Clinic offers services that include a special wellness program as well as traditional primary services, and there's easy access to the VA Hospital Center and veterans facilities in Temple (30 miles north of Georgetown). And since Austin's medical community is just twenty minutes away, you can rest easy about health care.

## When Grandkids Visit

Check out Inner Space Cavern, just 1 mile south of town, next to Interstate 35. The cavern was unknown until a construction crew working on the interstate broke through the earth and made the discovery. One of only seven commercially operated caves in Texas, the Inner Space Cavern tour takes about an hour and a half. You enter by cable car and are treated to special lighting and sound effects.

## Addresses and Connections

*Chamber of Commerce:* P.O. Box 346, Georgetown, TX 78627
*Senior Services:* 1704 Hart Street, Georgetown, TX 78626
*Newspaper: Williamson County Sun,* 709 South Main Street, P.O. Drawer 39, Georgetown, TX 78767

*Airport:* Austin Bergstrom International Airport, Austin
*Bus:* there are no local or intercity connections

## Georgetown Area Weather

| | In degrees Fahrenheit | | | | | |
| | Jan. | April | July | Oct. | Rain | Snow |
|---|---|---|---|---|---|---|
| DAILY HIGHS | 59 | 79 | 95 | 81 | 32" | 1" |
| DAILY LOWS | 39 | 58 | 74 | 59 | | |

## Georgetown Area Cost of Living

| (percentage of national average) | | | | |
| Overall | Housing | Medical | Groceries | Utilities |
|---|---|---|---|---|
| 96% | 91% | 96% | 90% | 90% |

# San Antonio

San Antonio is a big city, the ninth largest in the country and the third largest in Texas. It's also growing quickly, having increased its population from 785,000 in 1980 to almost a million twenty years later. A good portion of San Antonio's growth can be attributed to retirees.

Normally, I don't like recommending such a large city as a place to retire, but San Antonio is a special place, and you needn't live in the heart of the city in order to enjoy what it has to offer. The city keeps expanding in an outward ring, with neighborhoods that provide a small-town flavor. I can heartily recommend these residential/commercial areas. The neighborhoods are complete in themselves. The core of the city is convenient to any part of the circle and is easy to visit for special occasions, but not at all essential for everyday living.

A major consideration of San Antonio retirement is its climate. San Antonio enjoys what weather experts call a modified subtropical climate. Summer days are hot, with highs typically in the low nineties. Yet summer evenings are delightful, with temperatures dropping into the high sixties or low seventies, just right for shirtsleeve evenings and for sleeping without the annoyance of air-conditioning. Mild weather prevails during the winter, with afternoon temperatures above sixty degrees, even in the coldest months. Snow? Almost none; every three or four years San Antonio catches enough snow to measure (although in 1985 it snowed 13 inches). Rain? Enough to keep lawns and shrubbery green. San

Antonio marks the western boundary of naturally green vegetation, with plenty of trees growing wild in the countryside. When you drive south and west of San Antonio, you'll see a dramatic dryness, the beginning of the Great Southwest Desert that stretches from here to California.

Because the city is so big, there's plenty to do and see. Shopping at the ten-acre River Center Mall, a bewildering number of good restaurants, art shows, and downtown walking tours are just for starters. Also downtown you'll find San Antonio's pride and joy: the Alamo, site of the famous battle.

When Spanish settlers first arrived here, a Coahuilecan Indian village already occupied the banks of the beautiful river, site of present-day downtown San Antonio. The river, life giving and crystal clear, was shaded by large poplar trees (*alamo* in Spanish). The Native Americans called the river *Yanaguana,* or "refreshing waters." The Spanish settlers were so overwhelmed with the river's beauty that they chased away the natives, changed the name of the river to San Antonio, and began polluting it.

Happily, today this river is a symbol of San Antonio's progressive fight against urban decay. The Downtown River Project is a textbook example of how to remedy urban core blight. The city completely transformed the area—which was little more than a weed-choked garbage dump a few years ago—into an elegant shopping and restaurant complex. Soaring cypress and cottonwood trees grace the riverbanks, shading shops, restaurants, and hotels. Tourists and residents alike enjoy strolls, boat rides, and nightlife along the river. The project revitalized San Antonio's entire downtown section. The Coahuilecan tribe would be proud of the way their river has returned to its "refreshing waters" status.

## Great Northwest

Let's take a look at a single San Antonio neighborhood, one that is typical of several around the fringes of San Antonio. The Great Northwest is home to 4,000 families, many of them retired. Although other areas are equally nice, I choose to highlight the Great Northwest because it's a model residential community. An indication of this is that for the last several years, the Great Northwest has often been awarded first place in quality living by the National Community Association. What this means is that, like many San Antonio neighborhoods, residents maintain an active property owners' association that pulls the community together. Although this sounds like the neighborly thing to do, it goes much further, producing more than fun projects, crafts clubs, or Saturday-night potlucks. A good association can greatly improve the quality of life of the community.

The Great Northwest may not have a golf course, country club, stables, or lakes that some retirees might expect, but the area does have an Olympic-size pool, several tennis courts, and a twenty-acre park, all maintained by residents' yearly dues. The neighborhood doesn't have gates to keep out strangers. It doesn't need gates; people look out for each other, and if that's not enough, six private patrol cars police the area twenty-four hours a day.

This is not an age-restricted retirement community. One of the Great Northwest's charms is its mixed-generation composition. Many residents are on active military duty; others work in San Antonio's electronic industry, and so on. Many have toddlers, kids, and teenagers living at home. Now, ordinarily, teenagers can spell trouble for a neighborhood, because most general cussedness is caused by adolescents. But an active community association provides activities to keep them out of trouble. When the entire family participates in community affairs, when everybody knows their neighbors, and when their parents will hear about everything that happens, teenagers tend to behave.

Neighborhood shopping is convenient, with large malls and commercial centers liberally scattered around the beltway surrounding San Antonio. Downtown is a twenty-minute drive, and the largest, most complete medical facility in Texas is also twenty minutes from the Great Northwest.

## Military Retirement

Since its beginning as a Spanish presidio almost three centuries ago, San Antonio has sustained its strong military tradition. Three Air Force bases are located here: Brooks, Lackland, and Randolph, plus Fort Sam Houston, an Army post. Lackland Air Force Base is famous in military circles for having one of the finest medical facilities in the country. This alone is an attraction for military retirees and would bring them here even if San Antonio weren't such a nice place to live. Almost 70,000 service personnel and families and at least twice that many retirees live in the San Antonio area. This may well be the largest population of ex-military in the country. One retired Air Force colonel said, "Many military families arrange to make San Antonio their last tour of duty when they are reaching the end of their career. That's because they've already decided this is where they want to retire."

Every good-size town has its share of retirement complexes and life-care communities. But San Antonio has several for military personnel only. These are nonprofit organizations and do not receive direct government funding. I visited one on the western edge of San Antonio, called Air Force Village. Conveniently located across the highway from Lackland Air Force Hospital, this facility provides quality apartments or cottages for a pleasant lifelong environment. Residents—who must be retired Air Force officers—buy into the complex with a "founder's fee," which starts at $46,000 for a one-bedroom, one-bath unit, going up to $100,000 for a deluxe two-bedroom, two-bath, 1,100-square-foot apartment. Then, with a $400 or $500 fee (depending on the size of the quarters), the resident is entitled to maid service, physician visits, transportation, all utilities, and meals. If it's needed, home health care and food delivered to the apartment is provided, as well as twenty-four-hour nursing care.

## Recreation and Culture

This is the home of the San Antonio Spurs basketball team, the AA San Antonio Mission baseball team, the San Antonio Racquets tennis team, the San Antonio Iguanas hockey team, and the U.S. Modern Pentathlon Olympic team. The city administers 135 parks, with more than 6,535 acres and two municipal swimming pools. For saltwater fishing, a little more than a two-hour drive places you at the beach, in Corpus Christi or on the famous Padre Islands.

San Antonians enjoy a variety of cultural attractions and entertainment. There are several community theaters, the Symphony Society of San Antonio, as well as a number of museums and dance companies. Fiesta, a weeklong festival, occurs every April. It was originally staged as a memorial to the heroes of the Alamo and has grown to such huge proportions that there's hardly space to move downtown. To foster tourism, the city sponsors a multitude of events, going to great bother to provide interesting things to do, events that residents happily join. There's hardly a day in the year without something special happening. The city even dyes the river green for St. Patrick's Day. (Fish hate this and try to vacation in other rivers when St. Patrick's Day rolls around.)

## Real Estate

San Antonio, like Austin to the north, enjoys a low cost of living, several percentage points below the national average for large cities; utility costs are particularly favorable. A buyers' real estate market has kept prices well within the affordable range. Preferred residential areas flourish on the fringes of the city, with new subdivisions popping up everywhere. The central area and older sections offer the biggest bargains in real estate, sometimes as low as $30,000, but for heaven's sake, don't make a decision on price alone; most central areas are clearly not suitable for most retirees. Among other things, crime levels here can be somewhat elevated. Most newcomers prefer to live in the outer ring of newer subdivisions, near one of several large shopping centers. These areas have comfortably high levels of personal safety, as opposed to the inevitable higher crime rate found closer to a city's center. Most San Antonio area homes fall in the price range of $75,000 to $100,000, with an average size of 1,400 square feet. Town houses are priced anywhere from $60,000 to $80,000 for maintenance-free living.

One reason for the abundance of rentals and reasonable rents is the enormous military population that is always on the move. A few years ago, developers sized up this market and decided to increase the number of rentals. With abundant savings-and-loan money available, apartments and condos sprouted more quickly than tenants. The result was too many rentals. However, lately this happy condition of ridiculously low rents is changing, as more people move into the San Antonio area and fewer new apartments are constructed.

## Medical Care

Medical care in and around San Antonio is awesome. The University of Texas Health Science Center is located here, with schools in medicine, dentistry, and nursing, and research programs in cancer, cardiovascular problems, and other problems endemic to the elderly. This is one of only six sites in the nation that is approved for experimental cancer drugs. The South Texas Medical Center, a 700-acre complex, encompasses eight major hospitals, clinics, laboratories, and a cancer research and therapy center. There's also the world-renowned burn unit at Brooke Army Medical Center at Fort Sam Houston, which receives burn victims from all over the world.

## When Grandkids Visit

They might enjoy riding on the world's tallest, fastest, and steepest roller coaster. Nicknamed "The Rattler," its wooden framework clings to the side of a 100-foot-tall quarry wall in the theme park Fiesta Texas. The coaster begins its wild ride at the top of the cliff, then climbs an additional 70 feet into the air before dropping a record 160 feet. It zooms upward again, zipping through a limestone tunnel, then back downward at insane speeds of more than 70 miles per hour. Your grandkids will love it, but you will probably hate it. Maybe you should take them to the zoo instead.

## Addresses and Connections

*Chamber of Commerce:* 602 East Commerce, San Antonio, TX 78296
*Senior Services:* 107 Lexington Avenue, San Antonio, TX 78205
*Newspaper: San Antonio Express-News,* Avenue E at Third Street, San Antonio, TX 78205
*Airport:* San Antonio Municipal Airport
*Bus:* both city buses and Greyhound are readily available

## San Antonio Area Weather

| | In degrees Fahrenheit | | | | | |
|---|---|---|---|---|---|---|
| | Jan. | April | July | Oct. | Rain | Snow |
| DAILY HIGHS | 62 | 80 | 96 | 82 | 28" | — |
| DAILY LOWS | 40 | 59 | 74 | 59 | | |

## San Antonio Cost of Living

| (percentage of national average) | | | | |
|---|---|---|---|---|
| Overall | Housing | Medical | Groceries | Utilities |
| 89% | 83% | 95% | 88% | 79% |

# Bandera

Perhaps it's too small to be included under its own section (its population is less than a thousand), but Bandera is too nice to ignore. It has become a retirement haven for San Antonio residents who are familiar with the area and probably will draw retirees from other parts of the country, once Bandera becomes better known. Just a 26-mile drive from Kerrville, this community is one of the nicest, greenest, and most comfortable of all.

Situated on the Medina River, surrounded by oak-covered hills laced with winding creeks, Bandera has long been a favorite of San Antonio residents as a weekend getaway.

The town's carefully preserved Main Street is pretty much the same as it must have appeared in the nineteenth century, recalling memories of the days when Bandera was known as the "Cowboy Capital of the World." This was a staging area for Texas cowboys and their cattle herds to join up with drives traveling north along the Western Trail to Kansas and sometimes on to Montana. It's easy to imagine the *Lonesome Dove* crew moving their herd through here on their way north.

This historic Western tradition lives on in Bandera, and if you feel up to it, you can try your hand at herding longhorns at one of the nearby dude ranches, you "city slicker" you! On the other hand, if you're like most of us broken-down old travel writers, you'll be more likely to enjoy betting on horses than sitting on them. So stop off at Bandera's famous racetrack and place your bets; this thoroughbred and quarter-horse track draws throngs who pilgrimage here for the privilege of throwing money away on pari-mutuel betting. I understand there's going to be a track in San Antonio before long, but that won't detract from Bandera's charm.

Love of horses goes beyond watching them race. Many residents maintain stables on their property and exercise their animals on the many miles of horse trails in the 5,000-acre Hill Country State Natural Area. This happens to be the largest state park open to horseback camping. Having a stable on your property is a good way to ensure good resale value, too.

Bandera has yet another historical tradition: country-western and dance music. The Cabaret Dance Hall on Bandera's Western-style Main Street brings in music fans from all over the region. The list of past performers at the cabaret reads like a who's who in Texas country music.

This is very much a rural community, despite the sophistication of the racetrack and the many sumptuous homes. Residential property tends toward large lots and privacy.

## Medina and Camp Verde

For those who enjoy truly small-town living, consider Medina, not far from Bandera and 37 miles from Kerrville. It's slightly larger, but quieter, without the country music aspect of Bandera.

Another interesting place is Camp Verde, between Bandera and Kerrville, a location curiously connected with camels. Back in the 1850s, the U.S. Army experimented with camels for transportation. The Army established a camel route from Camp Verde that stretched all the way to Yuma, Arizona. And, no, I am not making this up.

## Bandera Area Weather

| | In degrees Fahrenheit | | | | | |
|---|---|---|---|---|---|---|
| | Jan. | April | July | Oct. | Rain | Snow |
| DAILY HIGHS | 62 | 78 | 92 | 79 | 30" | — |
| DAILY LOWS | 35 | 54 | 73 | 54 | | |

# The El Paso Region

West of the wooded, brushy foothills of the Texas Hill Country, the environment changes dramatically. Instead of 30 inches of rain every year, this truly western portion of Texas has to survive on a third or less of the moisture that blesses the Hill Country and east Texas. Of course, this gives the countryside a totally different look. Plants that grow here are different, having evolved to deal with 7 or 8 inches of annual rainfall and having learned to conserve precious water. For that reason, you can drive through long stretches of the state and see little evidence of human habitation. The occasional towns will usually be located on a river or near another source of water. That's not to say that the entire western part of Texas is pure desert; in some areas wheat fields thrive and a few other crops do quite well.

None of the aforementioned facts make the sparsely populated areas of west Texas bad places to retire. In fact, some people prefer small towns and the quiet solitude of wide-open spaces. But those who choose to move to small towns in west Texas for retirement usually have a particular reason to do so. (Perhaps they have relatives living here; perhaps they don't want relatives to find them; perhaps they're in the Witness Protection Program.) Look at it this way: There are usually good reasons why small towns in the semidesert portions of Texas stay small. On the other hand, a town like El Paso has a growing population. The countryside may be no different from locations a hundred miles away, but the environment is different. In the larger population centers you have shopping choices (more than one supermarket), you have entertainment and recreation choices (more than one movie theater), and you have access to better medical care. The city of El Paso is an example of a larger city that attracts retirees.

# El Paso

More than four centuries ago, in 1581, the first Europeans pushed their way north from Mexico and found an easy pass across the sometimes sluggish, sometimes wild Rio Grande. (Incidentally, Mexicans call the stream Rio Bravo, which means "wild river," instead of Rio Grande.) Early Spanish explorers named the crossing El Paso del Norte. When Mexico relinquished claim to the crossing, the U.S. Army established a post here to protect American settlers from marauding Comanches and to oversee the growing business of international trade between Mexico and the United States.

Over the ensuing years, El Paso grew from a dusty cow town into a modern city of a half million, the largest city on the American side of the 1,933-mile border. El Paso has several good things going for it. First, the climate is mild, with summers far cooler than those of the lower Rio Grande Valley. You can usually get out in July or August and play a game of golf without risking sunstroke. Low humidity and a 3,700-foot elevation make a world of difference. It's also a large city, with all the inherent amenities and benefits yet without the feeling of total urbanization found in similarly sized cities back East. You can live just a few minutes' drive from downtown El Paso yet not feel the pressures of a large city.

Another attraction for retirees is Ciudad Juárez, just across the Rio Grande. Juárez is more than just another border town like Reynosa or Matamoros; it is truly a city. It's even larger than El Paso, with an estimated population nearing a million. Juárez's downtown section, situated close to the border, is a bit grungy, with honky-tonks and bars, plus the inevitable border town curio and souvenir shops. But when you get away from the old downtown section you'll find modern areas with broad boulevards, good restaurants, and nice clothing stores.

Depending on the state of the economy, shopping in Juárez can be an experience in bargains and a challenge to your bargaining skills. Some commodities are always cheaper across the border, particularly items like booze, instant coffee, and some grocery items. At the time of this writing, the U.S. dollar maintains a favorable exchange rate against the Mexican peso, but inflation is narrowing the gap for those with dollars in their pockets. Many retirees make weekly forays across the border to take advantage of bargains. As long as the peso-dollar relationship remains favorable, Mexico will retain its status as a world-class shopping destination.

## Blending Cultures

El Paso has a delightful way of blending Mexican and Anglo cultures, something that doesn't occur in most border towns, from Texas to California. Instead of rigid social barriers separating them, you'll find a mellow blending of worldviews, language, and a refreshing mutual understanding. El Paso is a mixture of Texas and Chihuahua, with a surprising lack of prejudice and intolerance. Radio and TV announcers on both sides of the border switch between Spanish and English, never missing a beat. Restaurant menus on both sides of the border do much the same. El Paso restaurants typically offer dishes like pozole and chiles rellenos, and Juárez restaurants are famous for steak-and-lobster dinners and Chinese food. Years ago, when I worked for the *El Paso Times,* my favorite lunchtime restaurant served a great chicken-fried steak. Now, traditionally, chicken-fried steak is a Texas-Southern dish, but instead of the familiar milk gravy topping the steak, it came smothered with Mexican chile con queso sauce. (That's chopped green chiles in melted jack cheese. Delicious!)

Modern American and old Mexican charm blend to give El Paso neighborhoods a distinctive character. The downtown's wide streets branch out in all directions, and Interstate 10 moves traffic quickly and efficiently through the center of the city. As you move toward the outskirts, you can't help but be impressed with the area's neatness and cleanliness.

An area that my wife and I particularly liked is El Paso's northwest side. Still under development, the neighborhoods here sit on the sloping foothills, with views across the Rio Grande into Mexico. Homes are newly built, well maintained, and priced economically. Of course, the state's high property taxes offset the bargains somewhat, but the quality here is superb. For example, relatively new homes, tastefully designed, start at less than $80,000 and go for more than $200,000, depending on the neighborhood and the size of the homes.

## Military Town

That first military post on the Rio Grande established a continuing tradition of military presence in El Paso. Many civilians are employed at military installations here, and ex-military families make up a good percentage of El Paso retirees. The area's military installations play a big part in El Paso's everyday life and activities. Fort Bliss, in northeastern El Paso, is the home of the U.S. Army Air Defense Center and contributes a huge payroll to keep the economy level. Military families and support personnel live in all sections of the city and make the population very "middle America." When retirement time rolls around, Air Force and Army personnel quite readily include El Paso in their list of retirement possibilities. They remember the cleanliness and neighborliness of the city, as well as the affordable real estate. Of course, being military, post exchange privileges and medical facilities for retirees influence their final decisions.

Like any big town, El Paso has its problems, but the city seems to be getting a handle on crime. In recent years crime rates in El Paso have fallen dramatically. For example, burglary, the crime that affects seniors the most, has dropped by 22 percent. Overall, El Paso's crime rate is 25 percent below places like Dallas and other large Texas cities. As in any large population center, the vast majority of offenses are not the kind that involve senior citizens, and most criminal activity is concentrated in areas where retirees wouldn't want to live anyway. The nicer residential areas of El Paso appear to be as safe as most small towns.

## Santa Teresa and Horizon City

A quiet secret (one I discovered when interviewing a real estate broker who lives here) is the El Paso suburb of Santa Teresa. Actually, Santa Teresa is located in New Mexico, even though it's just fifteen minutes' driving time from El Paso's center. This little community offers the best of both worlds. Because it's just across the New Mexico state line, property taxes are much lower (by as much as a third), yet it's close enough to El Paso to enjoy its cultural and sports activities. The major community in Santa Teresa is gated, with homes costing from $80,000 to $300,000. The country club in the community charges an affordable membership fee and provides two eighteen-hole golf courses designed by Lee Trevino, twenty-four tennis courts, and a swimming pool. Other homes outside the gated community can be found for less than $100,000.

Another place to consider is Horizon City. Five miles east of El Paso city limits, this is reputed to be one of the fastest-growing communities in Texas. Just incorporated seven years ago, the town now has 4,000 residents. Horizon City is divided into two general neighborhoods. The first is Horizon Manor, where houses cost between $50,000 and $90,000. The second is Horizon Heights, with homes built around a golf course; houses on the fairway cost as much as $350,000.

## Recreation and Culture

Why retire in El Paso? A frequent answer to this question is the area's mild weather, which allows for healthy, year-round outdoor activities. Besides golf, tennis, and jogging, less vigorous spectator sports include bullfights across the river in Mexico and horse racing at Sunland Park in New Mexico, only fifteen minutes from downtown El Paso.

Golf is a year-round sport, with four eighteen-hole public courses and seven members-only layouts. The city has an unusually large number of tennis courts, which are scattered about the neighborhoods. Twenty-five public courts in all, eighteen of them lighted for night play, are joined by five private tennis courts to give El Paso residents lots of opportunity to hit the balls.

El Paso Community College, one of the largest in the nation, is even bigger than the University of Texas at El Paso, with almost 20,000 students. The school offers a variety of courses through its alternative education program, which is tailored for seniors, and its Weekend College program.

The El Paso Symphony Orchestra is the longest continuously running symphony orchestra in Texas. It's joined by El Paso Pro Musica, a concert choir, and a chamber orchestra. The Americana Museum maintains at least ten exhibits a year, promoting and displaying local and regional art, and the El Paso Museum of Art is the fine-arts museum of the region.

## Real Estate

The cost of living in El Paso falls 6 percent below the national average. Partly this is due to the exceptionally low cost of housing, which is almost 15 percent below average. These low real estate prices more than offset the higher Texas property tax structure. Utilities, too, are low, as is health care, both about ten points below average.

Most single-family neighborhoods feature brick, ranch-style homes, with low-maintenance landscaping. Latest figures show average sales prices at exceptionally low levels. These figures could be misleading, because they average in houses in exceptionally low-priced neighborhoods, places where many retirees might not want to live.

In El Paso's newer sections, away from the downtown area, you'll find a proliferation of apartment buildings, with more than one hundred apartment complexes throughout the city. Like many Texas cities that participated in the savings-and-loan jubilee, condo and apartment construction was overly enthusiastic, resulting in an oversupply. However, like many Texas cities, this bonanza for renters isn't quite as plush as it once was. New apartment construction has halted, and rents have crept up, almost to a normal level. Still, apartments are easy to find and are relatively affordable.

## Medical Care

El Paso is well supplied with medical facilities, with thirteen private hospitals and one public hospital. The William Beaumont Army Medical Center is one of the largest U.S. Army general hospitals in the nation, with 479 beds for area military personnel and veterans. It is also home to a branch of Texas Tech University School of Medicine, a full-time teaching facility for third- and fourth-year med students. The city and county also have a well-organized public health services program, with branches in various parts of the city.

## When Grandkids Visit

This might be an appropriate time to visit some military museums, since the military figures so prominently here. The Fort Bliss Museum has a reproduction of the way the fort looked in the 1850s. You'll see how soldiers lived back in the frontier days. Then visit the Army Air Defense Museum, also on the grounds of Fort Bliss, which has a slide show, films, and a display of antiaircraft weapons.

## Addresses and Connections

*Chamber of Commerce:* 10 Civic Center Plaza, El Paso, TX 79901

*Senior Services:* El Paso Senior Opportunities and Services, 100 North Oregon Street, El Paso, TX 79901

*Newspaper:* El Paso Times, Times Plaza, El Paso, TX 79900

*Airport:* El Paso Airport, a major transportation hub
*Bus:* the area is well served by a city bus system and Greyhound

## El Paso Area Weather

| | In degrees Fahrenheit | | | | | |
| | Jan. | April | July | Oct. | Rain | Snow |
|---|---|---|---|---|---|---|
| DAILY HIGHS | 58 | 79 | 96 | 79 | 8" | 6" |
| DAILY LOWS | 30 | 49 | 70 | 49 | | |

## El Paso Area Cost of Living

| | (percentage of national average) | | | |
| Overall | Housing | Medical | Groceries | Utilities |
|---|---|---|---|---|
| 94% | 84% | 94% | 101% | 83% |

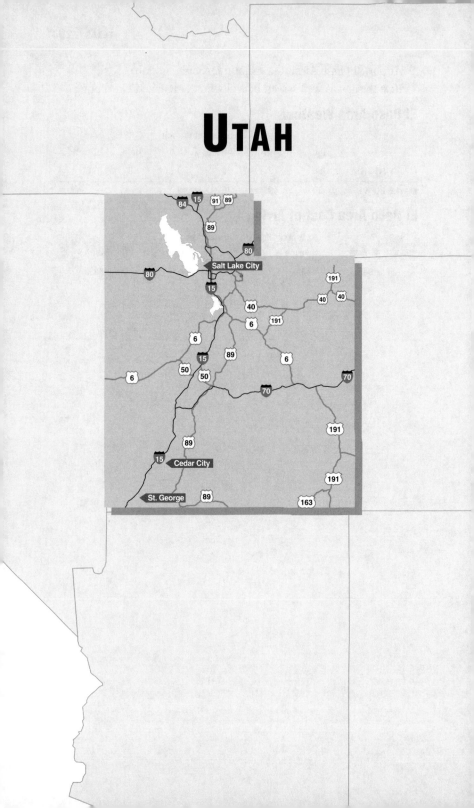

# UTAH

Utah offers some of the nation's most spectacular landscapes, with fantastic canyons carved in brilliant red stone, lush mountain forests teeming with wildlife, and sapphire lakes brimming with trout. Few places in the world can compete with Utah when it comes to sheer beauty. Zion and Bryce Canyon National Parks, in the southern portion of the state, will absolutely take your breath away, while Capital Reef and the Canyonlands up north are unmatched for sheer desert and mountain beauty. Anyone contemplating a motoring trip out West will never be disappointed by detouring through these areas.

Utah isn't all national parkland and scenic wonders, however. The state is also famous for uninhabited stretches of desert and alkaline flats dotted with sagebrush. Parts of the Great Salt Lake Desert receive less than 5 inches of rain a year. To balance out the landscape, the high, north-central region of the state receives considerable rain, sometimes up to 40 inches a year. That's as much as what falls on most Eastern and Midwestern states. Utah's best-known landmark, of course, is the Great Salt Lake. Actually an inland sea, the water is so salty that most ocean fish couldn't live in it. In the midst of a desert, hundreds of miles from the Pacific Ocean, it seems strange to see swarms of seagulls and pelicans. Even in the drier, desertlike regions of the state, wildlife is surprisingly plentiful, including ducks, deer, elk, and mountain lions.

Because the desert and canyon lands are chronically short of water, few people choose to live here. Therefore, the most scenic and dramatic panoramas are located in isolated and unpopulated wilderness. That's part of the charm. You'll find just a few scattered farms and an occasional village in the most gorgeous parts of Utah. Most people prefer to live in areas where there's more rain—places where rainfall averages at least 15 inches a year.

Those who are not familiar with the state need to understand Utah's unique social structure before deciding to retire here. Especially in smaller towns, religion has a strong influence on everyday living—even greater than in Southern Bible Belt communities. In many, if not most, small towns there is only one church: the Church of Jesus Christ of Latter-Day Saints (also known as the LDS, or Mormons). Occasionally, there'll be an alternative, perhaps a Baptist or Catholic denomination in town, but in all cases, non-Mormons are in the minority. Social life and everyday activities are often entwined in some way with the Mormon church. Many other religious denominations do thrive in the larger cities, which is why most non-Mormons seek out places like Salt Lake City, Cedar City, and St. George—places where the population is mixed. The larger the town or city, the larger the percentage of residents who are not LDS members. For example, there are only two Jewish rabbis in the state, both living in Salt Lake City, and the only synagogue outside Salt Lake City is in Ogden (with no rabbi).

Mormons are wonderfully warm and loving, showing deep concern for each other's welfare. With members of other faiths, Mormons can be polite but appear to be aloof. In my interviews with several Utah retirees, most non-Mormons affirmed that they haven't found religion much of a problem. "It's only a problem if you let it be one," said one newcomer to St. George. "We've had no trouble making friends, and our neighbors are quite gracious."

Are non-Mormons discriminated against? You'll hear yes and no to this question. One member of the church I interviewed disputed the existence of discrimination and explained it this way: "What many folks don't understand is that being a member of our church isn't just a 'Sunday' thing. Our everyday activities often involve the church in one way or another. So, when Mormon families in a neighborhood all get on a bus to go to a church activity, the uninvited neighbors could feel left out. We don't mean to snub our neighbors. It's just that they don't join in our church affairs any more than we participate in their church activities."

In this chapter, we'll take a look at just three areas for retirement. These are not the only places that might make good retirement destinations, but they are the only places I'm aware of where a substantial number of people from other states actually do retire and where non-Mormons aren't complete rarities.

# History

In 1540 an expedition from Mexico brought the first Spanish to explore what is now Utah. Francisco Coronado went to search for the "seven cities of Cibola" and their reputed strongholds of riches and gold-clad buildings, but the trek yielded no gold. The explorers did find three native tribes inhabiting the region: the Ute, Shoshone, and Paiute. They were nomadic, living by hunting small animals and gathering seeds. Utah obtained its name from the Ute tribe.

More than 200 years later, in 1776, two Franciscan missionaries, Francisco Silvestre Velez de Escalante and Francisco Dominguez, resumed exploration of southern and central Utah. Part of the route they blazed became known as the Old Spanish Trail. Yet the country remained relatively unexplored until 1824, when hardy fur trappers moved into northern Utah in search of rich hunting territory. Later, a few wagon trains made their way across the territory on their way to California, but it wasn't until after 1843, when John C. Frémont and Kit Carson explored the Salt Lake area, that a few settlers decided to put down tentative stakes in Utah.

Most early pioneers pushed on through the territory, their sights fixed on good pastures and timbered lands to be found in the lush lands of Oregon and California. The canyons and deserts of Utah offered little promise.

The settlement of Utah's shunned regions began in earnest when a group of persecuted Mormons, driven into exile from their Midwestern homes by mobs of murderous religious bigots, loaded their covered wagons and plodded west to seek lands no one else wanted. Those lacking horses and wagons carried their belongings in handcarts. All they wanted was a place where they could live unmolested, where they could worship in their own way. On July 24, 1847, a group of 148 pioneers, under the leadership of Brigham Young, chose a stop at the foot of the Wasatch mountain range as their promised land. Heroically, the disciplined and self-sufficient group turned the desert into a garden virtually overnight.

The hardy Mormon colony spread northward and southward from the original site, and only three years later, Utah's population had grown to about 11,000. By 1880 the populace had multiplied more than twelve times. The Mormon church directed this development, and almost all immigrants were church members.

In 1869, when the first transcontinental railroad was completed at Promontory, Utah, the state began to attract a steady influx of outsiders. More and more non-Mormons—known then, as today, as Gentiles—began settling in the area. The number increased with the introduction of manufacturing, around the end of the nineteenth century. Nevertheless, even today about 70 percent of the state's inhabitants are

## Utah Tax Profile

Sales tax:
**6.25%; drugs exempt**

State income tax:
**graduated from 2.3% to 7% from $750 to $7,500; federal income tax 50% deductible**

Property taxes:
**average 1% of market value**

Intangibles tax:
**none**

Social Security tax:
**half of benefits taxable for higher incomes**

Pension taxes:
**exclude up to $7,500, depending on income level**

Gasoline tax:
**19.5¢ per gallon**

active members of the Church of Jesus Christ of Latter-Day Saints. In smaller towns it's not uncommon to have 100 percent Mormon populations. An active social and political force in Utah, the church owns much property and manages many cooperative enterprises.

The desolate land that so many pioneers passed by as worthless and unyielding today produces a wealth of minerals, agricultural products, and manufactured goods. Large cities, comfortable towns, and small villages dot the landscape where nomadic tribes felt lucky to find a few handfuls of seeds. Yet some things haven't changed much from early pioneer days: Water is still scarce, and religion remains an integral part of everyday life.

# Cedar City

Most Utah communities present a pleasant, old-fashioned appearance, neat as a starched shirt. Whether or not Utah's high percentage of Mormons is the cause of the state's exceptionally low crime rate may be open for debate, but the fact is, tranquillity is the norm in most Utah locations. Cedar City is typical of Utah's small cities.

This university town of 22,000 offers many advantages for retirement living. Sheltered in the foothills, just a few miles from some of the most spectacular landscapes in the world, Cedar City combines the cultural

atmosphere of an active university with some of the best skiing and outdoor sports to be found anywhere. The 5,800-foot altitude guarantees a
vigorous, four-season climate. According to residents, the region usually
has four good snowfalls every winter, but warm afternoons and plenty of
sunshine make quick work of the white stuff.

Cedar City is located off Interstate 15, which gives it easy access to St.
George, 52 miles south, and to Salt Lake City, 250 miles north. Las Vegas
is little more than a three-hour drive. You might expect a small city like
Cedar City to be safe, and it is, exceptionally so. According to my calcu-
lations, only eight cities in the United States have lower crime rates than
Cedar City.

Because of its exciting variety of cultural presentations, Cedar City calls
itself the "Festival City." Now in its thirty-ninth season, the Shakespeare
Festival, which runs from the last week in June through Labor Day, with a
new fall season that runs from mid-September through mid-October, is
famous throughout the West and draws fans from far and wide. Each year
Southern Utah University presents four Shakespeare plays plus another
stage play and a musical. Another interesting festival is the yearly Jedediah
Smith High Mountain Rendezvous. This follows an old-time Western
theme, assembling trappers, traders, and mountain men for a nostalgic festival of frontier contests and camaraderie. Southern Utah University's campus is the focus of many other community events such as music festivals,
ballet performances, and the Utah Summer Games.

Even though a large majority of residents are Mormons, Cedar City
also has a comparatively large percentage of non-Mormons (there are
thirteen other churches in town). This is partly due to the workers who
have moved into the community, following the manufacturing companies that have relocated here.

## Recreation and Culture

A major attraction here is some of the West's best skiing, at Brian
Head, about 30 miles from Cedar City—close enough for easy day
trips. With 400 inches annually of Utah powder and fifty-three spectacular ski trails through red-rock scenery, Brian Head attracts downhillers
from as far away as Los Angeles. The facilities are also used as a summer
resort, with chairlift rides and community events such as the Fourth of
July celebration, an Octoberfest, and an annual kite-flying contest.

For golfers, there's Cedar Ridge, a public eighteen-hole course. Its par-seventy-one layout is enhanced by its surroundings of red cliffs and foothills. The city also has two tennis courts and a municipal pool.

In addition to the cultural opportunities already mentioned, continuing education at the university is encouraged. Retirees may audit any university class on a space-available basis for $10 (noncredit). The continuing education department also offers a variety of evening courses.

## Real Estate

Cedar City has a low cost of living, about 9 percent below nearby St. George. Housing costs are dramatically lower as well, about 23 percent less. According to local realtors, a lower-priced home in an acceptable neighborhood would sell for $71,000 and a high-end home for a little more than $150,000. The average price is around $102,000. Apartment rentals average $400.

## Medical Care

Valley View Medical Center is a forty-eight-bed, full-service facility with some secondary-level services. It has an intensive care/cardiac care unit. The city has forty-two doctors, seventeen dentists, and four chiropractors. Four home-health agencies and a new regional care center are located in Cedar City. A new, state-of-the-art hospital will open in 2002.

## When Grandkids Visit

Take a 21-mile drive to Cedar Breaks National Monument. A miniature version of Bryce Canyon, Cedar Breaks is considered by many to be even more colorful. The abrupt cliffs and fantastic formations are like a watercolor palette left in the rain, with ribbons of lavender and purple running into creamy gold and pink. Get there early, because every morning park rangers conduct nature walks. There are also hiking, picnicking, and camping areas.

## Addresses and Connections

*Chamber of Commerce:* 581 North Main, Cedar City, UT 84720

*Senior Services:* Cedar City Senior Citizens, 489 East 200 South, Cedar City, UT 84720

*Newspaper:* The Spectrum Daily News, 207 North Main, Cedar City, UT 84720

*Airport:* Cedar City Municipal, with commuter service to Salt Lake City

*Bus:* while there are no public transportation services, there is a senior bus for trips to the doctor, shopping, etc.; Greyhound and Trailways both pass through town; and taxi service and a town shuttle are available

## Cedar City Weather

|  | In degrees Fahrenheit | | | | | |
|---|---|---|---|---|---|---|
|  | Jan. | April | July | Oct. | Rain | Snow |
| DAILY HIGHS | 47 | 72 | 89 | 77 | 10" | 40" |
| DAILY LOWS | 28 | 44 | 66 | 48 | | |

## Cedar City Area Cost of Living

| (percentage of national average) | | | | |
|---|---|---|---|---|
| Overall | Housing | Medical | Groceries | Utilities |
| 93% | 77% | 91% | 106% | 77% |

# St. George

The largest city in southern Utah, St. George works hard to attract retirees and has acquired a strong reputation as a retirement community. It consistently receives top recommendations from national magazines and retirement guides, often ranking number one in the West. A day trip to Zion National Park, Bryce Canyon, and the Grand Canyon are attractions that prompt locals to refer to St. George as a great "jumping off" point. It certainly scores high on scenic values and appears to be a comfortable place to live.

Located on Interstate 15, a little more than two hours' drive from Las Vegas, St. George isn't as isolated as it might seem. The city's population of about 50,000 is large enough to provide adequate services, and the community stands on its own commercially.

St. George's picturesque surroundings are some of the more dramatic of any retirement destination described in this book. Stark red cliffs loom over the town, sometimes rising vertically from residents' backyards. You get the feeling that you're living in a Western movie set. In its own way, St. George is as spectacular as Sedona, Arizona, although on a smaller scale.

A combination of beauty, relatively mild winters, and great golfing draws more retirees from outside Utah than do other Utah communities. This is important for non-Mormons, because outsiders dilute the reli-

gious majority. As a matter of fact, St. George has twenty-four community churches besides those of the Mormon faith.

Settled in 1861 by 309 Mormon families, St. George was transformed
from a forbidding alkali flat into a livable town in the space of a decade.
Some original homes survive and are treated with reverence by local residents. Included in the list of old homes is Brigham Young's house, where
he spent some of his last years. Streets are wide and tree-lined, and
homes are as neat and orderly as Brigham Young would have wished.

St. George boosters like to refer to the area as Utah's "Dixie" out of
respect for the area's relatively mild winters. The truth is, the designation
"Dixie" derived not so much from the town's southernmost location in
the state as from the early-day cotton fields that brought prosperity to
the pioneer community. It's true that a lower elevation (only 2,840 feet)
blesses St. George with warmer winters than its nearby retirement coun-
terpart, Cedar City. The trade-off is warmer summer temperatures, yet
evenings are always cool enough to sleep under blankets.

The FBI ranks St. George as very safe. According to FBI figures, St.
George is in the top third of all recommended retirement locations in
terms of personal safety.

## Recreation and Culture

According to local boosters, St. George has more golf-course facilities
per capita than any place this side of Palm Springs. I'm not sure that's true,
but golfers do enjoy ten great courses—open year-round and within a fif-
teen-minute drive from town. There's even an 1,800-square-foot indoor
golf facility to help you find out why your slice is so messed up. St. George
is also home to the Huntsman World Senior Games, which attracts thousands of seniors from all over the country.

Dixie State College of Utah, which recently acquired four-year status, provides a cultural setting with music and theater productions, a Celebrity
Concert Series, the Jazz Ensemble, and the Southwest Symphony Orchestra.
The college serves the retired community with continuing education classes
tailored for senior citizens, with computer and Internet courses among the
most popular.

## Real Estate

A variety of properties and housing is available in this area. Homes
sell from $80,000 to more than $1.5 million. An older, more economi-

cal, three-bedroom house costs about $101,000, and the annual property tax on such a home is about $1,000. The average selling price of all homes here was $116,489 in early 2000. I suspect the higher prices reflect sales in the newer, upscale developments that are sprouting up around the area.

Several small towns nearby extend lower home prices for cost-conscious folks. In the southern section of St. George, the Bloomington and Bloomington Hills developments offer exceptionally well-designed homes, reminiscent of those in Arizona's Sun City projects.

## Medical Care

As the health care center for the surrounding area, St. George is noted for its top facilities, which offer quality care at a lower cost than the national average. The 137-bed Dixie Medical Center is a progressive, regional referral facility that serves the health care needs of nearly 100,000 residents in the tristate area of southern Utah, southern Nevada, and northeastern Arizona. Owned and operated by Intermountain Health Care, a private nonprofit system based in Salt Lake City, the hospital provides quality care to those with medical needs regardless of their ability to pay.

## When Grandkids Visit

An unforgettable place to visit is Zion National Park. This is the most spectacular scenic marvel of all Utah's fantastic settings. Massive, multi-colored cliffs and deep canyons; hiking trails through a petrified forest; waterfalls; and desert wildlife make this a must-visit. Be sure to bring your camera.

## Addresses and Connections

*Chamber of Commerce:* 97 East St. George Boulevard, St. George, UT 84770

*Senior Services:* 245 North 200 West, St. George, UT 84770

*Newspaper: The Spectrum,* 275 East St. George Boulevard, St. George, UT 84770

*Airport:* the local airport offers SkyWest commuter flights with two daily flights to Los Angeles

*Bus:* no local bus, but there is Greyhound service and the St. George Shuttle to the Las Vegas airport

## St. George Area Weather

| | Jan. | April | July | Oct. | Rain | Snow |
|---|---|---|---|---|---|---|
| | In degrees Fahrenheit | | | | | |
| DAILY HIGHS | 54 | 77 | 101 | 81 | 8" | trace |
| DAILY LOWS | 27 | 44 | 68 | 46 | | |

## St. George Area Cost of Living

| | | (percentage of national average) | | |
|---|---|---|---|---|
| Overall | Housing | Medical | Groceries | Utilities |
| 102% | 101% | 96% | 107% | 95% |

# Salt Lake City

In 1847 Brigham Young led a following of 148 Mormons westward across the plains and mountains in search of a new home free from religious persecution. When the travelers looked down from mountains overlooking the broad valley of the Great Salt Lake, Brigham Young announced that this was the Promised Land where they would live. His wife, Clara Decker Young, said of that moment, "I cried, for it seemed to me the most desolate in all the world." It was a broad plain, bordered to the north and east by snow-capped mountains and by the Great Salt Lake to the southeast. The city sits at an altitude of 4,300 feet.

The hardy settlers set to work that same day, laying out a city, tilling the soil, and transforming dry, desolate land into farmlands. Within a few months they were harvesting crops and building what was to become today's beautiful Salt Lake City. Wide streets and boulevards were part of the pioneers' design. The impressive LDS (Mormon) Temple, constructed from granite quarried from nearby canyons and surrounded by beautiful gardens, became the city's central focus and the world capital of the Church of Jesus Christ of Latter-Day Saints.

At first the city's growth depended on the inflow of Mormon converts from Europe and America. California's gold rush of 1849 added settlers who decided to abandon their journey west and stay here. Later, industrial and business expansion attracted non-Mormons—who now make up almost half the county's population. This makes for a more cosmopolitan community than is found in most areas of Utah. Salt Lake City today is the capital of Utah and is one of the largest cities in the

Rocky Mountain region, with a population of more than 173,000.

Other buildings of note in the city are those of the University of Utah, the State Capitol, the impressive City and County Building, the famous Utah Museum of Fine Arts, several large exposition buildings, and two former residences of Brigham Young. In Temple Square is the Seagull Monument, dedicated to the flights of seagulls that dramatically saved the first crops from a plague of locusts. Salt Lake City is known for neighborhoods that are neat and well kept with exceptionally safe conditions. Some downtown neighborhoods are showcases of pioneer and turn-of-the-twentieth-century homes, while the fringes of the city feature modern suburban neighborhoods.

## Recreation and Culture

Skiing in nearby Park City, home of the U.S. Ski and Snowboard Team and other winter sports, draws snow enthusiasts in the winter. Utah's snow is unusually dry powder—up to 400 inches a year—considered by many skiers to be the world's best. Seven ski resorts are less than an hour's drive of Salt Lake City.

The region's low humidity and abundance of sunshine makes golf a year-round sport, with eight courses open for play. *Golf Digest* ranked Salt Lake City as a number-one golf destination for big cities in the U.S.A. Hiking and bicycling in the nearby mountains are popular recreational activities. Salt Lake City is the home base of the Utah (formerly New Orleans) Jazz professional NBA basketball team. It also has its own hockey team and a Triple-A baseball Team.

Part of Salt Lake City's rich quality of life derives from its enthusiastic support of the arts. A haven for creative expression, residents have daily choices of performances, exhibits, and events for entertainment or enrichment. A world-class symphony orchestra, the Utah Opera Company, and one of the country's largest ballet companies attract professionals from around the world. And, of course, the world-famous Mormon Tabernacle Choir performs on Temple Square each week. Five major universities are within an hour's drive from Salt Lake City, plus several community colleges. The Utah Museum of fine Arts is located on the University of Utah campus, and many school performances and exhibits are open to the public.

## Real Estate

The overall cost of living in Salt Lake City is slightly below average, helped in part by exceptionally low utility costs (20 percent below average). A robust, diverse economy, attracting newcomers, has created an increase in real estate prices over the past few years. Nevertheless, median sales prices hover around the national average: about $135,000, with many quality homes priced in the $95,000 range. Despite this increase, Salt Lake continues to be an affordable place to live, ranking sixteenth among seventy-five major U.S. cities.

## Medical Care

Seven major medical facilities serve this area, making it one of the premier places for health care in the West. Altogether, Salt Lake City has thirteen hospitals. Provo is currently served by two excellent hospitals, providing more than 400 beds.

## Provo

Located about 40 miles south of Salt Lake City, the city of Provo often garners top ratings as a place to retire by retirement guides and magazines. Provo is also the home of Brigham Young University, one of the largest private universities in the country. As a general rule, towns with higher ratings for personal safety and low crime rates are smaller communities—below 20,000. Yet Provo, with 92,000 inhabitants, is hardly a small town, but it scores unusually high personal safety scores. It consistently scores in the top twenty-five safest places in the nation.

## When Grandkids Visit

You'll find most attractions have something to do with Mormon history, reflecting the religious emphasis by state and local governments. Not to be missed is the Hansen Planetarium and the Natural History Museum, with a nice collection of dinosaur skeletons. Neither institution has any particular religious bias in the displays. The dinosaurs are mostly nonsectarian.

## Addresses and Connections

*Chamber of Commerce:* 175 East 400 South, #600, Salt Lake City, UT 84111

*Senior Services:* 1992 South 200 East, Salt Lake City, UT 84115

*Newspapers: Salt Lake Tribune,* 143 South Main Street, Salt Lake City, UT 84111; *Deseret News,* 30 East 100 South, Salt Lake City, UT 84111
**Airport:** Salt Lake International, a major airline junction
**Bus/Train:** a city bus system, Greyhound, and Amtrak serve the area

## Salt Lake City Weather

|  | In degrees Fahrenheit | | | | | |
|---|---|---|---|---|---|---|
|  | Jan. | April | July | Oct. | Rain | Snow |
| DAILY HIGHS | 37 | 61 | 93 | 67 | 15" | 58" |
| DAILY LOWS | 20 | 37 | 62 | 39 | | |

## Salt Lake City/Provo Area Cost of Living

| (percentage of national average) | | | | |
|---|---|---|---|---|
| Overall | Housing | Medical | Groceries | Utilities |
| 98% | 100% | 88% | 99% | 80% |

# INDEX

# About the Author

John Howells and his wife, Sherry, spent many months traveling by automobile, motor home, and airplane gathering information to produce this book. They interviewed retired folks in every state of the Southwest, collecting experiences, advice, and valuable insights into successful retirement lifestyles.

John has written and coauthored several other books about retirement locations. Among them are *Where to Retire* and *Choose Costa Rica.* He also writes about retirement and travel for mature Americans in magazines such as *Consumers Digest* and *Where to Retire* magazine. He is a member of the board of directors of the American Association of Retirement Communities. John and his wife live in California and Costa Rica.